Connection to Nature, Deep Ecology, and Conservation Social Science

Connection to Nature, Deep Ecology, and Conservation Social Science

Human-Nature Bonding and Protecting the Natural World

Christian Diehm

Foreword by Holmes Rolston III

LEXINGTON BOOKS
Lanham • Boulder • New York • London

Published by Lexington Books
An imprint of The Rowman & Littlefield Publishing Group, Inc.
4501 Forbes Boulevard, Suite 200, Lanham, Maryland 20706
www.rowman.com

6 Tinworth Street, London SE11 5AL, United Kingdom

Copyright © 2020 The Rowman & Littlefield Publishing Group, Inc.

All rights reserved. No part of this book may be reproduced in any form or by any electronic or mechanical means, including information storage and retrieval systems, without written permission from the publisher, except by a reviewer who may quote passages in a review.

British Library Cataloguing in Publication Information Available

Library of Congress Cataloging-in-Publication Data

Names: Diehm, Christian, 1969- author.
Title: Connection to nature, deep ecology, and conservation social science : human-nature bonding and protecting the natural world / Christian Diehm ; foreword by Holmes Rolston III.
Description: Lanham, Maryland : Lexington Books, 2020. | Includes bibliographical references and index. | Summary: "This book explores human-nature connectedness through deep ecological philosophy and conservation social science. Emphasizing ecologically-inclusive identities, it argues that connection to nature is more important than many environmental advocates realize and that deep ecology contributes much to the increasingly pressing conversations about it"—Provided by publisher.
Identifiers: LCCN 2020039747 (print) | LCCN 2020039748 (ebook) |
  ISBN 9781793624208 (cloth) | ISBN 9781793624215 (epub)
Subjects: LCSH: Human ecology. | Nature—Effect of human beings on. | Deep ecology. | Nature conservation—Social aspects. | Environmental ethics.
Classification: LCC GF41 .D527 2020 (print) | LCC GF41 (ebook) | DDC 304.2—dc23
LC record available at https://lccn.loc.gov/2020039747
LC ebook record available at https://lccn.loc.gov/2020039748

Contents

Foreword *Holmes Rolston III*	vii
Acknowledgments	xi
Introduction: Connection to Nature and the Enduring Influence of Deep Ecology	1
1 Self-Realization and Identification with Nature	15
2 Ecological Identity Matters: Deep Ecology and Conservation Psychology	41
3 Connection to Nature and Environmental Values	67
4 We Belong Outside: Connectedness to Nature and Outdoor Experience	95
5 Loving More-than-Human Life: Connectedness to Nature, Deep Ecology, and Biophilia	119
Bibliography	139
Index	157
About the Author	163

Foreword

Some years back, Chris Diehm invited me to speak at his university. As it turned out, I first met his students on an afternoon walk in a nearby forest on a wintry Wisconsin day. Students were asking me questions about environmental ethics. This particular woods was full of oaks, and Chris was pointing out how you could tell the various oaks apart even in winter, if you looked carefully at bark and buds and found a few acorns or fallen leaves. There were eight or ten different oaks, white oaks, red oaks, and black oaks, and a couple might have been hybrids. I was shivering and, at the end of the walk, over coffee I suggested to the students that our walk was an icon or model of human-nature bonding, one where we experienced the intriguing detail of a local site simultaneously with concern for living well both locally and on the home planet.

This book is that experience writ large. When I gave my featured lecture on campus the next day, Chris's reputation for challenging thinking brought me a packed audience of some four hundred students and faculty. With this book, Chris is challenging as broad an audience as he can reach—including you, the reader—to think deeply about how you are connected to nature. "Connectedness with nature presents itself as a radical but necessary prerequisite for realizing desired conservation and environmental behavior outcomes."[1] Rid yourself of any "disconnect from nature."

"But," I find myself wanting to reply. Well, *humans are disconnected with nature through the kinds of connections they have.* No other species has power to jeopardize the planet. No other species has a "deep ecological philosophy." No other species can take the kind of walk I took with those students in the Wisconsin woods, pondering ancient natural history and what humans have done to displace it. So we have to spell out our uniqueness. Yes, we connect with nature, but humans are cultural animals, the only animal with a cumulative transmissible culture. Connecting with nature is necessary, but not sufficient to become human. Connecting with culture is necessary but not sufficient to become human. Man is "a political animal" (Aristotle). That's where Diehm needs his "social science," his "conservation social sciences."

Arne Naess, the famous Norwegian philosopher whom Chris once interviewed (as did I), helps with his focus on the notions of "self-realization" and "identification" with nature. Naess invites us to a "relational, total-field" view.[2] With *Homo sapiens* he says, "a life form has developed on Earth which is capable of understanding and appreciating its relations with all other life forms and to the Earth as a whole."[3] There is "something of ourselves in the other creature, or something of the other creature in ourselves."[4]

Humans, he says, "are the first kind of living beings we know of which have the potentialities of living in community with all other living beings. It is our hope that these potentialities will be realized."[5] We "seek what is best for ourselves, but through the extension of the self, our 'own' best is also that of others."[6] Botanists love and seek to conserve plants, but we do not think oak trees with their "own best" are potentially in reciprocating relationships with us. Naess did report that in his mountain hut he found himself "together as one entity" with tiny alpine flowers. "I have known the rocks at Tvergastein since I was very young, and they *look* at me. I *look* at them and they *look* at me."[7] Diehm has to twist and turn to show that this experience is in part inexpressible, but is not doublespeak. That is the genius of the book.

Once—on another afternoon before I spoke at Stevens Point—during a rainstorm with lightning, I visited the Leopold shack and listened to Nina Leopold Bradley reminisce about her father. Aldo Leopold finds an A/B cleavage in attitudes toward nature. The A side sees land, water, and forests as commodity, the B side as community. The cleavage continues with game versus wildlife, acre-feet of water versus rivers in ecosystems, timber versus forests, owning land versus sense of place, and humans as conquerors versus humans as citizens. Leopold urges us to love the landscapes in which we reside. The day before I had visited the original John Muir homestead where John Muir insisted, famously: "When we try to pick out anything by itself, we find it hitched to everything else in the Universe."[8] That sounds like deep interconnections. But—

I take an interest in bats, yet doubt that I can think like a bat. I am unable to hear well enough to catch insects flying in the dark, or to find my particular pup by echolocation in a cave and nurse it. Then again, I can understand *that*, maybe even (with some scientific studies) *how* bats do this. Is that my "own best" in others? I've watched pelicans in the Antarctic dive and catch fish in freezing water. They avoid the killer whales. They are hungry, I suppose, but my capacities for indwelling empathy end there. It seems crazy to seek the "own best" of malaria parasites or the polio virus.

Once every few years, fishermen in the Indian and South Pacific oceans drag up a coelacanth in their nets. This is a very rare and weird fish, a huge fish with a tiny brain, with a history spanning from the age of the dinosaurs sixty-five million years ago; it is a creature long thought extinct. I saw one once, pickled, when I spoke at Rhodes University, Grahamstown, South Africa. After the talk, an ichthyologist came up and invited me to visit the South African Institute for Aquatic Biodiversity, which calls itself the "scientific home of the coelacanth." Researchers first rediscovered the oddball fish on a fishing trawler in port there in 1938. I have no idea how to identify with a coelacanth. I don't think they are much interrelated with everything else. I do wish to protect them, but is this somehow in my wider self-interest?

I start by protesting: This Promethean force-fitting of every possible conservation good into something good for us in our place goes sour, analogously to the way that force-fitting the conservation of goods for the many peoples of the world into goods for us Americans, or the conservation of goods for Americans into what is good for me and my family, goes sour. No matter how much we enlarge the circle with increasing enlightenment, eventually the curve comes back to us and reveals the underlying motivation as self-interest, even if always with entwined destinies with whatever else there is on Earth.

But then again, challenged by Diehm and Naess, I too twist and turn, torn between the natural world I seek to enjoy and the classic self-defeating character of self-interest. The wild fauna and flora have a good of their own: they are located in a good place, they are desired for their own sake, and appreciating them is my flourishing. That is a win-win situation. Oppositely, losing them is losing the quality of life that comes based on them, as well as their being lost in their own right; that is a lose-lose situation. We win when we assume responsibility for heritages that are greater than we are. Some things have to be won together.

Humans can and ought to inherit the Earth; we become rich with this inheritance only as we oversee a richness of planetary biodiversity that embraces and transcends us. We are not choosing this inheritance for our happiness, but our happiness is bound up with it. We are in significant part constituted by our ecology. There are essential cultural ingredients to happiness, but they now are conjoined with this ecological birthright, my biophilia. Repudiating the natural world in which we reside, repudiating our ecology, is itself unsatisfying. Not choosing these ecological goods in order to gain authentic happiness, therefore, is a logical, empirical, psychological impossibility.

Read this book. Get the gestalt. If that is not already your conviction, I predict it will be by the time you finish reading!

Holmes Rolston III,
Colorado State University

NOTES

1. Matthew J. Zylstra et al., "Connectedness as a Core Conservation Concern: An Interdisciplinary Review of Theory and a Call for Practice," *Springer Science Reviews* 2, no. 1–2 (December 2014): 119, cited in the Introduction.

2. Arne Naess, "The Shallow and the Deep, Long-Range Ecology Movement. A Summary," *Inquiry* 16, no. 1–4 (1973): 95, cited in the Introduction.

3. Arne Naess, *Ecology, Community and Lifestyle: Outline of an Ecosophy*, trans. and rev. David Rothenberg (Cambridge: Cambridge University Press, 1989), 166, cited in chapter 1, note 24.

4. Arne Naess with Per Ingvar Haukeland, *Life's Philosophy: Reason and Feeling in a Deeper World*, trans. Roland Huntford (Athens: University of Georgia Press, 2002), 114, cited in chapters 1 and 3.

5. Arne Naess, "Self-Realization: An Ecological Approach to Being-in-the-World," in *Deep Ecology for the Twenty-First Century: Readings on the Philosophy and Practice of the New Environmentalism*, ed. George Sessions (Boston: Shambhala, 1995), 239, cited in chapter 1.

6. Naess, *Ecology, Community and Lifestyle*, 175, cited in chapter 1.

7. Arne Naess, "'Here I Stand': An Interview with Arne Naess," interview by Christian Diehm, *Environmental Philosophy* 1, no. 2 (Fall 2004): 9, 14.

8. John Muir, *My First Summer in the Sierra* (Boston: Houghton Mifflin Company, 1911), 211.

Acknowledgments

Work on this book began with a sabbatical leave from my teaching position in the Department of Philosophy at the University of Wisconsin–Stevens Point. I am immensely thankful to the many people who facilitated this extended research period, including my always supportive departmental colleagues, and then-dean of UWSP's College of Letters and Science, the late Chris Cirmo. I am likewise grateful to Kendra Liddicoat and other colleagues in and the Human Dimensions division of UWSP's College of Natural Resources who gave helpful initial direction and provided research leads for several parts of the book. A similar acknowledgment is due to Rob McDonald, lead scientist for The Nature Conservancy's Global Cities program, who oversaw most of the research that went into chapter 4 while I served as a fellow with The Nature Conservancy from 2016 to 2017. Working with Rob and other Conservancy staff expanded the scope of this project significantly, and provided several opportunities to present research to Conservancy administrators and team members, all of which have measurably improved my work. I have also been fortunate to present portions of this project at other venues, including UWSP's "LIFE" program coordinated by Pat and Jim Keir, UWSP's "Faculty Forum" coordinated by Robert Sirabian, and several meetings of the International Society for Environmental Ethics, which have always resulted in productive exchanges. Notable, too, among those who have helped this book come into existence are the many students I have had in recent years, including those who took Advanced Environmental Ethics in the spring of 2018, and those who read several draft chapters of this text as part of their coursework. They gave the kind of feedback that only a lively and passionate group of college students could give. Two other former students, Stacie Brey and Jenika Marion, deserve special credit for first introducing me to the field of conservation psychology and for ultimately catalyzing this entire undertaking. Last, but by no means least, are those people most close who have enabled my work in countless ways, including Grant Diehm, Tianna Kline, and Ann Hanson. Without you none of this would be possible.

Introduction

Connection to Nature and the Enduring Influence of Deep Ecology

A recent review essay titled "Connectedness as a Core Conservation Concern" analyzed over three hundred sources on the subject of human connectedness to nature. The broad array of literature the essay surveyed addressed an equally broad array of questions about this phenomenon, including how to define it, how to promote it, what prevents it, and what, if anything, ultimately results from it. Encapsulating one of the main themes of this substantial collection of research, the review's authors assert that "the Western disconnect from nature is central to the convergent social-ecological crises and is primarily a problem in consciousness." They also claim that connectedness with nature "presents itself as a radical but necessary prerequisite for realizing desired conservation and environmental behavior outcomes."[1]

Such statements capture a number of sentiments that have been voiced with increasing frequency, and intensity, in environmental writing in recent years. Yet the idea that promoting a sense of connection to nature represents a "radical" conservation strategy, or indeed that people could "disconnect" from nature in the first place, might at first sound rather odd. That humans are connected to nature appears to be a truth so self-evident that it would never need saying, and the possibility of forgetting such a basic truth seems too remote to be worth entertaining. Nevertheless, even among social scientists who approach the subject empirically, it is not uncommon to hear it claimed that we would do well to be reminded of this seemingly basic fact about ourselves as the prospect of human-nature disconnection has steadily exited the realm of possibility and entered everyday reality.[2]

How such a disconnect could arise is, to be sure, a matter of some debate. Perhaps it reflects the influence of intellectual traditions that cast us as separate from the natural world. Maybe it is a result of the striking trends toward urbanization and diminished outdoor experience that put into practice what those traditions assert in principle.³ Whatever the reasons might be, growing numbers of environmental advocates are worried that we are losing sight of something fundamental about ourselves, and that this spells trouble for nature.

The current concern about human-nature connectedness that these remarks convey is without a doubt the product of multiple factors, among which would have to be counted early work done in this area by philosophers associated with the "deep ecology" movement. Deep ecology theorists have for a long time argued that our conceptions of ourselves in relation to nature—or whether we really think of our relations to nature at all—are key factors in understanding how we actually end up relating to it. To date, there has been very little discussion of the relevance of deep ecological philosophy to the contemporary conversation about connectedness to nature, or of how this school of thought can be linked to the academic developments that this conversation has sparked.

The primary aim of this book is to forge such links, largely through the pursuit of two related goals. First, it seeks to develop a distinctive interpretation of deep ecological philosophy, one that not only facilitates its integration into current conversations about connectedness to nature, but that also addresses some of its most troubling criticisms. Second, it essays to demonstrate the ways in which deep ecological theory does in fact contribute to these conversations by helping us to understand more precisely what a sense of connection to nature entails, what its attitudinal and behavioral effects might be, and how it might be nurtured and developed. Before embarking upon these tasks, however, it will be helpful to make some initial terminological and conceptual clarifications regarding this area of environmental thinking, and to offer some preliminary comments about why it represents a viable point of departure for an exploration of connection to nature.

DEEP ECOLOGICAL THEORY AND THE DEEP ECOLOGY MOVEMENT

The term "deep ecology" was first introduced by Arne Naess in 1972 in an attempt to characterize what he saw as a distinctive faction emerging within the environmental, or "ecology," movement.⁴ Unlike so-called "shallow" environmentalism—which focused on securing human welfare in affluent countries—Naess argued that a newer "deep" ecology movement had appeared, one that embraced far more sweeping values of diversity, complexity, political decentralization, and the equality of human and nonhuman beings. First among this new movement's distinguishing features, however, was a "[r]ejection of the man-in-environment image in favour of *the relational, total-field image*."⁵ The core of this competing image, Naess went on to explain, is the idea that relations with nature are an essential part of what it means to be human, or are a part of our "basic constitutions" as human beings.[6] In his estimation, then, one of the most notable characteristics of this novel sort of ecological advocacy was its acceptance of a thoroughly interrelational understanding of human existence, a nondualistic view of ourselves as inextricably connected to, rather than separate from, the more-than-human world around us.

As thinkers like Naess continued to develop the theoretical aspects of this unique type of environmentalism, they also began to distinguish more carefully between the beliefs held in common by its advocates, and the idiosyncratic views, or "ecosophies," of the theorists and activists affiliated with it.[7] Deep ecology's supporters, they stressed, were united not by their adherence to any particular philosophical outlook, but by their commitment to certain general ideals that were potentially compatible with any number of more basic theoretical commitments. What they argued, in other words, is that "deep ecology" is not so much an ideology as it is an ideologically pluralistic social and political *movement*, one with "multiple roots" instead of a singular unified conceptual foundation.[8]

In this way, early deep ecology theorists came to conclude that the real "heart" of deep ecology is a conceptually midrange assortment of values, policy positions, and lifestyle principles that its supporters tend to hold, principles that are distinct from whatever more logically foundational beliefs they might otherwise espouse.[9] And while the question of what exactly these midrange principles are has been subject to debate, most deep ecology supporters seem to accept the collection first assembled by Naess and George Sessions in 1984.[10] This eight-point "platform" of the deep ecology movement appears in slightly modified forms throughout the deep ecology literature, but originally included the following:

1. The well-being and flourishing of human and nonhuman life on Earth have value in themselves (synonyms: inherent worth, intrinsic value, inherent value). These values are independent of the usefulness of the nonhuman world for human purposes.
2. Richness and diversity of life forms contribute to the realization of these values and are also values in themselves.
3. Humans have no right to reduce this richness and diversity except to satisfy vital needs.
4. Present human interference with the nonhuman world is excessive, and the situation is rapidly worsening.
5. The flourishing of human life and cultures is compatible with a substantial decrease of the human population. The flourishing of nonhuman life requires such a decrease.

6. Policies must therefore be changed. The changes in policies affect basic economic, technological, and ideological structures. The resulting state of affairs will be deeply different from the present.
7. The ideological change is mainly that of appreciating life quality (dwelling in situations of inherent worth) rather than adhering to an increasingly higher standard of living. There will be a profound awareness of the difference between big and great.
8. Those who subscribe to the foregoing points have an obligation directly or indirectly to participate in the attempt to implement the necessary changes.[11]

Not surprisingly, environmental theorists have had much to say about these eight points. What is most important for our purposes, though, is the way in which they differ from the characterization of deep ecology that Naess first offered in 1972. Specifically, nowhere in any of the platform statements does one find mention of the "relational, total-field image" that figured so prominently in Naess's earlier account of "deep" versus "shallow" ecologies. This notable difference has led commentators like Frederic Bender to claim, correctly it seems, that the eight-point platform "decouples deep ecology from nondualism."[12] The 1984 platform formulation omits assertions of human-nature connectedness from the cluster of principles said to define the deep ecology movement, and relocates them within the more particular viewpoints of those theorists who happen to embrace them. The net effect, then, of casting the platform in this defining role is that it forces the conclusion that it is inaccurate to describe deep ecology as a position emphasizing a relational view of human beings, or that includes any special concern about human connectedness to nature.[13]

But while it may be that, properly speaking, the heart of the deep ecology movement is the eight-point platform, it is still the case that at the heart of Naess's own view—dubbed "ecosophy T"[14]—there remains a deep affirmation of human-nature connectedness of precisely the sort he described in the 1970s. Indeed, Naess's environmental thought has always expressed serious apprehension about human disconnection, or "alienation," from nature, and it has always placed a corresponding emphasis on the root importance of human-nature bonding, or "identification" with the natural world.[15] Moreover, although Naess himself would be the first to point out that his own philosophical outlook is not equivalent to deep ecology per se, it is nevertheless true that the central features of his ecosophy have been adopted by many (arguably most) leading deep ecology theorists. In fact, there is such a high degree of conceptual convergence among theorists in the deep ecology movement that a number of commentators have argued, against some deep ecologists' objections, that "deep ecology" does refer to a relatively well-defined theoretical position, the main features of which are those that, not coincidentally, were first articulated by Naess.[16]

There is a sense, therefore, in which it is correct to say that deep ecology has no stated position on the subject of connection to nature. In another sense, however, claims to this effect are misleading, since connectedness to nature is one of the most prominent themes in the work of many of the deep ecology movement's most prominent intellectual figures. Deep ecological *theory* undoubtedly does stress human–nature connectedness, even if the *platform* does not, and the theoretical explorations of this phenomenon by academically oriented deep ecology advocates began well before contemporary interest in this subject fully blossomed.

Hence while it is important not to conflate the deep ecology movement with the work of individual deep ecology theorists, it is equally important not to ignore these theorists' collective focus on human-nature bonding and interdependence, or the collective contributions they are able to make to discourses of human-nature connectedness. It is with this understanding, then, and in the spirit of these latter recommendations, that the present investigation intends to take up with the work of theorists in the deep ecology movement. A relational outlook on humans and nature is precisely what animates the writings of many deep ecology theorists, and it is precisely this dimension of deep ecological thought that brings it into such close association with the contemporary conversation about connectedness to nature.

THE DEATH OF DEEP ECOLOGY?

One of the most substantial preliminary challenges faced by the project proposed here is that, despite the genuine thematic affinities just highlighted, the status of deep ecological thought among environmental activists and academics has waned significantly in recent years. Perhaps the clearest indication of this is in a 2014 special issue of *The Trumpeter*, a journal with close ties to the deep ecology movement and a reputation as a leading forum for explorations of deep ecological theory and practice.[17] The special issue's call for papers noted the current perception within environmental circles that deep ecology has "dissipated as a force of environmental theory in the 21st century." Prospective contributors were thus asked straightforwardly, "So whatever happened to deep ecology? Is it dead?"[18]

Although the authors who wrote in response to these prompts offered a range of more or less supportive remarks, present consensus among academics seems to be that the answer to the second of these questions could be, at best, only a weakly qualified yes. Kate Booth, for example, whose own work is quite sympathetic to that of deep ecology theorists, wrote in her entry on "Deep Ecology" in 2018's *Encyclopedia of Global Environmental Governance and Politics* that:

> It is fair to say that deep ecology's heyday is well and truly past and it is possible to dismiss it as a small and largely irrelevant blip in western environmental thought. The baton of its core thinkers has not been passed onto a new generation and the profile of deep ecological writings has diminished. Its critics have moved onto other things, and deep ecology, if referenced at all, is skated over as an example of a problematic relic of western modernity.[19]

Expressing roughly the same sentiment, David Keller's entry on deep ecology in 2008's *Encyclopedia of Environmental Ethics and Philosophy* cites the extensive criticisms to which deep ecologists' work has been subjected, and claims that "together, these various critiques have contributed to a significant consensus that Deep Ecology has reached its logical conclusion and has exhausted itself."[20]

Of course, it is possible that these comments overstate the case against deep ecology to some degree, as the tremendous influence that it had at the end of the twentieth century has not dissipated entirely, and discussions of deep ecology do still regularly appear in a variety of academic and popular venues.[21] A 2015 study of environmentally active students in Australia, for example, investigated whether or not their outlooks resonated with the major themes of deep ecological thought, and reported affirmatively that "secondary school students in environmental clubs align with the principles of deep ecology."[22] Consistent with this finding, Md. Munir Hossain Talukder's 2018 book *Nature and Life: Essays on Deep Ecology and Applied Ethics* opens by saying that "many environmental organizations and activists find the deep ecological approach worthwhile,"[23] and later adds that the notion of identification with nature that appears in much deep ecological literature "deserves special consideration to overcome the ecological crisis."[24] Even more recently, scientists Nathan Lima and Cristiano Moura, citing the need for people "to connect with other beings," have called for science educators to find ways to transition "science education into deep ecological education."[25]

At the very least, such ongoing efforts across multiple disciplines signal what Keller aptly describes as deep ecology's "enduring influence and importance."[26] Yet, these signals aside, it is undeniable that deep ecology's place in environmental thought has become harder to discern in the past few decades. By all accounts, interest in and attention to the deep ecology movement have noticeably declined. Somewhat curiously, though, these declines have occurred at the same time as interest in the subject of connection to nature that is so central to deep ecological philosophy has steadily grown. Truly, as our opening comments have already indicated, this growth has been so pronounced that connectedness to nature can now rightly be counted as one of the dominant concerns of contemporary conservationists. But how might this peculiar circumstance be explained?

One of the answers to this question, I think, and certainly one of the beliefs that animates the present inquiry, is that concentrated attention on the major themes of deep ecological philosophy has shifted, somewhat quietly, into fields other than philosophy. That this would occur is, to be sure, nothing startling. As Booth has observed, "Many of the ideas core to deep ecology have emerged and evolved in parallel to deep ecology, in other fields," and thus she herself contends that deep ecology "can be understood as part of a significant cultural shift that continues to unfold in more robust and nuanced ways."[27] A similar sort of unfolding seems to be what the editors of the special issue of *The Trumpeter* had in view when, in their call for papers, they asked not only if deep ecology was "dead," but if it might have been "transformed and dispersed into other branches of environmental theory."[28]

Precisely what disciplinary transformations deep ecological thought might be undergoing, or where the cultural shifts it has contributed to are taking place, are open to discussion. It is clear, however, that a tremendous amount of research in what some scholars now call the "conservation social sciences"[29]—including especially environmental psychology, environmental sociology, and environmental education—overlaps substantially with the philosophical work done by Naess and other deep ecology theorists. It is certain, too, that some of this overlap is indebted, in one way or another, to the groundwork these philosophical theorists first laid. Social scientists Paul Stern and Thomas Dietz, for instance, explicitly acknowledge Naess, Sessions, and Bill Devall in their attempts to study what they label, following deep ecologists, people's "biospheric" value orientations.[30] In like fashion, psychologists Elizabeth Nisbet, John Zelenski, and Steven Murphy cite Naess as an important influence on their creation of the "Nature Relatedness Scale," a tool that many researchers use today to measure people's degree of felt connection to the natural world.[31]

This cross-disciplinary influence is a promising indicator of deep ecology's continuing vitality in various contemporary fields of environmental research. But the integration of deep ecological theory into these fields, as well as the integration of these research areas into philosophical treatments of deep ecological thought, are to date incomplete. Researchers outside of philosophy most often do not attend to the details of deep ecological theorizing, and philosophical treatments of deep ecology have not yet seriously engaged with the work being conducted in the conservation social sciences.[32] What is required, therefore, is a more synthetic project than has so far been attempted, one that proceeds not only with an eye to deep ecological philosophy, but also with an understanding of research being conducted in those fields in which its principal themes are now most actively investigated.

This book makes an attempt at exactly the sort of integrative project just described. Although its approach is primarily philosophical and grounded in a careful reading of the works of deep ecology theorists, it is also closely informed by, and engages at length with, work being done in the conservation social sciences. Proceeding in this fashion, its chapters collectively present the argument that a sense of connection to nature is indeed more important than many academics, conservationists, and environmental advocates might previously have realized, and that deep ecological thought has much to add to the increasingly pressing conversations about it.

PLAN OF THE BOOK

The theoretical foundations of the argument to follow are presented in chapter 1. This chapter provides a detailed review of the concepts of Self-realization and identification with nature as they have been articulated in the works of deep ecology theorists, and distinguishes between two types of identification that can be discerned therein. These I refer to as "identification-as-belonging" and "identification-as-kinship," neither of which are typically distinguished in deep ecological literature, and both of which typically appear in conjunction with the notion of Self-realization. Against the most common criticism of deep ecological thought—namely, that it relies on an egoist moral psychology and supports only some variant of anthropocentric environmental ethics—it is argued that while deep ecological theory can indeed be construed in this way, it can also be interpreted along lines that are much more other-oriented than this. The contention is also made, however, that the basis of this perennial criticism of deep ecological thought is the commitment many theorists make to the norm of Self-realization, and that keeping these alternative lines of interpretation open therefore requires refraining from that commitment. Accordingly, subsequent chapters shift attention away from a discussion of Self-realization and onto what deep ecology theorists have had to say about identification with, or connectedness to, nature.

Chapter 2 begins the work of bringing deep ecological philosophy into dialogue with conservation social science. Focusing on the field of "conservation psychology," it explains the conceptual overlap between deep ecologists' ideas about identification with nature and social scientists' concepts of "place attachment" and "environmental identity." After showing how research into the pro-environmental effects of both of the latter constructs largely confirms what deep ecology theorists hypothesize about identification, it demonstrates how work in the social sciences also contributes to the resolution of two of the most significant philosophical problems deep ecology theorists have faced regarding their views on human-nature connectedness. This latter portion of the chapter involves a discussion of the ways in which the findings of social scientists indicate that connectedness to nature is not inevitably linked to an ethic of self-interest, and that personal forms of connection to nature ought not to be disparaged in favor of an emphasis on transpersonal ones.

Chapter 3 offers an extended analysis of the relationship between identification with nature and environmental values. It first explains how the process of identification-as-kinship tends to promote value orientations that are not only nonanthropocentric, but also individualistic. It then discusses the issue of "moral extensionism" in environmental ethics, and contends that the kinship-based view that emerges from deep ecological theorizing does not necessarily run afoul of critiques of extensionist thinking as some environmental philosophers might be inclined to believe. Next it examines the process of identification-as-belonging, and claims that this process, unlike kinship-identification, tends to promote nonanthropocentric outlooks that are holistic, or that emphasize the intrinsic value of ecological collectives. It also considers the concern that deep ecological notions of belonging promote forms of holism that are reductive of difference, and argues that Naess's thought offers a model of self-other relations that is sensitive both to the limits of the Self and to the relative distinctness of others. The chapter concludes by arguing against an objection to the notion of intrinsic value that might be thought to apply to the analysis it provides, and by defending the phenomenon of identification from the criticism that is not a valid source of belief in nature's intrinsic value.

It is worth noting here that while chapter 3 engages with one of the most widely debated topics in environmental philosophy, it differs from the approach to this topic most commonly taken by environmental ethicists. In keeping with the style of Naess and other deep ecology theorists, as well as the approach typical of the social sciences, its primary focus is not on prescribing the particular value orientations it discusses. Rather, it seeks to highlight one of the background conditions—that is, people's sense of connection to nature—that promotes and lends intelligibility to the environmental values people adopt, and to explain the relationship between this background condition and some of the different value orientations environmental ethicists have articulated.

While chapters 2 and 3 deal with the behavioral and attitudinal *effects* of connectedness to nature, chapter 4 investigates one of its potential *sources*, and it begins with a review of what is known as "significant life experiences" research. This body of literature reveals the influential role that outdoor experience has tended to play in the life-paths of many dedicated conservationists, and provides insight into some of the features that such experience typically displays. This chapter also enlists the work of conservation psychologists to show that part of the reason why outdoor experience has such influence is that it promotes connectedness to nature, thus illuminating a link between outdoor experience, connection to nature, and pro-environmental behavior. The discussion then turns to the writings of deep ecology theorists, and shows that much of what these theorists have written about the role and significance of time outdoors compares favorably to the available social scientific research. It also reviews one of the most robust critiques of deep ecologists' ideas about nature experience, and argues that deep ecological thought is not committed to an ideal of the outdoors as rugged, rural, and elitist, but rather to the belief that time outdoors is a pathway both to greater connection to nature, and to the view that environmentalists ought to work toward greater access to nature for increasingly urban human populations.

Chapter 5 compares and contrasts the work of deep ecology theorists with the "biophilia hypothesis" as it is developed in the work of Stephen R. Kellert. Following an overview of Kellert's distinctive version of the biophilia hypothesis, the chapter describes how deep ecological and biophilic theories converge on their mutual affirmation of the import of human connectedness to, and contact with, nature. It notes, however, that these schools of thought diverge insofar as deep ecologists stress connectedness to nature in conjunction with nonanthropocentric environmental ethics while Kellert frames it as the basis of biophilic anthropocentrism. It argues that even though Kellert is right to encourage deep ecologists and other environmental advocates to pay greater attention to the therapeutic and restorative benefits of time in nature, his adoption of anthropocentric ethics is problematic. It then makes the case that Kellert's writing actually undergirds nonanthropocentric views more so than anthropocentric ones, that the analyses of deep ecological thought in previous chapters help reveal why Kellert himself misses this conclusion, and that biophilic thought should indeed pivot in the nonanthropocentric direction that deep ecology theorists presumably would usher it. The chapter concludes with a defense of the preceding analysis from Kellert's own pragmatically inspired objection to it, arguing that the nonanthropocentric outlooks that tend to be promoted by feelings of connection to nature are as pragmatically effective, if not more so, than any others.

NOTES

1. Matthew J. Zylstra et al., "Connectedness as a Core Conservation Concern: An Interdisciplinary Review of Theory and a Call for Practice," *Springer Science Reviews* 2, no. 1–2 (December 2014): 119.

2. For a recent example of such research, see Ansgar Johannes Gräntzdörffer, Angela James, and Doris Elster, "Exploring Human-Nature Relationships amongst Young People: Findings of a Quantitative Survey between Germany and South Africa," *International Journal of Environmental and Science Education* 14, no. 7 (2019): 417–24. Further discussion of social scientific analyses of connection to nature is provided in chapter 2.

3. Discussions of these issues are found in Christopher D. Ives et al., "Reconnecting with Nature for Sustainability," *Sustainability Science* 13, no. 5 (2018): 1389–97; James R. Miller, "Biodiversity Conservation and the Extinction of Experience," *Trends in Ecology and Evolution* 20, no. 8 (August 2005): 430–4; Val Plumwood, *Feminism and the Mastery of Nature* (London: Routledge, 1993); Carolyn Merchant, *The Death of Nature: Women, Ecology and the Scientific Revolution* (San Francisco: Harper, 1983); Lynn Townsend White, Jr., "The Historical Roots of Our Ecologic Crisis," *Science* 155 (1967): 1203–7.

4. Arne Naess, "The Shallow and the Deep, Long-Range Ecology Movement. A Summary," *Inquiry* 16, no. 1–4 (1973): 95–100. Though this essay appeared in 1973, as Naess explains on p. 95, it is based on a lecture he delivered in Budapest in 1972.

5. Ibid., 95.

6. Ibid.

7. Naess's "The Shallow and the Deep" gestures toward this distinction, but does not develop it in the sort of explicit detail that is characteristic of later discussions of the deep ecology platform. The term "ecosophy" appears in this essay on p. 99.

8. Naess has discussed this point in numerous publications. One of his early articulations of it is found in "The Deep Ecological Movement: Some Philosophical Aspects," *Inquiry* 8, no. 1–2 (1986): 10–31.

9. See Andrew McLaughlin, "The Heart of Deep Ecology," in *Deep Ecology for the Twenty-First Century: Readings on the Philosophy and Practice of the New Environmentalism*, ed. George Sessions (Boston: Shambhala, 1995), 85–93.

10. George Sessions, "Basic Principles of Deep Ecology," *Ecophilosophy* VI (May 1984): 5.

11. Arne Naess, "The Deep Ecological Movement," 14.

12. Frederic L. Bender, *The Culture of Extinction: Toward a Philosophy of Deep Ecology* (Amherst: Humanity Books, 2003), 408, 448.

13. Bender's response to this issue is to suggest a revision to the platform, as he explains in *The Culture of Extinction*, 445–50.

14. Arne Naess, *Ecology, Community and Lifestyle: Outline of an Ecosophy*, trans. and rev. David Rothenberg (Cambridge: Cambridge University Press, 1989).

15. These are constant themes across much of Naess' published work, but receive some of their most well-known treatments in "Identification as a Source of Deep Ecological Attitudes," in *Deep Ecology*, ed. Michael Tobias (San Diego: Avant Books. 1985), 256–70; "Self-Realization: An Ecological Approach to Being-in-the-World," in *Deep Ecology for the Twenty-First Century*, 225–39; and *Ecology Community and Lifestyle*.

16. Warwick Fox, for example, believes that Naess's ecosophy "constitutes the most interesting and significant" way in which one could characterize deep ecology,

and that, from a conceptual or theoretical standpoint, it is precisely a commitment to Naess's philosophical approach that "distinguishes deep ecologists from other ecophilosophers" (Warwick Fox, *Toward a Transpersonal Ecology: Developing New Foundations for Environmentalism* [Albany: State University of New York Press, 1995], 145). See also Eric Katz, Andrew Light, and David Rothenberg, "Deep Ecology as Philosophy," introduction to *Beneath the Surface: Critical Essays in the Philosophy of Deep Ecology*, ed. Eric Katz, Andrew Light, and David Rothenberg (Cambridge: The MIT Press. 2000), ix–xxiv.

17. See Home Page, *The Trumpeter*, accessed December 26, 2019, http://trumpeter.athabascau.ca/index.php/trumpet.

18. "CFP—Whatever Happened to Deep Ecology?," International Society for Environmental Ethics, accessed December 2, 2019, https://enviroethics.org/2014/03/28/cfp-whatever-happened-to-deep-ecology/. For further discussion of the theme of the special issue, see Nathan Kowalsky, "Whatever Happened to Deep Ecology?," *The Trumpeter* 30, no. 2 (2014): 95–100.

19. Kate Booth, "Deep Ecology," in *Encyclopedia of Global Environmental Governance and Politics*, ed. Philipp H. Pattberg and Fariborz Zelli (Northhampton, MA: Edward Elgar Publishing, 2015), 92.

20. David Keller, "Deep Ecology," in *Encyclopedia of Environmental Ethics and Philosophy*, vol. 1, ed. J. Baird Callicott and Robert Frodeman (Detroit: Macmillan Reference USA, 2009), 210.

21. In addition to the sources cited below, recent treatments of deep ecological thought include Cary L. Klemmer and Kathleen A. McNamara, "Deep Ecology and Ecofeminism: Social Work to Address Global Environmental Crisis," *Affilia: Journal of Women and Social Work* (2019): 1–13, https://doi.org/10.1177/0886109919894650 ; Richa Bhardwaj, "Deep Ecology: Origins, Influences and Relevance," *Writers Editors Critics* 9, no. 1 (March 2019): 65–71; Knut J. Ims, "Quality of Life in a Deep Ecological Perspective: The Need for a Transformation of the Western Mindset?," *Society and Economy* 40, no. 4 (2018): 531–52; Teea Kortetmäki, "Is Broad the New Deep in Environmental Ethics?: A Comparison of Broad Ecological Justice and Deep Ecology," *Ethics and the Environment* 21, no. 1 (Spring 2016): 89–108; Tony Lynch and Stephen Norris, "On the Enduring Importance of Deep Ecology," *Environmental Ethics* 38, no. 2 (Spring 2016): 63–75; Helen Kopnina and Brett Cherniakdoi, "Cultivating a Value for Non-Human Interests through the Convergence of Animal Welfare, Animal Rights, and Deep Ecology in Environmental Education," *Education Sciences* 5 (2015): 363–79, https://doi.org/10.3390/educsci5040363.

22. Annette Gough and William Smith, "Deep Ecology as a Framework for Student Eco-Philosophical Thinking," *Journal of Philosophy in Schools* 2, no. 1 (2015): 38.

23. Md. Munir Hossain Talukder, *Nature and Life: Essays on Deep Ecology and Applied Ethics* (Newcastle upon Tyne: Cambridge Scholars Publishing, 2018), xi.

24. Ibid., 31.

25. Nathan Willig Lima and Cristiano Moura, "Stop Teaching Science: A Philosophical Framework to Depart from Science Education into Deep Ecological Education," in *Re-Introducing Science: Sculpting the Image of Science for Education*

and Media in Its Historical and Philosophical Background, ed. Fanny Seroglou and Vassilis Koulountzos (Proceedings of the 15th International History, Philosophy and Science Teaching Conference, July 15–19, 2019), 7.

26. Keller, "Deep Ecology," 210.

27. Booth, "Deep Ecology," 92.

28. "CFP—Whatever Happened to Deep Ecology?," International Society for Environmental Ethics.

29. Nathan J. Bennett and Robin Roth, eds., *The Conservation Social Sciences: What?, How? and Why?* (Vancouver, BC: Canadian Wildlife Federation and Institute for Resources, Environment and Sustainability, University of British Columbia, 2015).

30. Paul C. Stern and Thomas Dietz, "The Value Basis of Environmental Concern," *Journal of Social Issues* 50, no. 3 (1994): 70.

31. Elizabeth K. Nisbet, John M. Zelenski, and Steven A. Murphy, "The Nature Relatedness Scale: Linking Individuals' Connection with Nature to Environmental Concern and Behavior," *Environment and Behavior* 41, no. 5 (2009): 715–40.

32. For an example of one of the integrative attempts coming from the social sciences, see Elizabeth Ann Bragg, "Towards Ecological Self: Deep Ecology Meets Constructionist Self-Theory," *Journal of Environmental Psychology* 16, no. 2 (1996): 93–108.

Chapter 1

Self-Realization and Identification with Nature

When Norwegian philosopher Arne Naess first introduced the term "deep ecology" to the academic world, he did so with reference to what he called the "relational, total-field" view of human existence. His point, in short, was that deep ecology advocates do not typically operate on the belief that humans and other organisms are utterly independent sorts of things. Their tendency, instead, is to regard all organisms, including we human ones, as "knots in the biospherical net or field of intrinsic relations."[1] What Naess proposed, in other words, was that among the more notable features of this "deeper" sort of environmentalism was an equally deep sensibility about the connectedness of humans and nature.

In keeping with Naess's estimation, Joanna Macy and Molly Brown later wrote that deep ecology, viewed both as an activist movement and an intellectual undertaking, arose from the perceived need to explore the question, "What does it mean or matter to be interdependent with all Earthly life?"[2] And although no mention of such interdependence appears in the deep ecology platform as Naess and George Sessions eventually came to formulate it in the 1980s, it is undoubtedly true that questions of human-nature connectedness have always been prominent in the theoretical explorations of deep ecology's supporters. The theme of human-nature connection is so pervasive in deep ecological literature, in fact, that some scholars argue that it ought to be regarded as one of the defining features of the deep ecology perspective, and included among its platform principles.[3] But why, exactly, do deep ecology theorists place such emphasis on this particular issue, and what, precisely, do they propose regarding it?

To answer these questions requires examining the eco-philosophies, or "ecosophies," of deep ecology supporters, many of which are deliberately styled after the position first articulated by Naess.[4] Naess's writing in this area is both prolific and widely discussed, yet understanding his "ecosophy T," as well as the roles that its core concepts play in the writings of other deep ecology theorists, is no easy task.[5] In this chapter, therefore, we set out to explore this challenging territory, focusing on the notions of "Self-realization" and "identification" with nature. In doing so, we will be attempting not only to clarify these two key ideas that have been so crucial to the intellectual development of the deep ecology movement, but also to explain in a preliminary way how we ourselves intend to make use of them going forward.

SELF-REALIZATION

The clearest evidence of the significance of the idea of Self-realization in Naess's thinking is that it serves as the "ultimate norm" of ecosophy T.[6] That it is a "norm" means, of course, that its primary function is prescriptive, or that it entails a value judgment about what it is that humans ought to do. That it is an "ultimate" norm indicates that, although it helps to ground other prescriptions Naess makes, it is not itself derived from any deeper or logically more basic premises.[7] For Naess, Self-realization is a genuinely foundational principle, the truth of which rests on a "rock bottom" intuition of its fundamental import.[8]

While many factors contributed to Naess's adoption of Self-realization as such a principle, his nearest intellectual influences in this regard were Mahatma Gandhi, Baruch Spinoza, and the teachings of certain eastern religious traditions.[9] The term "Self-realization" is in fact borrowed from Gandhi, and Naess's 1974 text *Gandhi and Group Conflict* presents Gandhi's outlook in a manner nearly identical to his own subsequent formulations of ecosophy T.[10] Yet despite this debt to Gandhi, Naess typically attributes his conception of Self-realization to Spinoza.[11] Just one year after his book on Gandhi appeared, he published a study of Spinoza that links the idea of Self-realization to Spinoza's notion of *conatus* or "striving."[12] This link, which Naess routinely makes elsewhere in his writings, is asserted unequivocally in *Ecology, Community and Lifestyle*, where he says that "[h]istorically, I trace the conception [of Self-realization] back to Spinoza's *perseverare in suo esse*, to persevere in one's own (way of) being."[13]

What, then, does Naess take Self-realization to be? To begin, it is evident that he does not interpret it in some minimalistic way as a bare effort to remain alive, or as a stark "struggle for existence." Instead, he sees it as a developmental process that, while not exclusive of self-preservation, also goes well beyond it. As he explains:

> The traditional way of expressing what is common to all species of life, is to point to a basic striving, that of self-preservation. This term is misleading,

however, in so far as it does not account for the dynamics of expansion and modification. There is a tendency to realize *every* possibility for development, to explore all possibilities of change within the framework of the species and even to transgress its limits.[14]

The equation here of Self-realization with a "tendency to realize *every* possibility for development" is illuminating, and helps to clarify why Naess also sometimes characterizes it as a movement toward "perfection."[15] Both comments indicate that Self-realization involves the increasing development, enhancement, or improvement of a being in all of the dimensions of existence that are available and most essential to it. For this reason it could alternatively be referred to as Self-*actualization*, since this term, too, conveys the crucial point which is that Naess envisions Self-realization as a matter of seizing upon existential potential and making it actual, or "getting out what is latent in the nature of a being."[16] As he sums it up, "'[r]ealizing inherent potentialities' is one of the good, less-than-ten-word, clarifications of 'self-realization'."[17]

These comments already indicate that Naess thinks of Self-realization not only as something for which humans ought to strive, but also as something toward which we (and other beings) are naturally so inclined. The problem that quickly arises, though, is that even if we can be said to have such an inclination, how we conceive of ourselves, and what we take our full potential to be, can be distorted or skewed in any number of ways. "The concept of self-realization," Naess readily admits, "as dependent upon insight into our own potentialities, makes it easy to see the possibilities of ignorance and misunderstanding in terms of what these potentialities are."[18]

In particular, Naess expresses concern about what he calls the "'ego-trip' interpretation" of Self-realization that he and many other deep ecology supporters think predominates in the West.[19] Underlying this view is what we might call an "ontologically isolationist" vision of who and what we are, a kind of "skin-in" account of ourselves as entities fundamentally discrete, separate, or detached from others. It is premised, that is, upon an extremely narrow, highly individualistic or atomistic conception of humans as beings whose basic characters, needs, and interests make no essential reference to realties regarded as "external" to ourselves. To encourage people to "actualize themselves" in this context would seem, therefore, to amount to nothing more than promoting a narcissistic focus on each person's exclusive drives, desires, and achievements. As Naess is keenly aware, "[i]n the prevalent individualistic and utilitarian political thinking in Western industrial states, the terms 'self-realisation,' 'self-expression,' 'self-interest' are used for . . . 'ego-realisation.' One stresses the ultimate and extensive incompatibility of the interests of different individuals."[20]

The main flaw Naess finds in this position is that its view of Self-realization is obstructed by an exceedingly limited estimation of the true range of human potential. Drawing on models in the social sciences, he posits that there are actually three increasingly inclusive areas of human identity, including the "ego," the "social self," and the "ecological Self."[21] Whereas the "ego" correlates with the narrow, individualistic aspects of self just described, the "social" and "ecological" dimensions of ourselves are inextricably relational, and have to do with our inherent ties to other people and to the natural world, respectively. Of course, Naess takes the latter, ecological aspect of Selfhood to be the most comprehensive (as indicated by the capital "S"), and although he believes that traditionally our developmental ideals have "largely ignored" this area of human existence, in ecosophy T it is brought to the fore. "We may be said," he writes, "to be in, and of, Nature from the very beginning of our selves. Society and human relationships are important, but our self is much richer in its constitutive relationships."[22]

Hence, in sharp contrast to an individualistic, ego-centered view of humans, Naess holds that our connections with others, both human and other-than-human, can and do comprise core dimensions of our Selves. Consequently, while he does not deny that we have certain idiosyncratic aspects or individualized needs, he also contends that to think that our existential potential, and thus our Self-realization, begins and ends with this "presupposes a major underestimation of the richness and broadness of our potentialities."[23] Humans, he says, "are the first kind of living beings we know of which have the potentialities of living in community with all other living beings. It is our hope that these potentialities will be realized."[24]

Thus it is that by positing a wide and comprehensive model of Self that Naess is able to argue for a wide and inclusive conception of Self-realization. If we are, in our very being, socially and ecologically relational, then we cannot view the actualization of our potentials as taking place in isolation from, or solely in competition with, the like actualization of potential in human and other-than-human others. To take such a stance would be, in a word, Self-defeating, since it would be to ignore the ways in which the flourishing of others is requisite for our own ability to thrive in the relational aspects of our Selves. Like Gandhi, then, whose emphasis on Self-realization combined with his "metaphysical postulate announcing the essential or ultimate oneness of all living beings"[25] implies that "[o]ne's own self-realization must therefore somehow include that of others,"[26] Naess holds that our Self-realization, rather than being exclusive of others', is instead thoroughly reliant upon them. There is always, he says, a "dependency of A's Self-realisation upon B's,"[27] a situation wherein "[o]ur self-realization is hindered if the self-realization of others . . . is hindered."[28]

IDENTIFICATION WITH NATURE

It remains, however, that when Naess raises the possibility of people misconstruing their existential potential, or mistakenly thinking that the norm of Self-realization licenses ego-trips, he touches on an issue of tremendous import for theorists in the deep ecology movement. Simply establishing that social and ecological relations constitute vital aspects of human life does not, in itself, guarantee that people will acknowledge these dimensions of themselves, or factor them into their attempts at Self-realization. Precisely because of this, therefore, these theorists often take it as a crucial task to encourage people to expand their awareness of the networks of relationships in which they exist, or an awareness of their connectedness to nature. Deep ecology theorists think it is imperative, in other words, that people develop an "ecological consciousness," and they often describe this in terms of what Naess calls "identification" with nature.[29]

Identification thus stands as the counter to "alienation" from nature, that pernicious failure to appreciate the degree to which we are related to or bound up with entities in the more-than-human world. The difficulty here, though, is that supporters of the deep ecology movement do not always understand this failure, or how identification serves to correct it, in exactly the same ways. In what follows, then, we will examine two different forms of identification that deep ecology theorists have articulated by seeking to comprehend not only what each entails, but also how, ultimately, each relates back to the norm of Self-realization.[30]

Identification-as-Belonging

When many theorists in the deep ecology movement discuss identification with nature, they contrast it with viewpoints that, in one way or another, set humans *apart from* the natural world. Ecologist Christopher Uhl, for example, in his book *Developing Ecological Consciousness*, says that many of our traditional Western notions about humans foster in us a "separation consciousness,"[31] meaning that they promote an overarching perception of ourselves as beings who are fundamentally disconnected from nature and ontologically discrete entities who stand outside and above more encompassing biospheric or ecological realities. Such "dysfunctional notions of self and false ideas about humanity's place in the order of things"[32] as Frederic Bender calls them, draw sharp boundaries between humans and nature, and assert that we *Homo sapiens* are, at bottom, misfits in a natural or material world to which we do not really belong.[33]

These sorts of dualistic, basically "separatist" viewpoints thus depict humans as existentially homeless, alien, and out of place on planet Earth.

Yet as ecologically disorienting as these pictures of ourselves surely are, they are just as surely not the only ones possible, and deep ecology theorists argue that they can be righted through a process of identification with nature. Accordingly, this process is said to require cultivating a sense of ourselves as beings thoroughly immersed in and essentially related to the environing natural world, resulting in a sense that we are not ecological outsiders, and are products of and participants in an ecological realm that grounds us and continually shapes who we are. In short, to identify with nature in this way entails developing a sense of *belonging to* or *community with* the more-than-human world, and, therefore, it can be called "identification-as-belonging."[34]

Analyses of the kind of ecological sensibility just described are not hard to come by in the literature of the deep ecology movement. The remarks by Naess at the opening of this chapter indicate a conception of humans as "knots in the biospherical net or field of intrinsic relations."[35] Warwick Fox, drawing on the image of the "tree of life," succinctly expresses what identification-as-belonging involves when he says that to identify widely with nature is to come to a "deep-seated realization that we and all other entities are aspects of a single unfolding reality."[36] Uhl, like Fox, encourages us to recognize that "[o]ur species, *Homo sapiens*, represents one bud on one branch" of the tree of life.[37] "This profound revelation," he says, "that we are not separate from, but part of, life's web . . . has the capacity to awaken us to our true place in the Earth community."[38]

Freya Mathews encapsulates these ideas by saying that most deep ecology theorists subscribe to an "interconnectedness thesis," and it is no coincidence that in advancing this thesis many contend that their relational ontology is more in keeping with contemporary science—especially the science of ecology—than is our traditional, individualistic one.[39] As J. Baird Callicott has explained, scientific ecologists variously portray natural systems as food chains, trophic webs, communities of life, or streams of energy flowing through organisms; in doing so they make use of, and lend some degree of scientific credibility to, the broader notions of interconnectedness, interdependence, and the relational character of things.[40] Scientific ecology has developed these themes so effectively, in fact, that in their seminal text *Deep Ecology: Living as if Nature Mattered* Bill Devall and George Sessions cite it as one of the principal wellsprings of ecological consciousness in the West. "The major contribution of the science of ecology to deep ecology," they write, "has been the rediscovery within the modern scientific context that everything is connected to everything else."[41]

Hence it may be that ecological science offers one of the most coherent explanations of the sort of perspective deep ecology theorists are advocating when they advocate identification-as-belonging. Nevertheless, identification is typically thought to require something beyond just an intellectual acceptance of certain scientific facts about ourselves. More than this, it requires an existential affirmation of who we are, a felt commitment to the truth that we are essentially ecological entities. In Uhl's words, "it is not sufficient to understand, intellectually, our connectedness to Earth; we have to live this relationship, experience it, embody it."[42] Consequently, while the findings of ecologists and other scientists are often said to be able to help motivate or validate identification with nature, these findings are not necessarily regarded as its sole or primary source.[43]

By way of a general summary, then, we could say that to achieve a sense of identification-as-belonging is to come to the lived awareness that we are a part of nature, and nature is a part of our Selves. Yet how this awareness comes about, as well as the range of others to which it extends, can vary in subtle but significant ways. To clarify some of this potential variability, therefore, Fox makes an additional distinction between "personal" and "transpersonal" subtypes of identification (table 1.1) and, given that these figure implicitly or explicitly in the works of many deep ecology theorists, we will do well to take a moment to describe them here.[44]

Personal identification, as the name suggests, refers to a sense of connectedness with others resulting from firsthand encounters with them.[45] This is, as Fox observes, "the way in which most of us think of the process of identification,"[46] and indeed many of us would find it fairly easy to specify entities with which we identify in this way. When I was a young boy, for example, my brother and I spent many hours exploring certain sections of the Gunpowder River in northern Maryland. There was, however, one place to which we were especially drawn. Marked by the presence of a large, elongated rock jutting out of the riverbed—which we christened "Whale Rock" due to its unmistakable shape and size—it was for many years a hub of our childhood activity. But Whale Rock was much more than a spot on the map we were fortunate enough to frequent; it was a dynamic player in the events that shaped our growing attitudes toward ourselves and the world,

Table 1.1 Varieties of Identification with Nature Articulated by Deep Ecology Theorists

	Personally Based	Transpersonal
Identification-as-belonging	A sense of belonging to or community with aspects of nature one has encountered personally	A sense of belonging to or community with aspects of nature one has not encountered personally
Identification-as-kinship	A sense of similarity or kinship with aspects of nature one has encountered personally	A sense of similarity or kinship with aspects of nature one has not encountered personally

Source: Author created.

as much a formative part of our daily lives as any of our human associates. So it happened that, through these personal experiences, my brother and I came to have deep feelings of connectedness and belonging associated with that place. We came, that is, to see the rock and the river as companions and contributors to who we are, which is what Fox expresses when he says that personal identification with others leads us to "experience these entities as part of 'us,' as part of our identity."[47]

In contrast to this more intimate type of identification, transpersonal identification results in a sense of community in relation to entities we have not contacted personally.[48] Of course, as a type of identification, transpersonal identification still has a felt effect on our lived experience of ourselves and nature. It can, however, be characterized as "more impartial" than personally based identification in that it results in feelings of interconnectedness that are not limited, or "partial," to beings we come across in our everyday experience.[49] In this way, transpersonal identification provides, as Fox puts it, "a lived sense of an overall scheme of things" in which one can "feel a sense of commonality with all other entities (whether one happens to encounter them personally or not)."[50]

Not surprisingly, deep ecology supporters offer an array of suggestions as to how such an inclusive sense of identification with nature might be attained, from doing theoretical work in the sciences, to participating in grassroots workshops, to experimenting with psychedelic drugs.[51] However it comes about, accounts of transpersonal identification, like accounts of personal identification, are easy to find in the writings of deep ecology supporters. Naess speaks of identifying with "all life forms and with the greater units: the ecosystems and Gaia, the fabulous old planet of ours."[52] Similarly, Devall and Sessions describe identification as including "not only me, an individual human, but all humans, whales, grizzly bears, whole rain forest ecosystems, mountains and rivers, the tiniest microbes in the soil, and so on."[53] Often, gaining such a wide sense of identification with others is depicted as proceeding from our immediate surroundings to that of nature-at-large. Bender, for example, explains how we might engage in a "mindfulness practice" through which we recognize our "interdependence with other living beings locally, with regional and global ecosystems, and ultimately with Earth's ecosphere as a whole."[54] Likewise, Naess says that "from identifying with 'one's nearest,' higher level unities are created through circles of friends, local communities, tribes, compatriots, races, humanity, life, and, ultimately . . . unity with the supreme whole."[55]

Identification-as-Belonging and Self-Realization

In our discussion to this point, we have seen that no matter what subtype of identification-as-belonging is at issue, Naess and other deep ecology theorists encourage this process because they regard it as key to the development of a more inclusive, ecologically oriented sense of Self. We have seen, too, that this stress on identification is typically associated with a deeper commitment to the ultimate norm of Self-realization. What we have not yet examined, though, are the details of the relationship between these two pivotal concepts. How, precisely, do theorists in the deep ecology movement connect Self-realization to identification-as-belonging?

Perhaps the easiest way to answer this question is to consider Naess's formal definition of identification as a "process through which the interest or interests of another being are reacted to as our own interest or interests."[56] What this indicates, in brief, is the belief that an expanded sense of Self issues in a comparably expanded sphere of attention and concern. If, as the process of identification-as-belonging reveals, we cannot be isolated from nature, if we are inescapably a part of the natural world, then neither, it appears, will we be able to isolate what is in our interests from what is in the interests of those other-than-human entities with which we are so fundamentally intertwined. "When my identity is interconnected with the identity of other beings," Devall explains, "then my experience and my existence depends on theirs. Their interests are my interests."[57]

With this dovetailing of interests, however, it seems obvious that we would, in turn, come to desire the flourishing of other-than-human entities, since Self-realization, as a basic inclination that we have, intuitively prompts us to seek what is conducive to the actualization of our potentials, or the promotion of our interests. As Naess puts it neatly in *Ecology, Community and Lifestyle*, we "seek what is best for ourselves, but through the extension of the self, our 'own' best is also that of others."[58] Thus, he proposes that if we can, through identification, in some way bridge the perceived divide separating ourselves and the more-than-human world, then so too will we be able to bridge the perceived divide between what promotes our own Self-realization and what promotes that of other-than-human beings.[59]

In a more detailed illustration of this cluster of ideas, Naess begins by asking:

> What is the practical importance of this conception of a wide and deep ecological self? When we attempt to defend nature in our rich industrial societies, the argument of our opponents is often that we are doing it to secure beauty, recreation, and other non-vital interests for ourselves. Our position is strengthened if, after honest reflection we find that the destruction of Nature (and our place) threatens us in our innermost self. If so, we are more convincingly defending our vital interests, not merely something "out there." We are engaged in self-defense. And to defend fundamental *human* rights is vital self-defense.[60]

Especially noteworthy in this is the way Naess distances himself from positions that consider nature's protection to be a matter of safeguarding certain ostensibly trivial human interests. When one identifies with nature, its conservation is not equivalent to protecting something "external" to oneself that, as such, could only be viewed as being of secondary importance (as outdoor recreation or aesthetic experience of nature is often thought to be). One is instead promoting something of primary significance indeed: the vital interests of one's ecological Self.

In light of this, it should be evident why deep ecology supporters often speak of the destruction of nature as Self-destructive, and nature's defense as Self-defense. Mathews says that when we expand our sense of self we realize that when we destroy the environment, "we are destroying what is in fact our larger self."[61] Bender echoes this sentiment in his comment that "[s]ince we are all connected, we harm ourselves whenever we unduly harm our fellow beings."[62] In a clear example of personal identification, forest activist John Seed recounts a time when he identified so deeply with a rainforest that he came to feel that he "was literally part of the rainforest defending herself."[63] Somewhat in contrast, John Livingston expresses the same Self-defensive stance on the basis of transpersonal identification, writing that "when I say that the fate of the sea turtle or the tiger or the gibbon is mine, I mean it. All that is in my universe is not merely mine; it is me. And I shall defend myself."[64]

Hence, whereas we might think that environmentally friendly actions involve self-sacrifice, many deep ecology theorists point out that with an expanded sense of Self we will come to see that these actions involve no such sacrifice at all. Furthermore, it appears that one of the consequences of identification is that actions on behalf of others become as natural as the inclination to care for ourselves, and therefore do not require moral exhortation to be performed. This idea is stressed repeatedly by Naess, who says that through identification, benevolent acts require no moralizing, "just as we don't need morals to make us breathe."[65] In Kantian terms, our ecological Self acts "beautifully" but not "morally": rather than feeling obligated to help others because it is our duty, we help them because of the basic inclination to care for everything that is a part of our extended Self, our basic urge toward Self-realization.[66] "Thus," Naess claims, "everything that can be achieved by altruism—the *dutiful, moral* consideration of others—can be achieved, and much more, by the process of widening and deepening ourselves."[67]

Identification-as-Kinship

It is fitting that, thus far, our attention has been focused on identification-as-belonging, as this is surely the type of identification that figures most prominently in the writings of deep ecology theorists. We noted earlier, however, that this is not the only form of identification that appears therein. Found particularly (if not exclusively) in Naess's works, there is at least one other broad type of identification that has been articulated, one that is seldom differentiated from identification-as-belonging, but which nevertheless is both distinctive and important to recognize.[68] Our current task, then, is to disentangle the meaning of this alternative conception of identification before considering how it, too, can be connected back to the norm of Self-realization.

In the book-length interview *Is It Painful to Think?*, Naess claims that his use of the term "identification" stems from an experience he had while performing a laboratory experiment.[69] He was looking through a microscope at a slide when a flea suddenly jumped into the chemical solution he was examining. It struggled violently for several minutes to free itself, but was unable to escape. Eventually it died. "Its movements were dreadfully expressive," Naess recalls, and he remembers feeling "a painful sense of compassion and empathy." He says, though, that his concern for the flea was not the most elementary aspect of his experience. Even more fundamental than the compassion he felt, and actually what made it possible, was "identification" with the flea. His response to the flea's plight, he says, "was *not* basic, rather it was a process of identification: that 'I saw myself in the flea'."[70]

Now, given what was said above about identification-as-belonging, the claim that identification entails "seeing oneself" in another may seem somewhat curious. It is, however, a claim that Naess makes in many places. In *Life's Philosophy* he explains that, through identification, "we recognize something of ourselves in the other creature, or something of the other creature in ourselves."[71] In *Ecology, Community and Lifestyle*, he gives the example of some children killing insects with bug spray, and an adult posing to them the question, "perhaps those animals might, like you, prefer to live rather than to die?" The adult's comment, Naess thinks, might bring about an "instance of momentary identification" in which the children are able to "see and experience spontaneously and immediately the insects as themselves, not only as something different but in an important sense like themselves."[72]

The way in which these passages portray identification is markedly different from the way in which it is typically characterized by deep ecology theorists. Here, the term "identification" does not refer to developing a sense of *interconnectedness* or *belonging*, but to becoming aware of some form of *similarity* or *likeness* between ourselves and others. On this telling, to identify with other-than-human beings is less about having a sense of community than a sense of commonality with them; it is to recognize them as bearing a certain resemblance to ourselves, to see ourselves as "akin" to them in some way. This form of identification might therefore be called "identification-as-kinship," since it involves catching sight of *commonality* or *similitude* between ourselves and other-than-human entities.[73]

Before going further, it is worth observing that although thinkers other than Naess appear not to place much emphasis on identification-as-kinship, Naess himself arguably takes it to be identification's most definitive form. In "Identification as a Source of Deep Ecological Attitudes," for instance, he presents kinship-identification as the principal link between ecosophy T and the belief that all living things have intrinsic value.[74] Even more straightforwardly, he asserts in the essay "Self-Realization" that his encounter with the flea represents a "paradigm situation" of identification.[75]

Of course, part of the reason why Naess's experience was a paradigmatic instance of identification is that it was not solely a matter of his having an intellectual grasp of similarities between himself and the small insect. Rather it was, as he often says, a "spontaneous" event, one that included the same kind of lived or felt awareness that we mentioned in reference to identification-as-belonging.[76] Like that other type of identification, therefore, kinship-identification is not reducible to the possession of formal, abstract information about commonalities between human and other-than-human beings, though such knowledge undoubtedly can inspire, encourage, and reinforce it.

Ordinarily, Naess is somewhat vague about what, exactly, is the commonality or kinship that this type of identification recognizes. He does, however, make a number of intriguing suggestions in this area. In *Life's Philosophy* he says that what identification discovers in others ranges from physical abilities and vulnerabilities that we share, to our common social activities and needs.[77] Elsewhere he says that identification is strongest when others are suffering, presumably because witnessing others suffer forcefully conveys to us that their lives, no less than our own, are imbued with feeling and purpose.[78] Shortly after making this comment, he mentions the intense identification people felt with Antarctic penguins that had been harmed by the pesticide DDT. These people, Naess believes, understood that humans and penguins alike are "expressions of life."[79] In one of his most provocative statements on the subject, he says that to identify with others could be to understand that there is in them "that part of God that lives in all that is living."[80]

Collectively, such remarks reinforce the idea that identification-as-kinship is a core component of Naess's ecosophy. They also imply that this form of identification, like identification-as-belonging, has both "personal" and "transpersonal" subtypes (table 1.1). Naess's identification with the flea, for example, rooted as it was in his direct witnessing of the animal's demise, obviously aligns with what Fox terms personal identification. Such firsthand interaction presumably was not a factor, though, for the vast majority of those who identified with penguins in Antarctica. Cases like this, therefore, appear to involve transpersonal kinship-identification, since they reveal how people can come to feel a deep sense of commonality with and concern for other-than-human beings despite the fact that they have never, and in all likelihood will never, encounter them in their immediate, day-to-day experiences.

Having all of this in mind, it should be evident that identification-as-kinship operates as a corrective to certain dualistic ideas about humans and nature. But unlike identification-as-belonging, the most basic function of identification-as-kinship is not to give us a better sense of our place in nature by situating us within more encompassing ecological realities. Rather, it counters the dualistic notion that human and other-than-human beings are utterly different, "separate" sorts of things by giving us insight into the various points of continuity that exist between us. In this way, kinship-identification can rightly be described as a process that counters alienation and "reconnects" us with the more-than-human world not by framing us as part of the larger natural order, but by working against the mistaken presumption that we are radically distinct from, instead of deeply continuous with, our other-than-human kin.

Identification-as-Kinship and Self-Realization

With this understanding of identification-as-kinship in view, it remains for us to examine how it is connected to the norm of Self-realization. We might initiate this inquiry, though, by asking first about the broader significance of kinship-identification itself. Why, that is, does Naess contend that an awareness of commonality with other-than-human entities matters for environmentalism? What, in his estimation, is the importance of this type of identification?

At one point when discussing his experience with the flea, Naess reiterates that the opposite of identification is alienation, and he asserts that "[i]f I had been alienated from the flea, not seeing intuitively anything even resembling myself, the death struggle would have left me feeling indifferent."[81] This statement captures well Naess's belief that alienation from others inhibits our ability to become emotionally invested in their well-being: absent any sense of commonality with entities other than ourselves, we are left with no way of feeling our way into their situations. But, if alienation is reversed by identification-as-kinship, such felt attentiveness might not only be unobstructed, but may indeed be actively facilitated. As Naess explains, "It is a necessary, but not sufficient condition of empathy and sympathy that one 'sees' or experiences something similar or identical with oneself."[82] Thus, he holds that it is the awareness of continuity or kinship with others that gives us an intimation of what their circumstances are like, which in turn makes it possible for us to feel with them their joys and their sorrows.[83]

Because it enables such genuine fellow feeling, however, Naess contends that the deeper eco-philosophical value of identification-as-kinship has to do with the way in which it promotes the development of our ecological Selves. He argues that, with kinship-identification, our self comes to "include" others since we come to experience their well-being as intertwined with our own: we find ourselves pained by their pain and uplifted by their flourishing; the joys and sorrows they feel, we feel in some sense as well.[84] Similar to identification-as-belonging, therefore, what is said to result from identification-as-kinship is an expanded sense of Self, one in which we understand our own well-being to be bound up with that of others, including those that are other-than-human.

For this reason kinship-identification, like identification-as-belonging, can be defined as a "process through which the interest or interests of another being are reacted to as our own interest or interests."[85] And here, as before, this widening of the Self and associated overlapping of interests is thought to have consequences vis-à-vis Self-realization: since kinship-identification gives us to experiencing others' interests as intertwined with our own, our inclination toward Self-realization—which urges us to seek what promotes our interests—now inclines us also to promote the interests of other-than-human beings. Hence it again comes about that, by weakening the perceived divide between ourselves and other-than-human beings, identification helps to weaken the perceived divide between what promotes our and others' Self-realization.[86]

It appears, moreover, that since kinship-identification can tap into our impulse toward Self-realization, it carries many of the same ethical implications that we described in relation to identification-as-belonging. Specifically, it would seem not only that the defense of other-than-human beings with whom we identify in this way could be described as a form of "Self-defense," but also that any such attempts to protect nature would arise, as Naess says, "because of a spontaneous urge to do so."[87] When we develop our ecological Selves via identification-as-kinship, then, environmentally sensitive behavior becomes something in which we readily engage not because we feel compelled to do so by formal moral principles, but as a natural result of our empathetic sense of connection to others alongside our desire for Self-realization.

IDENTIFICATION, SELF-REALIZATION, AND SELF-INTEREST

Having completed our review of the notions of Self-realization and identification with nature as Naess and other deep ecology theorists have articulated them, we are now in position to step back and examine what is perhaps the most common criticism of the unique eco-philosophical perspective to which these ideas give rise. In doing this, we will be able not only to formulate a preliminary response to one of the foremost challenges that Naess and other theorists in the deep ecology movement have faced, but also to provide a sketch of the conceptual orientation that will guide our own analyses in subsequent chapters.

As we start this more critical discussion, it is important to remember that even though deep ecology theorists tend to associate Self-realization and identification with nature very closely, these are distinct ideas that play distinct roles in the philosophies of those who utilize them. Self-realization refers to the basically good, deep-seated drive that we and other beings have to actualize our existential potential. Identification, on the other hand—whether as belonging or as kinship—is the means through which we develop awareness of our connectedness to others, or a more inclusive sense of Self.[88] These ideas come together at the point where deep ecology theorists observe that it is possible for us to have an overly narrow conception of the end toward which Self-realization motivates us to strive. If our sphere of identifications is restricted, we may find ourselves limited to the ego-oriented identity that Naess describes, and consequently pursue our Self-realization in ways that are exclusive or destructive of others. If, however, we extend our sphere of identifications to illuminate the relational aspects of our Selves, then we may come to construe, and pursue, our good in ways that more adequately take the goods of others into account.

This line of thinking is assuredly one that many have found compelling. However, it has also received its fair share of criticisms; among the most persistent of these is that the ethic it entails is simply a variant of anthropocentric self-interest. The contention, that is, is that the foundational place that many deep ecology theorists accord to Self-realization and the expansion of the self through identification with nature generates an environmental outlook in which nature's protection stems not from a desire to protect others who are recognized as being worthy of moral concern, but from a desire to protect our Selves.[89]

One especially powerful version of this critique is found in Val Plumwood's *Feminism and the Mastery of Nature*. In this text, Plumwood argues that Naess and other theorists of deep ecology have failed to "question the structures of possessive egoism and self-interest," and thus end up assuming such egoism as their starting point. Once this assumption is made, she says, these theorists can see no way to encourage responsible behavior other than to have us expand our sense of self to include others. Hence their advocacy of Self-realization and identification with nature, far from entailing a critique of human egoism, is really just "an enlargement and an extension" of it, a way to "allow for a wider set of concerns while continuing to allow the self to operate on the fuel of self-interest (or Self-interest)."[90] Eric Katz summarily expresses the same idea, saying that although "the interests of the individual from within the deep ecological perspective will not be the narrow egoistic interests of ordinary human life," it is still the case that on this account "the focus and goal of the preservation of natural processes is the maximization of human interests."[91]

This is a serious criticism, no doubt. When looked at carefully, though, it seems obvious that the problem it flags is not mainly the result of deep ecology theorists' interest in identification with nature. It results, rather, from the way in which they posit Self-realization as an ultimate norm, and to see why this is the case we need only remember that this norm is meant to prescribe (and describe) what is ostensibly our most fundamental goal and, correspondingly, our motive for action. Accordingly, any link to Self-realization will presumably require us to frame the moral motivations of those who have undergone this process in self-oriented terms, to interpret their actions as expressions of a desire for some sort of Self-enhancement, Self-fulfillment, or Self-actualization. No matter what else supporters of the deep ecology movement may want to say about human identity or connectedness to nature, therefore, as long as their claims remain tethered to the principle of Self-realization, it appears that they will remain exposed to the charge that they implicitly or explicitly appeal to a self-centered or egoist moral psychology.[92]

If we were to set aside the norm of Self-realization, however, and examine the phenomenon of identification with nature by itself, we would quickly find that there are dimensions of this process that do not fit so easily within a self-referential ethical framework. Identification-as-kinship, for example, is something that by Naess's own account is primarily a matter of reshaping our perceptions of others in ways that facilitate heightened ethical concern for them. This is in fact the point he illustrates when he discusses the adult who encounters children killing insects with bug spray. In that scenario, the adult's intent is for the children to discover something about the insects that they otherwise seem to have missed, and to see other-than-human beings as similar to themselves where before they saw either something alien, or something that they had given no notice to at all prior to the moment of identification.[93] The most basic aim of this kind of identification, therefore, is not to have us view others as part of our Selves, but to have us come to regard others in ways that elicit for them the same sort of felt concern and respect that we have for ourselves.

That Naess goes on to frame this shift in terms of Self-realization surely indicates his commitment to this norm. But it also tends to stress an *effect* of our kinship-identification with other-than-human beings (our feeling personally connected to and impacted by their suffering or flourishing) at the risk of obscuring its *cause* (our genuine concern for and investment in their well-being, made possible by our sense of commonality with them). It certainly is worthwhile to consider the motivational implications of this process for ourselves. Yet is only afterward, so to speak, that kinship-identification has these implications, and that they emerge is because this form of identification enables us to care for others deeply—so deeply, in fact, that our very Self is implicated. The most appropriate ethical model for this sort of identification, then, would not be that of a form of self-interest that expands to incorporate the goods of others, but a form of concern for others that is not exclusive of the good of the Self—a model that, not coincidentally, closely resembles the care-based perspectives adopted by some ecofeminists, including Plumwood.[94]

Something similar might be said of identification-as-belonging, as this process, too, can be interpreted along less self-centric lines than deep ecology theorists usually offer. One possibility here would be to understand the shift in perspective that this type of identification involves as a reversal of the way in which we often marginalize the contributions that other-than-human entities make to our lives, a tendency that Plumwood aptly calls "backgrounding." This downplaying of the significance of other-than-human activities, she explains, helps to foster not only our sense of disconnection from nature, but also our sense that other-than-human beings are inessential, unimportant, and ultimately inferior to ourselves.[95] In contrast to this, identification-as-belonging promotes our awareness of the vital relations that always exist between ourselves and nature, and thus it can be viewed as a process that refuses the background status of other-than-human beings and elevates our assessment of their worth.

The starting point for such a revised appraisal would, it is true, still be a reflection on ourselves. But it is not unreasonable to think that the more we reflect on the unique ways in which others contribute to our lives, the more we become sensitive to and appreciative of the unique ways-of-being they themselves embody. Thomas Hill has suggested that "[t]ypically, . . . as we become more and more aware that we are parts of the larger whole we come to value the whole independently of its effect on ourselves."[96] Whatever defense of nature might proceed on this basis, therefore, would not be most accurately cast as a form of Self-defense. It would be best viewed, instead, as a form of concern for others that grows out of our maturing sense of Self-in-relationship, one that opens us to the uniquely valuable gifts, characters, and capabilities of other-than-human beings.

These cursory remarks do not, of course, answer every question here. Much more needs to be said about the ethical and attitudinal aspects of identification, and this is one of the main tasks of the next two chapters. For the moment, though, the takeaway is that those who identify with nature may have a variety of motives for protecting it that do not necessarily amount to some kind of expanded egoism, or "ecologically enlightened" self-interest. What is required for these alternative motives to come more sharply into focus, however, is that one does not automatically posit that the most basic value, or our most basic impulse, is the actualization of our Selves. Holding back from this ultimate normative commitment to Self-realization, one is able to keep open these more other-oriented possibilities for understanding ethical relationships that a sense of connectedness to nature harbors, many of which are discernible in the works of deep ecology theorists themselves.[97]

CONNECTED TO OTHERS

At the conclusion of this opening analysis, it should quickly be mentioned that although we have discussed identification-as-belonging and identification-as-kinship separately, this should not be taken to mean that these processes are mutually exclusive, or that they are in no way mutually reinforcing. Quite the opposite, it is entirely likely that a sense of belonging to the natural world promotes the recognition of various commonalities between ourselves and other-than-human existents, just as a sense of kinship with other-than-human beings promotes a sense of belonging to the more-than-human natural world. That these may be different processes with potentially different implications does not mean that, as they are actually lived, they do not occur together in highly integrated ways.

Additionally, nothing in the preceding is meant to suggest that Self-realization is not something for which human beings should strive, or that the development of our existential potential is not in many cases a very good thing. What we have tried to assert, instead, is simply that the project of Self-realization is not necessarily the only, or the most fundamental, dimension of our encounters with the natural world. To engage with others recognized as such, and as deserving of our concern and respect, is just as vital to ethical life, and the point being accentuated here is that despite the emphasis Naess and other deep ecology theorists place on realizing our Selves, their equal emphasis on the role and impact of identification with, or connection to, nature leaves ample room for an appropriately more other-oriented ethical discourse, one that balances its claims about the importance of fulfilling our human potentials with a genuine appreciation of what is other-than-human.

To be sure, a great deal remains to be said about the significance of connectedness to nature. One of the most basic issues to be addressed, however, concerns whether or not environmentally inclusive self-understandings matter for environmentalism as much as deep ecology supporters would have us believe. Does identification with nature really shape our outlooks and actions, our attitudes and behaviors, as dramatically as deep ecology theorists suggest? Is the development of an "ecological Self" truly as impactful as they assert? Such questions, it might seem, could lead only to conjecture and philosophical guesswork. Thanks to recent developments in the social sciences, however, their answers are becoming considerably less speculative than we might think.

NOTES

1. Arne Naess, "The Shallow and the Deep, Long-Range Ecology Movement. A Summary," *Inquiry* 16, no. 1–4 (1973): 95.

2. Joanna Macy and Molly Young Brown, *Coming Back to Life: The Updated Guide to the Work That Reconnects* (Gabriola Island, BC: New Society Publishers, 2014), 43.

3. Frederic L. Bender, *The Culture of Extinction: Toward a Philosophy of Deep Ecology* (Amherst: Humanity Books, 2003), 445–50.

4. For an early explanation of the term "ecosophy," see Naess, "The Shallow and the Deep," 99.

5. Naess discusses "ecosophy T" in numerous places, including *Ecology, Community and Lifestyle: Outline of an Ecosophy*, trans. and rev. David Rothenberg (Cambridge: Cambridge University Press, 1989). See also Arne Naess, "The Deep Ecological Movement: Some Philosophical Aspects," *Inquiry* 8, no. 1–2 (1986): 10–31.

6. This is indicated in many places throughout Naess's writing, and is discussed in detail in *Ecology, Community and Lifestyle*, chapter 3.

7. Naess, *Ecology, Community and Lifestyle*, 74. See also Arne Naess, "'Here I Stand': An Interview with Arne Naess," interview by Christian Diehm, *Environmental Philosophy* 1, no. 2 (Fall 2004): 16.

8. Naess, "'Here I Stand'," 16.

9. Warwick Fox, *Toward a Transpersonal Ecology: Developing New Foundations for Environmentalism* (Albany: State University of New York Press, 1995), 103–14; Alan Drengson, "The Life and Works of Arne Naess: An Appreciative Overview," introduction to *The Ecology of Wisdom: Writings by Arne Naess*, ed. Alan Drengson and Bill Devall (Berkeley: Counterpoint, 2008), 35; David Landis Barnhill and Roger S. Gottlieb, eds., *Deep Ecology and World Religions: New Essays on Sacred Ground* (Albany: State University of New York Press, 2001).

10. Naess, *Gandhi and Group Conflict: An Exploration of Satyagraha* (Oslo: Universitetsforlaget, 1974), 52–55. See also Fox, *Toward a Transpersonal Ecology*, 107.

11. In a general acknowledgment of the profound impact of Spinoza on his thought, Naess writes that "[n]o great philosopher has so much to offer in the way of clarification and articulation of basic ecological attitudes as Baruch Spinoza" ("Spinoza and Ecology," *Philosophia* 7, no. 1 [1977]: 54). See also Arne Naess, "Spinoza and the Deep Ecology Movement," in *The Ecology of Wisdom*, 230–51. For a more recent analysis of the relationship between Spinoza and deep ecological thought, see Eccy de Jonge, *Spinoza and Deep Ecology: Challenging Traditional Approaches to Environmentalism* (London: Routledge, 2016).

12. Naess, *Freedom, Emotion, and Self-Subsistence: The Structure of a Central Part of Spinoza's Ethics* (Oslo: Universitetsforlaget, 1975), 96–97.

13. Naess, *Ecology, Community and Lifestyle*, 166.

14. Ibid. In another condensed statement of these ideas, Naess declares that every being "strives to preserve *and* develop its specific essence or nature" ("Spinoza and Ecology," 48, emphasis added).

15. It is for this reason that Naess says that, in ecosophy T, "the term 'Self-realisation' is used to indicate a kind of perfection" (*Ecology, Community and Lifestyle*, 84).

16. Arne Naess, "Identification as a Source of Deep Ecological Attitudes," in *Deep Ecology*, ed. Michael Tobias (San Diego: Avant Books, 1985), 264.

17. Arne Naess, "Self-Realization: An Ecological Approach to Being-in-the-World," in *Deep Ecology for the Twenty-First Century: Readings on the Philosophy and Practice of the New Environmentalism*, ed. George Sessions (Boston: Shambhala, 1995), 226.

18. Naess, "Self-Realization," 230.

19. Ibid.

20. Naess, *Ecology, Community and Lifestyle*, 85

21. Naess, "Self-Realization," 226; "'Here I Stand'," 13.

22. Naess, "Self-Realization," 226.

23. Ibid., 230.

24. Ibid., 239. With *Homo sapiens* he says, "A life form has developed on Earth which is capable of understanding and appreciating its relations with all other life forms and to the Earth as a whole" (*Ecology, Community and Lifestyle*, 166).

25. Naess, *Gandhi and Group Conflict*, 52–53.

26. Ibid., 42. Naess also links this to Gandhi's philosophy of nonviolence (Ibid., 53).

27. Naess, *Ecology, Community and Lifestyle*, 172.

28. Naess, "Self-Realization," 226. See also Arne Naess, "The Deep Ecological Movement," 80; Fox, *Toward a Transpersonal Ecology*, 105.

29. The term "ecological consciousness" is used fairly widely in the literature of the deep ecology movement and beyond. See, for example, Christopher Uhl, *Developing Ecological Consciousness: The End of Separation*, 2nd ed. (Lanham: Rowman & Littlefield, 2013); Bill Devall and George Sessions, *Deep Ecology: Living as if Nature Mattered* (Salt Lake City: Gibbs Smith, 1985); John Rodman, "Four Forms of Ecological Consciousness Reconsidered," in *Deep Ecology for the Twenty-First Century*, 121–30. Bill Devall uses the language of "identification" in *Simple in Means, Rich in Ends: Practicing Deep Ecology* (Salt Lake City: Peregrine Smith Books, 1988), 49.

30. The discussions of "identification as belonging" and "identification as kinship" that follow are adapted from my earlier work in this area, first published in Christian Diehm, "Identification with Nature: What It Is and Why It Matters," *Ethics and the Environment* 12, no. 2 (Autumn 2007): 1–22.

31. Uhl, *Developing Ecological Consciousness*, 181.

32. Bender, *The Culture of Extinction*, 393.

33. Ibid., 19–21, 397–400; Uhl, *Developing Ecological Consciousness*, 181.

34. Naess himself uses the related language of "ecospheric belonging" in *Ecology, Community and Lifestyle*, 168.

35. Naess, "The Shallow and the Deep," 95.
36. Fox, *Toward a Transpersonal Ecology*, 252.
37. Uhl, *Developing Ecological Consciousness*, 79.
38. Ibid., 80.
39. Freya Mathews, "Conservation and Self-Realization: A Deep Ecology Perspective," *Environmental Ethics* 10, no. 4 (Winter 1988): 349. Regarding the claim that deep ecology theorists align their notions of interconnection with natural science, see Fox, *Toward a Transpersonal Ecology*, 254; Uhl, *Developing Ecological Consciousness*, 78.

40. J. Baird Callicott, "The Metaphysical Implications of Ecology," in *In Defense of the Land Ethic: Essays in Environmental Philosophy* (Albany: SUNY Press, 1989), 101–14. As Callicott puts it in this essay, ecological science has "made plain to us the fact that we are enfolded, involved, and engaged within the living, terrestrial environment" (101).

41. Devall and Sessions, *Deep Ecology*, 85. The perceived alliance of scientific ecology with the deep ecology movement helps explain why some deep ecology theorists cite Aldo Leopold as a philosophical ally. Not only did Leopold articulate an environmental ethic that relied explicitly on ecological insights, but he also thought these insights could facilitate our coming to see ourselves as part of a more-than-human community comprised of "soils, waters, plants, and animals, or collectively: the land." This expanded "community concept," he claimed, "changes the role of *Homo sapiens* from conqueror of the land-community to plain member and citizen of it" (*A Sand County Almanac with Essays on Conservation from Round River* [New York: Ballantine Books, 1970], 239–40). Bender thus claims that Leopold's thought prompts a basic change in perspective, or "gestalt shift," in which "the dualistic 'I,' framed as standing outside nature looking in, is suddenly reframed as just one part of the biotic pyramid." "The land ethic," says Bender, "frames the biotic community (the ecosphere) as everyone's encompassing self, or Self, since we are the ecosphere, since we belong to the ecosphere, and since we are dependent upon the ecosphere" (*The Culture of Extinction*, 370–71).

42. Uhl, *Developing Ecological Consciousness*, 80.

43. As Naess explains, "The norms and tendencies of the Deep Ecology movement are not derived from ecology by logic or induction. Ecological knowledge and the life-style of the ecological field-worker have *suggested*, *inspired*, and *fortified* the perspectives of the Deep Ecology movement" ("The Shallow and the Deep," 98). See also Devall and Sessions, *Deep Ecology*, 69; Fox, *Toward a Transpersonal Ecology*, 246–7.

44. This distinction is discussed in detail in Fox, *Toward a Transpersonal Ecology*, chapter 8. Not all thinkers in the deep ecology movement use this same terminology, of course, or make this distinction explicitly, but the general distinction that Fox is trying to capture with it can be found expressed in various ways in the works of numerous theorists.

45. Fox, *Toward a Transpersonal Ecology*, 249.
46. Ibid.
47. Ibid., 250. It is possible that, in some of his examples of personal identification, Fox has in mind something like what I call below "identification-as-kinship."

I think, though, that the sense of identification to which he appeals most often is identification-as-belonging.

48. Of course, there is a sense in which all forms of identification can be described as "transpersonal" insofar as they involve developing a sense of self that outstrips one's narrow, individualistic ego (see Devall, *Simple in Means*, 42). Here, however, I am following Fox and restricting the meaning of transpersonal identification to a type of identification that is "not primarily a function of the personal contacts or relationships of this or that particular person" (*Toward a Transpersonal Ecology*, 250).

49. Fox, *Toward a Transpersonal Ecology*, 256.

50. Ibid., 257.

51. See Fox, *Toward a Transpersonal Ecology*, 258; Joanna Macy and Pat Fleming, "Guidelines for a Council of All Beings Workshop," in John Seed et al., *Thinking Like a Mountain: Towards a Council of All Beings* (Gabriola Island, BC: New Society Publishers, 1988), 97–116. On the relationship between deep ecology and psychedelic drug use, see the special issue of the bulletin of the Multidisciplinary Association for Psychedelic Studies, "Psychedelics and Ecology," edited by David Jay Brown (*MAPS Bulletin* 19, 1 [2009], accessed October 15, 2017, https://maps.org/news-letters/v19n1/v19n1-maps_bulletin_spring_2009.pdf). For recent evidence of a link between a sense of connection to nature and psychedelic drug use, see Hannes Kettner et al., "From Egoism to Ecoism: Psychedelics Increase Nature Relatedness in a State-Mediated and Context-Dependent Manner," *International Journal of Environmental Research and Public Health* 16, no. 24 (2019), https://doi.org/10.3390/ijerph16245147.

52. Naess, "Self-Realization," 235.

53. Devall and Sessions, *Deep Ecology*, 67.

54. Bender, *The Culture of Extinction*, 424.

55. Naess, "Identification as a Source," 263. Exemplifying the importance of truly expansive, cosmological identification, Mathews proposes a new term to indicate the widest possible self that might be attained: beyond the "ecological" Self lies the "cosmic" self ("Conservation and Self-Realization," 352).

56. Naess, "Identification as a Source," 261.

57. Devall, *Simple in Means*, 69. See also David Rothenberg, "Ecosophy T: From Intuition to System," introduction to *Ecology, Community and Lifestyle*, 11.

58. Naess, *Ecology, Community and Lifestyle*, 175.

59. Devall and Sessions, too, discuss the importance of Self-realization, and say that that with a wide sense of Self we will come to see that "if we harm the rest of Nature then we are harming ourselves" (*Deep Ecology*, 68).

60. Naess, "Self-Realization," 232.

61. Mathews, "Conservation and Self-Realization," 354.

62. Bender, *The Culture of Extinction*, 400.

63. John Seed, "To Hear Within Ourselves the Sound of the Earth Crying," introduction to *Thinking Like a Mountain*, 6.

64. John A. Livingston, *The John A. Livingston Reader* (Toronto: McClelland and Stewart, 2007), 146. Devall, too, claims that through identification we come to realize that "[c]onservation is thus self defense" (*Simple in Means*, 70).

65. Naess, "Self-Realization," 233.
66. See Naess, *Ecology, Community and Lifestyle*, 85; "Identification as a Source," 264.
67. Naess, "Self-Realization," 226. For examples of other deep ecology theorists who stress these points, see Devall, *Simple in Means*, 43; Fox, *Toward a Transpersonal Ecology*, 204–7.
68. One writer who has noted this other form of identification is Val Plumwood, *Feminism and the Mastery of Nature* (London: Routledge, 1993), 180–81 and 216–17, note 8.
69. David Rothenberg, *Is It Painful to Think?: Conversations with Arne Naess* (Minneapolis: University of Minnesota Press, 1993), 178–79.
70. Naess, "Self-Realization," 227.
71. Arne Naess with Per Ingvar Haukeland, *Life's Philosophy: Reason and Feeling in a Deeper World*, trans. Roland Huntford (Athens: University of Georgia Press, 2002), 114.
72. Naess, *Ecology, Community and Lifestyle*, 171–72.
73. By kinship or similarity is not meant sheer physical resemblance. As Naess says, a "process of identification is created by the very fact of your feeling something of yourself in something else. Not that it need resemble yourself, but there is something about it that you recognize in yourself" (Naess with Haukeland, *Life's Philosophy*, 113–14).
74. In "Identification as a Source" Naess writes that identification "tells me: if *I* have a right to live, *you* have the same right" (266). The context of this comment is clearly that of a discussion of identification-as-kinship. In that respect, it is very different from Devall and Sessions's discussion of "biocentric equality" in *Deep Ecology*, since their analysis centers on identification-as-belonging (66–69).
75. Naess, "Self-Realization," 227.
76. See Naess, "Identification as a Source," 261, and "'Here I Stand'," 12.
77. Naess with Haukeland, *Life's Philosophy*, 114–15.
78. Naess, "Identification as a Source," 264.
79. Ibid., 265.
80. Naess with Haukeland, *Life's Philosophy*, 114.
81. Naess, "Self-Realization," 227.
82. Naess, "Identification as a Source," 262.
83. Through this sort of identification, Naess says, "[t]he road is . . . opened . . . for delight in the well-being of others and sorrow when harm befalls them" (*Ecology, Community and Lifestyle*, 175).
84. This is illustrated in a comment Naess made in a public debate with Alfred Ayer. During their conversation, Naess explained what he meant by identification with others with the hypothetical example of making a hurtful comment to Ayer. The result of such a remark, he said, might be "moment of identification" with Ayer, a situation in which there was "'one' hurt, which was not yet 'my' experience." The reference to "one hurt" indicates that, with identification, Naess would in some sense share in Ayer's experience, to be pained by what pained Ayer (Arne Naess, Alfred Ayer, and Fons Elders, "The Glass Is on the Table: The Empiricist versus Total

View," in *Philosophical Dialogues: Arne Naess and the Progress of Ecophilosophy*, ed. Nina Witoszek and Andrew Brennan [Lanham: Rowman & Littlefield, 1999], 20). In this debate, as elsewhere, Naess does not distinguish between identification-as-kinship and identification-as-belonging. It is almost certain that he draws on both concepts at various times when speaking to Ayer. In the comment cited, however, it is clear that he is talking about an empathic response to Ayer, based on what I have been calling identification-as-kinship.

85. Naess, "Identification as a Source," 261.

86. "[T]hrough genuine self-love," as Naess says, identification issues in "the love of a widened and deepened self" ("Self-Realization," 229).

87. Naess, "Identification as a Source," 264.

88. "Our Self," Naess says, "is that with which we identify" ("Identification as a Source," 261).

89. See, for example, John Nolt, *Environmental Ethics for the Long Term: An Introduction* (New York: Routledge, 2015), where he writes that "Deep ecology motivates concern for other living beings by assimilating it to concern for ourselves" (164). For other versions of this critique, see Janice Birkeland, "Ecofeminism: Linking Theory and Practice," in *Ecofeminism: Women, Animals, Nature*, ed. Greta Gaard (Philadelphia: Temple University Press, 1993), 13–59; Marti Kheel, "From Heroic to Holistic Ethics: The Ecofeminist Challenge," in *Ecofeminism: Women, Animals, Nature*, 243–67; Peter Reed, "Man Apart: An Alternative to the Self-Realization Approach," in *Philosophical Dialogues*, 181–97; Jim Cheney, "Eco-Feminism and Deep Ecology," *Environmental Ethics* 9, no. 2 (Summer 1987): 115–45.

90. Plumwood, *Feminism and the Mastery of Nature*, 179. See also Val Plumwood, "Nature, Self, and Gender: Feminism, Environmental Philosophy, and the Critique of Rationalism," *Hypatia* 6, no. 1 (Spring 1991): 3–27. Marti Kheel raises this same objection in relation to Aldo Leopold specifically and deep ecologists generally in "From Heroic to Holistic Ethics," 250–55.

91. Eric Katz, "Against the Inevitability of Anthropocentrism," in *Beneath the Surface: Critical Essays in the Philosophy of Deep Ecology*, ed. Eric Katz, Andrew Light and David Rothenberg (Cambridge: MIT Press, 2000), 34.

92. This same point is made by Andrew Dobson in "Deep Ecology: A Study in the Philosophy of the Green Movement . . . But Philosophy Is Not Enough," *Cogito* 3, no. 1 (Spring 1989): 45.

93. In *Life's Philosophy*, Naess expresses this same concern, entreating us "to learn about the similarities between human beings and other living creatures" (115).

94. See, for example, Plumwood, *Feminism and the Mastery of Nature*; Val Plumwood, *Environmental Culture: The Ecological Crisis of Reason* (London: Routledge, 2002); Karen Warren, *Ecofeminist Philosophy: A Western Perspective on What It Is and Why It Matters* (Lanham: Rowman & Littlefield, 2000); Josephine Donovan and Carol J. Adams, eds., *Beyond Animal Rights: A Feminist Caring Ethic for the Treatment of Animals* (New York: Continuum, 1996).

95. See Plumwood, *Feminism and the Mastery of Nature*, and Plumwood, *Environmental Culture*.

96. Thomas E. Hill, Jr., "Ideals of Human Excellence and Preserving Natural Environments," *Environmental Ethics* 5, no. 3 (Fall 1983): 218.

97. In the context of an analysis quite different from the present one, Harold Glasser raises the possibility that the idea of "wide-identification" may be more important to the ecosophies of many deep ecology theorists than the norm of Self-realization (see "On Warwick Fox's Assessment of Deep Ecology," *Environmental Ethics* 19, no. 1 [Spring 1997]: 74–79).

Chapter 2

Ecological Identity Matters
Deep Ecology and Conservation Psychology

Conservation psychology is a relatively new idea in the social sciences. Psychologists have, of course, studied people's interactions with their environments for some time, and environmental psychology has been an established field for at least a half-century. Conservation psychology, by contrast, emerged as an identifiable research area only as recently as the late 1990s and early 2000s. Deliberately fashioned after the model of conservation biology, conservation psychology distinguishes itself from environmental psychology in part by the heightened attention it pays to people's relations to natural (as opposed to built) environments, and in part by its overtly value-laden mission of promoting environmental protection.[1] Like environmental psychology, though, and somewhat unlike the related field of eco-psychology, conservation psychology takes a more empirical and less therapeutic approach to understanding the human-nature interactions it sets out to explore.[2] Hence this burgeoning field has been defined as "the scientific study of the reciprocal relationships between humans and the rest of nature, with a particular focus on how to encourage conservation of the natural world."[3]

Deep ecology, on the other hand, despite its misleading moniker, is not a branch of the natural sciences. It is, rather, a branch of the modern environmental or "ecology" movement that crystallized in the early 1970s, the main tenets of which were encapsulated roughly one decade later in its eight-point "platform" statement.[4] Those familiar with this particular branch of environmentalism are well aware that deep ecology has never claimed for itself a single, unified conceptual foundation. Still, many who express support of the deep ecology platform also express agreement with the eco-philosophy of Norwegian philosopher Arne Naess. Arguably, the hallmark of Naess's environmental thought is its contention that environmental problems are most likely to be solved not by traditional philosophical approaches to ethics, but by developing an understanding of our "ecological Selves," or deeper awareness of the true extent of our connectedness to nature. With Naess, therefore, many deep ecology theorists assert that the most promising way to foster pro-environmental attitudes and behaviors is for us to reconceive who and what we really are, to "identify" with nature and affirm our inextricable connectedness to our other-than-human kin.

Stated thusly, it seems clear that the ecosophies of Naess and other theorists in the deep ecology movement involve a number of basically "psychological" assumptions. Indeed, in *Toward a Transpersonal Ecology*, Warwick Fox says that most deep ecology theorists are "not concerned with the question of the *logical* connection between the fact that we are intimately bound up with the world and the question of how we should behave, but, rather, with the *psychological* connection between this fact and our behavior." The key assumption deep ecology theorists make in this regard, Fox says, is that if people can attain an ecological sense of Self, then they will "naturally be inclined to care for the unfolding of the world."[5]

With all of this in view, it seems reasonable to presume that conservation psychologists and deep ecology theorists would have much to offer each other. To date, though, while many conservation psychologists indicate a familiarity with the writings of deep ecology supporters, philosophers interested in the deep ecology movement have not surveyed in any detailed way the relevance of conservation psychology for their own conversations.[6] This situation is understandable; however, it is also unfortunate nonetheless, since the findings of conservation and environmental psychologists present a unique opportunity to evaluate the central claims of deep ecological philosophy in light of a growing body of social scientific research. Our aim in this chapter, then, is to take advantage of this opportunity by considering not only whether or not conservation psychology substantiates some of the key assertions deep ecology theorists have made, but also how it might help us navigate some of the philosophical debates these assertions have sparked.

HUMAN-NATURE BONDING

As we saw in the preceding chapter, deep ecology theorists have articulated several ways in which people might come to feel more connected to nature, forming "ecological identities," or environmentally oriented senses of ourselves. We have seen, too, that for the most part they tend to discuss all of these relationships under the blanket heading of "identification" with nature (table 1.1). Conservation and environmental psychologists, by contrast, employ a considerably more diverse lexicon to describe the human-nature affiliations they study. For our purposes, however, the most significant of these affiliations are "place attachment" and "environmental identity."

Place Attachment

Place attachment is without question a complex phenomenon, and there is still a good deal of academic debate about how best to conceptualize it.[7] In the most general sense, social scientists take it to refer to "the bonding that occurs between individuals and their meaningful environments."[8] These "meaningful environments" include both built and natural settings, and indeed a great deal of what has been written on this subject has focused on the built environment. But as researchers have become increasingly conservation-minded, they have also increasingly come to explore place attachment in relation to the natural world. In doing so, they have found that such human–nature bonding has multiple facets, and therefore they often treat it as consisting of "place dependence" and "place identity" subdimensions.

Place *dependence*, as the name suggests, describes a functional reliance that people have on places in order to meet specific goals. It is thus closely related to the physical characteristics or amenities that an area possesses (e.g., accessible resources, water features, hiking trails, etc.) which can facilitate or impede people's engagement in desired activities.[9] Place identity, on the other hand, while not unrelated to place dependence, signifies a less utilitarian or pragmatic bond that forms between people and places. This type of connection involves, in the words of Jerry Vaske and Katherine Kobrin, "a psychological investment with a setting that has developed over time," one that is characterized in part by people's feeling that they belong to a given locale and that important aspects of themselves are embedded within it.[10] Consequently, as Suzanne Bott, James Cantrill, and Eugene Myers summarize the literature in this area, place identity can be regarded as "a relationship in which, through personal attachment to a geographically locatable place, a person acquires a sense of belonging and purpose in that place, which gives meaning to life."[11]

As one would expect, these theoretical constructs that researchers employ to understand people's attachments to natural places are reflected in and further clarified by the sorts of survey questions they ask to assess them. Hence place *dependence* is typically measured by inquiring into people's level of agreement with statements like, "This place is the best place for what I like to do," and, "I wouldn't substitute any other area for doing the types of things I do at this place." In turn, place *identity* is appraised by examining people's ratings of statements such as "I identify strongly with this place," and "I feel that this place is a part of me."[12]

These last survey items, in particular, begin to make clear the striking resemblance between the place *identity* dimension of place attachment and what deep ecology theorists would call personally based forms of identification-as-belonging. In short, such identification entails having the sense that we are not separate from but are fundamentally connected to the natural world, or the feeling that we are "a part of" nature rather than "apart from" nature. Additionally, to say that this sense of connection is personally based means that it occurs in relation to other-than-human entities with which we have had firsthand experience (table 1.1). This type of identification therefore appears to be precisely what Bott, Cantrill, and Myers refer to above when they define place identity as a "personal attachment to a geographically locatable place" that leads to "a sense of belonging and purpose" therein. What both social scientists and deep ecology theorists are describing here, that is, is a place-bonding process that affords us a sense that we are not ecological outsiders to a specific locale, but that we are deeply connected to and at home within it (table 2.1).

Not surprisingly, the writings of deep ecology theorists are replete with examples of this phenomenon. Naess frequently discusses the personal connections he feels to the area around his mountain hut in Norway, and has even written an extended reflection on the subject titled, "An Example of a Place: Tvergastein."[13] Likewise, in *Simple in Means, Rich in Ends*, Bill Devall speaks of the "sense-of-place" that he developed in relation to the great redwood forests near his home in the pacific northwestern region of the United States.[14] Our own example of Whale Rock similarly well illustrates the kind of intimate attachment and personal bonding to a particular area that characterizes place identity.

Still, deep ecology theorists have not contented themselves merely with describing place attachment. They also prescribe it.[15] Then again, so do some conservation psychologists. But whereas the former make this prescription based on a presumed link between identification-as-belonging and pro-environmental behavior, the latter do so based on the available empirical evidence, much of which supports the deep ecological hypothesis. A number of studies, in fact, have found that people who are more significantly attached to natural places show a greater propensity to engage in place-specific pro-environmental behaviors than those who are less so.[16] The not-so-startling conclusion of this research, in other words, is that the more people feel

Table 2.1 Varieties of Identification with Nature and Correlates in Conservation Psychology

	Personally Based	Transpersonal
Identification-as-belonging	Place attachment/Place identity	Environmental identity[a]
Identification-as-kinship		

Source: Author created.
[a] Conceptual overlap occurs with related constructs, for example, "Connectedness to Nature."

attached to specific natural settings, the more likely they will be to act in ways they believe will protect those settings.

In conjunction with these remarks, it is interesting to note that a number of studies in this area have found that while place *identity* has correlated positively with various pro-environmental measures, place *dependence* has not. A survey conducted at Mono Basin Scenic Area in California, for instance, discovered that visitors who were place-identified expressed increased support for user fees, yet the same was not true of those who were only place-dependent.[17] Similarly, a survey of campers at Ningaloo Marine Park in Australia found that place identity was the only dimension of place attachment that correlated with any of the pro-environmental behaviors the study assessed, and this correlation strengthened as the degree of time and commitment required by the behaviors also escalated.[18] In one of the better-known studies in this area, research conducted along the Appalachian Trail found that as hikers' place identity increased, so did their negative perceptions of social and environmental trail conditions (e.g., trail crowding, erosion, and litter). Hikers with lower place identity and higher place dependence, however, were less likely to see any of the conditions as problematic.[19]

It may be, then, that more utilitarian bonds of dependence upon places do not foster pro-environmental behaviors in the way that bonds of belonging or identity do.[20] There is some evidence, too, as several deep ecology theorists have postulated, that place identity encourages not only place-specific pro-environmental action, but also more general sorts of environmental concern.[21] Vaske and Kobrin, in a study of teenagers participating in natural resource work programs, found that the teens' identification with their worksites tended to spill over into more broadly focused conservation behaviors.[22] A similar effect is reported by Elizabeth Halpenny, whose survey of visitors to Point Pelee National Park in Canada revealed that increased place attachment, and especially place identity, corresponded with pro-environmental intentions not only inside the park, but elsewhere as well. Halpenny thus speculates that "as individuals build increased awareness, understanding, and attachments to nature-based contexts, which may form and confirm their sense of identity associated with these places, their attachment to natural settings may convert to a commitment to the environment in general."[23]

These examples notwithstanding, not all analyses of place attachment have produced such positive results. On the contrary, in several notable instances, researchers have found that people's place-bonds were actually a factor in their opposition to certain ostensibly environmentally friendly projects.[24] Illustrating some of the potential drawbacks here, James Cantrill cites a case in which wildlife officials in Michigan wanted to limit motorized access to a wetland to aid recovery of the gray wolf (*Canis lupus*), but were met with strong resistance from local recreationists. Having previously assessed rural Michiganders' attachments to place, Cantrill proposes that "for long-term residents of the region, the value of ecosystem services provided by a previously extirpated top-line carnivore may have been trumped by an emergent sense of self-in-place that placed a premium upon the use of the landscape for social activities." The result, Cantrill says, was a "less-than-satisfactory wildlife management situation."[25]

Environmental Identity

This last example warrants further examination, and we will have occasion to revisit it later. For the time being, though, perhaps the best that can be said about place attachment, or personally based identification-as-belonging, is that its significance for environmentalism is promising but not entirely clear. But this is not the only kind of human-nature bonding in which conservation psychologists and deep ecology theorists have expressed interest. They have also considered less place-specific ecological identities, and while psychologists have utilized neither a common vocabulary nor common assessment tools to explore these more broad-based attachments, much of what they have said is captured in the concept of "environmental identity."[26]

In one form or another, the idea of environmental identity has been a subject of academic discussion for many years.[27] It was not until 2003, however, that it was formalized by conservation psychologist Susan Clayton, who introduced it as "one part of the way in which people form their self-concept: a sense of connection to some part of the nonhuman natural environment, based on history, emotional attachment, and/or similarity, that affects the ways in which we perceive and act towards the world."[28] Reiterating these ideas, Clayton says elsewhere that to have such an environmentally oriented outlook is to have "a sense of self as conceptually interdependent with or connected to the natural world,"[29] and she suggests that this type of self-understanding "should imply an increased perception of similarity with, and moral standing accorded to, nonhuman natural entities."[30] On her account, then, environmental identity is something that leaves us with "a sense of connection, of being part of a larger whole, and with a recognition of similarity between ourselves and others."[31]

Understood in this manner, the concept of environmental identity is obviously similar to that of place attachment, since such attachment in relation to nature also entails the felt sense that who we are is fundamentally bound up with the more-than-human environment. Unlike place attachment, though, environmental identity is less a matter of our feeling connected to specific places than of our having an overarching perception of ourselves as intertwined with nature. In Clayton's words, "[a]n identity rooted in a specific place . . . is conceptually distinct from a more general sense of connection to the natural world. One important distinction . . . is that the latter should have implications for entities associated with nature and yet not affiliated with a particular place."[32]

Considering that environmental identity involves viewing ourselves as essentially connected to broader ecological realities, it appears to overlap substantially with the deep ecological notion of identification-as-belonging.[33] Yet environmental identity is not characterized solely by feelings of belonging or interconnection; it concurrently brings with it an "increased perception of similarity" with other-than-human entities, and in this respect it also resembles what we have referred to as identification-as-kinship. This type of identification, which is especially important to Naess's thought, involves becoming aware of certain likenesses between ourselves and others, or realizing that we share various points of similarity or commonality with our other-than-human kin (table 1.1). As it turns out, then, rather than corresponding exclusively with either one of the two broad types of identification that deep ecology theorists have articulated, environmental identity evidently incorporates elements of both (table 2.1).

Conservation psychologists have, of course, devised various means of determining whether or not people possess such an ecologically oriented sense of self, and many of these measures confirm that both belonging and kinship are integral to it.[34] Stephan Mayer and Cynthia Frantz's "Connectedness to Nature Scale," for example, asks people if they agree not only with statements such as "I think of the natural world as a community to which I belong," but also with assertions like "I recognize and appreciate the intelligence of other living organisms," and "I feel that all inhabitants of Earth, human, and nonhuman, share a common 'life force'."[35] Likewise, items on Clayton's "Environmental Identity Scale" ask people to record their agreement with indicators of belonging like "I think of myself as a part of nature, not separate from it," as well as with indices of their perceived kinship with other-than-human entities, such as "I feel that I have a lot in common with other species," and "Sometimes I feel like parts of nature—certain trees, or storms, or mountains—have a personality of their own."[36]

No matter which type of identification is stressed in conjunction with environmental identity, though, the fact that the bonding it involves is less particularistic than that of place attachment suggests that it is "trans-personal" rather than personally based. As Fox explains, transpersonal identification extends our spheres of inclusion beyond the range of our personal interactions, thereby issuing in feelings of community or commonality with others whom we have not encountered firsthand.[37] Hence when Clayton says that environmental identity has "implications for entities associated with nature and yet not affiliated with a particular place" she is, along with many theorists in the deep ecology movement, indicating just this more sweeping sensibility that one might attain, one that is not necessarily detached from idiosyncratic experiences of place, but that ultimately provides a wider-reaching sense of relationship to the natural world (table 2.1).

Now to be sure, researchers' interest in this phenomenon is not merely theoretical, and there are indeed some remarkable parallels between the findings of social scientists and what deep ecology supporters argue is the practical significance of such inclusive identification with nature. Clayton, for example, reports a strong correlation between environmental identity and "eco-centric" values,[38] or value orientations that include the idea that nature should be protected "for its own sake."[39] Arriving at essentially the same conclusion, a number of studies have found that people with higher levels of connectedness to nature have a greater tendency to hold what Paul Stern and Thomas Dietz have dubbed "biospheric" values,[40] meaning that they believe that "nonhuman aspects of the environment should be valued in their own right" rather than solely for their individual or social utility.[41]

Closely related to this is research that also confirms a link between identification with nature and pro-environmental behaviors. Again and again, surveys show that people with broadly inclusive ecological self-concepts, unlike those whose senses of self are more individualistic, have an increased likelihood of participating in an array of "green" activities, including everything from recycling and bike riding, to voting for politicians who are solid on environmental issues and boycotting companies that are not.[42] One study even found that an environmentally inclusive self-construal predicted willingness to cooperate with other people and with nature in a commons dilemma.[43] Accordingly, as Jan Stets and Chris Biga summarize their own work on this topic, it surely does appear that "the more ecocentric the environment identity, the more environmentally friendly are the environmental attitudes and behavior."[44]

Lastly, it is worth noting that some studies report a further positive correlation between biospheric value orientations and pro-environmental behaviors that are "self-determined." What these studies have found, that is, is that people who value nature noninstrumentally are quite often self-motivated to act on its behalf, whereas those with more utilitarian mindsets tend to be willing to engage in environmental causes only when externally prompted.[45] These findings, taken together with the correlations just mentioned between environmental identity, biospheric values, and pro-environmental behaviors, may well lead us to say, with Naess, that "identification makes the efforts of simplicity joyful and there is not a feeling of moral compulsion."[46]

BIOSPHERIC VALUES AND ENLIGHTENED SELF-INTEREST

To this point our examination has focused on how conservation psychology addresses some of the principal claims deep ecology theorists have made about identification with nature and pro-environmental attitudes and behaviors. And although it is true that the social science on this subject is still limited in certain ways, the evidence gathered thus far does weigh rather heavily in support of what these philosophical theorists have proposed.[47] At the outset, though, we suggested that this is not the only way in which psychological research might contribute to philosophical investigations in this area. Beyond this, it seems that it could also help philosophers navigate certain debates in which deep ecology theorists have been involved, or evaluate some of the criticisms they have faced. Let us turn, then, to explore this additional facet of the relationship between deep ecology and conservation psychology, beginning with a look at one of the most serious charges that has been leveled against deep ecological thought.

Among environmental ethicists, probably the most widespread critique of the philosophical position we have been discussing is that it presumes some version of an egoist moral psychology. In specific, the charge is that deep ecology theorists assume that we humans seek primarily to promote our own well-being, or further our self-development, and that consequently we will act in environmentally friendly ways only if we feel that doing so will somehow aid in these efforts. Therefore, the argument continues, these thinkers promote ecological identities in an attempt to convince us that, since we are interdependent with the natural world, whenever we act to benefit nature we really benefit ourselves. The sort of environmentalism that deep ecology theorists actually advocate, critics say, does not involve expanding our concern for others who are recognized as being worthy of respect, but merely expanding our sphere of self-concern, via an ecologically expanded sense of Self.[48]

As argued in the last chapter, the main reason why deep ecology theorists are exposed to this criticism is that they commonly embrace the norm of "Self-realization," or the idea that the most fundamental goal toward which we and other living things can and ought to strive is to actualize our existential potential.[49] This normative commitment, in turn, routinely leads them to describe the pro-environmental activities of those who identify with nature as being motivated by a desire to promote, protect, or defend themselves. Naess, for instance, says that "if the 'self' is widened and deepened . . . protection of free nature is felt and conceived as protection of ourselves."[50] In a similar vein, Fox writes in an early essay that the "message of deep ecology is that we ought to care as deeply and compassionately as possible about [the fate of the earth]—not because it *affects* us but because it *is* us."[51]

Of course, conservation psychologists do not, as a rule, make any special commitment to the norm of Self-realization. Even so, they sometimes frame pro-environmental behaviors in precisely the same self-referential terms that deep ecology theorists employ. Steven Arnocky, Mirella Stroink, and Teresa DeCicco assert that with a broadly ecological sense of self, "one is likely to care for and actively protect the environment because the entire ecosystem is considered an integral part of the person. Therefore, they are in a way, protecting the self by actively protecting the environment."[52] Mayer and Frantz, too, say that "if people feel connected to nature, then they will be less likely to harm it, for harming it would in essence be harming their very self."[53] Clayton likewise proposes that "an environmental identity can serve to transform the motive for environmental behavior; when one shares an identity with another, promoting their welfare is selfish rather than altruistic."[54]

On the surface, these comments appear to vindicate the claim that the approach to environmental problems taken by deep ecology theorists remains somehow self- or human-centered. The problem, however, is that they seem not to reflect the results of conservation psychologists' own inquiries into the relationship between environmental identity and environmental *values*, results that show fairly clearly that those who identify with nature typically do not relate to it on the basis of concern for themselves. In fact, as we saw before, researchers regularly report a correlation between environmental identity and "biospheric" or "eco-centric" perspectives, both of which are conceptually and operationally defined specifically in opposition to egoistic or anthropocentric orientations that predispose people to value nature in terms of how it benefits themselves or other human beings.[55] The conclusion toward which this research points, therefore, is not that identification prompts us to realize that protecting nature is really in our own interests; it is, rather, that this sort of human–nature bonding fosters genuinely other-oriented sensibilities about why it is that nature matters.

In conjunction with this, we might observe that more than one study has found that people high in environmental identity approach ecological problem-solving differently than those with less inclusive self-construals. In the commons dilemma cited earlier, Arnocky, Stroink, and DeCicco found that respondents with ecological identities were more likely than others to engage the scenario by drawing on beliefs such as "I feel responsible for the well-being of the land and ecosystem."[56] Similarly, a survey conducted by Clayton discovered that those who were more strongly identified with nature placed greater emphasis on the principles of "responsibility to other species" and "the rights of the environment" when responding to environmental conflict cases.[57] At least part of what these studies show, therefore, is the heightened degree to which people who identify with nature view nature itself as morally significant and thereafter bring this perception to bear on their practical deliberations.

Such outcomes thus give every indication that, as Wesley Schultz et al. express, "[p]eople who include aspects of nature within their cognitive representation of self tend to be concerned about more than just *me*."[58]

What, then, can be said about the role of identity in this? Why might it be that a genuine concern for other-than-human beings would accompany our having a sense of connectedness to and kinship with them? Such questions require some degree of speculation, it is true, but one possibility is simply that broad-based environmental identities are particularly well suited to foster these more egalitarian sorts of moral sensibilities. As psychologists have known for some time, collective identities do not always pair with nonhierarchical or "horizontal" perceptions of others.[59] Still, numerous ecophilosophical texts, as well as the works of many conservation psychologists, suggest that viewing ourselves as akin to and connected with other-than-human entities makes it difficult for us to conceive of ourselves as morally superior to them.[60] Among the most relevant research findings on this subject is Clayton's detection of an association between environmental identity and what has been called "horizontal collectivism," meaning that people who were identified with nature in this way expressed not only a sense of relatedness to other-than-human beings, but also a more egalitarian sensibility about who these others were and how their relations with them were configured.[61]

Another possible explanation for why other-oriented ethical views correlate with ecological identities is one that may have been first proposed by Naess himself. In his discussions of identification-as-kinship, Naess argues that having a sense of similarity with other-than-human beings allows us to empathize or sympathize with them, which encourages a kind of self-other intertwining in which we come to rank their well-being among our own primary interests.[62] Lending some credence to this line of thought, Wesley Schultz conducted an experiment which revealed that people's expressions of biospheric concerns increased significantly after they participated in an activity where they were asked to take the perspectives of other-than-human animals. In explanation of this, Schultz suggests that the perspective-taking exercise facilitated empathy, and "temporarily increased the extent to which participants viewed themselves as interconnected with nature." The general conclusion that Schultz draws, therefore, is that "any activity that reduces an individual's perceived separation between self and nature will lead to an increase in that individual's biospheric concern."[63]

A final potential response here has to do with the way in which an ecologically inclusive identity influences how we attend to and interpret information about the more-than-human world. As Clayton explains, "Identities tend to generate cognitive schemas that affect the way people organize and process information."[64] Hence the development of an ecological sense of Self is likely to alter not only the degree to which we focus on environmental issues, but also how we frame those issues, evaluate their significance, and respond to them behaviorally.[65] Such cognitive and behavioral shifts could, assuredly, be related to the fact that an environmental identity gives us to realize that what impacts nature often impacts ourselves. It appears equally likely, however, that there is a reciprocal relation wherein these shifts are both driven by and help to promote a sincere investment in the well-being of other-than-human entities, further encouraging exactly the sorts of other-regarding sentiments that those who identity with nature commonly express.

PLACES VERSUS THE ENVIRONMENT?

In all probability, much of what has just been said about environmental identity is also true of place attachment. Due to certain gaps in the literature, though, it is at present difficult to evaluate this presumption carefully.[66] Current research on place attachment is immediately relevant, however, to another debate in which some deep ecology theorists have been involved; it is one that is less frequently discussed, but is no less important to an understanding of connectedness to nature than that which we have been reviewing.

In *Toward a Transpersonal Ecology*, Fox argues that personally based identification with nature is problematic insofar as the attachments that result from it are constrained by the extent of our firsthand interactions. Thus, it seems to promote our being "partial" to, or morally biased in favor of, those other-than-human entities with whom we are most directly acquainted. Transpersonal identification, on the other hand, is said to avoid fostering such an exclusionary moral outlook, precisely because it entails a more inclusive sense of bonding with other-than-human entities.[67] Fox contends, therefore, that although personal identification need not be wholly disparaged, environmentalists should advocate for a broader sense of interconnection with nature that can contextualize and moderate the moral favoritism that our personal experience inevitably generates. He believes, that is, that while personal identification is "an inescapable aspect of living and . . . plays a fundamental role in human development,"[68] transpersonal identification should be prioritized as a "corrective to the partiality and problems of attachment that are associated with personally based identification."[69]

In response to this, some ecofeminist philosophers have claimed that Fox's position repeats a patriarchal gesture that valorizes the abstract and universal at the expense of the concrete and particular. Marti Kheel, for example, asserts that Fox's thought reflects "the familiar masculinist quest to escape the unpredictable world of particularity for something more distant, enduring, and abstract."[70] Similarly, Val Plumwood argues that Fox treats particularity as "corrupting and self-interested," and shows a related preference for more abstract and impersonal forms of association with others.[71] Such a disparaging take on personal relations, she says, not only potentially "breeds moral blindness or indifference" to individual other-than-human beings,[72] but also leads Fox to espouse a view that "cannot allow . . . for the deep and highly particularistic attachment to place" that motivates many contemporary conservationists' involvement in environmental causes.[73]

Given the conceptual parallels we have drawn, this dispute can rightly be said to concern the relative merits of place attachment and environmental identity, particularly as these may involve different sorts of "in group" or "out group" biases.[74] Expressed in these terms, Fox's contention is that if our only attachments are to particular places, we will tend to situate other parts of nature outside our moral purview, and thus either ignore the larger ecological issues that impact them, or perhaps even strive to protect our cherished places at their expense. It appears, moreover, that conservation psychologists may be inclined to agree with Fox on this point, especially in light of those studies mentioned before which indicate that place-protective attitudes can sometimes fuel opposition to pro-environmental efforts. Indeed, in a statement that calls to mind the idea that place attachment occurs in relation to "geographically locatable" spaces, Clayton says that one of the advantages of an environmental identity is that it has "no fixed geographic boundaries."[75] She even suggests, as Fox does in regard to transpersonal identification, that because of its less geographically restricted character, this wider self-construal could provide us with a "superordinate" set of commitments to the environment, commitments that could cut across our more local identity-related attachments and help minimize whatever conflicts that they might produce.[76]

Despite initial appearances, however, a number of findings related to place attachment counsel against taking an overly skeptical attitude toward it. Scannell and Gifford, for instance, observe that people often express affinity for places because of the opportunities for *social* interaction they afford, and their research has found that such "civic place attachment" does not correlate with pro-environmental behaviors in the way that "natural place attachment" does.[77] To this can be added that place *dependence* may be less effective at fostering pro-environmental concerns than place *identity*. Hence, in cases like that wherein rural Michiganders opposed recreational closures intended to aid gray wolf recovery, it is entirely plausible that such opposition was driven not by protective attitudes toward a natural area per se, but by people's desire to continue the social and recreational activities they conducted therein. What this research points out, in other words, is that place-based hostility toward environmental projects may not so much reveal the inadequacies of personal identification with nature as highlight the all-too-familiar phenomenon of social and recreational interests overriding environmental ones.

Of course, there is no guarantee that attachment to natural places will always serve conservation goals. A study on the Big Island of Hawaii, for instance, found that natural place attachment was negatively correlated with behaviors aimed at controlling the invasive albizia tree (*Falcataria moluccana*), and qualitative interviews revealed the likely cause to be that the study's participants regarded the species as a part of the biophysical landscape to which they had bonded.[78] But cases like this need not necessarily be interpreted as instances in which place attachment must be checked by more generalized forms of environmental concern. Rather, they demonstrate the potentially differing roles that people's attachments to various features of natural environments (e.g., the native or introduced components thereof) might play in motivating their behavior, and highlight the challenges of promoting people's bonding to ecologically healthy landscapes in a world where local lands are increasingly disturbed.[79]

Arguably more germane to this conversation are the many indications conservation psychologists give that place attachment could itself be vital to the development of more general environmental sensibilities.[80] Clayton, for example, believes that personal bonds with nature factor into environmental identities, and therefore her Environmental Identity Scale includes items such as "I feel that I have roots to a particular geographic location that had a significant impact on my development."[81] In concert with Clayton, many psychologists who speak favorably of environmental identities also propose that place-specific activities are useful for promoting them,[82] and at least one recent study apparently corroborates this relationship.[83] Even more telling is research conducted by Stephen Zavestoski at a workshop sponsored by the Institute for Deep Ecology. Through questionnaires and interviews, Zavestoski discovered not only that workshop participants were quite high in what he calls "ecological identity,"[84] but also that most of them "had either special places in nature, a place that had been special to them but was developed or destroyed, or a particular experience in nature that was significant in developing concern for nature."[85]

It seems, therefore, that Plumwood is right to say that a "deep and highly particularistic attachment to place" underlies many people's engagement in environmental issues. It also seems that there is a more balanced relationship between personal and transpersonal identification than Fox's writing usually conveys.[86] Where Fox depicts identification as a process whereby, ideally, a broad-based ecological consciousness moves inward to hold our personal attachments in check, the remarks above suggest that it is better viewed as one whereby our concrete bonds with nature move outward to connect us to others who are increasingly distant.[87] Thus, we could say that while the propensity of place attachment to grow beyond its geographic bounds is something to be welcomed, we need not envision this as a matter of transcending our personal affiliations with other-than-human entities, or inscribing them in a globalized perspective that somehow constrains their ethically harmful potential. Our personal attachments to nature remain important even as they expand into more encompassing moral sensibilities, which is, perhaps, what Naess signals when he writes that "from identifying with 'one's nearest,' higher level unities are created through circles of friends, local communities, tribes, compatriots, races, humanity, life, and, ultimately . . . unity with the supreme whole."[88]

ORIENTING OURSELVES TO NATURE

Altogether, then, the preceding analysis shows that conservation psychology does indeed have substantial contributions to make to philosophical inquiries into deep ecological thought. It also shows fairly convincingly that there is a great deal of merit in the ecosophies articulated by Naess and other supporters of the deep ecology movement. As these thinkers have claimed, and social scientists have begun to confirm, various forms of human–nature bonding have crucial roles to play both in promoting nonanthropocentric values and in motivating pro-environmental behaviors. The overarching theme that emerges from this interdisciplinary examination is, quite simply, that ecological identities matter, and probably much more than most of us have hitherto imagined.

Of course, to say that identification with nature matters in these ways is not to say that it in some way dictates or commands what we think and do. Environmental attitudes and behaviors rooted in a sense of connectedness to nature are not closed to reflection and deliberation, nor are they impervious to information and evidence. As both deep ecology theorists and conservation psychologists would be quick to observe, our self-construals function less as strict determinants of thought and action than they do as headings or orientations that incline us to make sense of and comport ourselves toward the world in certain ways. Hence while it is true that an ecological sense of self impacts how we receive and respond to information, it is also true that the specifics of what we come to believe in, care about, and do are shaped by myriad additional considerations—something that subsequent chapters surely will demonstrate.[89]

In exploring these connections between the writings of conservation psychologists and deep ecology theorists, we have not addressed every concern that arises in relation to an environmental perspective that takes connectedness to nature seriously. Many of these concerns, interestingly enough, derive not from academic theory but from the changing character of modern life itself. Human beings are becoming increasingly mobile, urbanized, and experientially disconnected from a natural world that is itself becoming increasingly managed, manipulated, and ecologically disturbed. What impacts might these changes have on our ability and willingness to connect with others who are other-than-human? To what lengths will we be inclined to go to rectify harms done to the environment, or restore places that have been degraded, if these are the only places we have ever known? What will we ultimately value and seek to protect as living nature becomes more and more compromised, and less and less conspicuous in our lives?

These are troubling questions, no doubt, many of which intersect with the subject of environmental values that has been broached several times already. This subject, as much as any other, motivates many deep ecology theorists' emphasis on identification with nature, and the exploration of questions about nature's value has in fact been a focal issue for environmental philosophers of nearly every sort. In the next chapter, therefore, we will examine in greater detail the relationship between identification with nature and environmental values in an attempt to understand more fully the phenomenon of connectedness to nature by understanding more thoroughly the ways in which it orients our evaluative attitudes.

NOTES

1. Carol D. Saunders, "The Emerging Field of Conservation Psychology," *Human Ecology Review* 10, no. 2 (2003): 138–39; Susan D. Clayton and Carol D. Saunders, "Environmental and Conservation Psychology," introduction to *The Oxford Handbook of Environmental and Conservation Psychology*, ed. Susan D. Clayton (Oxford: Oxford UP, 2012), 1–3.

2. See Clayton and Saunders, "Environmental Psychology and Conservation Psychology," 4; Peter H. Kahn, Jr., "The Next Phase for Ecopsychology: Ideas and Directions," *Ecopsychology* 5, no. 3 (September 2013): 164.

3. Saunders, "The Emerging Field of Conservation Psychology," 138. See also Susan Clayton and Gene Meyers, *Conservation Psychology: Understanding and Promoting Human Care for Nature* (West Sussex: Wiley-Blackwell, 2009), chapter 1.

4. George Sessions, "Basic Principles of Deep Ecology," *Ecophilosophy* VI (May 1984): 5.

5. Warwick Fox, *Toward a Transpersonal Ecology: Developing New Foundations for Environmentalism* (Albany: SUNY Press, 1995), 246–47. Alan Drengson and Yuichi Inoue make essentially the same point about Naess when they write that "Naess advocates a psychological rather than a moralistic approach to environmentalism" (Introduction to *The Deep Ecology Movement: An Introductory Anthology*, ed. Alan Drengson and Yuichi Inoue [Berkeley: North Atlantic Books, 1995], xxii).

6. A relatively early, and thorough, treatment of deep ecological thought in relation to environmental psychology can be found in Elizabeth Ann Bragg, "Towards

Ecological Self: Deep Ecology Meets Constructionist Self-Theory," *Journal of Environmental Psychology* 16, no. 2 (1996): 93–108.

7. See Kalevi M. Korpela, "Place Attachment," in *The Oxford Handbook of Environmental and Conservation Psychology*, 148–63.

8. Leila Scannell and Robert Gifford, "Defining Place Attachment: A Tripartite Organizing Framework," *Journal of Environmental Psychology* 30, no. 1 (2010): 1.

9. Jerry J. Vaske and Katherine C. Kobrin, "Place Attachment and Environmentally Responsible Behavior," *The Journal of Environmental Education* 32, no. 4 (2001): 17; Joanna Tonge et al., "The Effect of Place Attachment on Pro-Environment Behavioral Intentions of Visitors to Coastal Natural Area Tourist Destinations," *Journal of Travel Research* 54, no. 6 (2015): 731; Roger L. Moore and Alan R. Graefe, "Attachments to Recreation Settings: The Case of Rail-Trail Users," *Leisure Sciences* 16, no. 1 (1994): 20; Daniel R. Williams and Jerry J. Vaske, "The Measurement of Place Attachment: Validity and Generalizability of a Psychometric Approach," *Forest Science* 49, no. 6 (2003): 831; Korpela, "Place Attachment," 149.

10. Vaske and Kobrin, "Place Attachment and Environmentally Responsible Behavior," 17. See also Williams and Vaske, "The Measurement of Place Attachment," 831; Tonge et al., "The Effect of Place Attachment," 731; Elizabeth A. Halpenny, "Pro-Environmental Behaviours and Park Visitors: The Effect of Place Attachment," *Journal of Environmental Psychology* 30, no. 4 (2010): 410; Harold M. Proshansky et al., "Place-Identity: Physical World Socialization of the Self," *Journal of Environmental Psychology* 3, no. 1 (1983): 57–83; Harold M. Proshansky, "The City and Self-Identity," *Environment and Behavior* 10, no. 2 (1978): 155.

11. Suzanne Bott, James G. Cantrill, and Olin Eugene Myers, Jr., "Place and the Promise of Conservation Psychology," *Human Ecology Review* 10, no. 2 (2003): 106.

12. See, for example, Williams and Vaske, "The Measurement of Place Attachment," 835; Daniel R. Williams and Joseph W. Roggenbuck, "Measuring Place Attachment: Some Preliminary Results," paper presented at the session on Outdoor Planning and Management, NRPA Symposium on Leisure Research, San Antonio, Texas (1989); Steve Semken, "Place Attachment Inventory (ASU) 1.3," accessed November 5, 2014, http://serc.carleton.edu/NAGTWorkshops/assess/activities/semken.html.

13. Arne Naess, "An Example of a Place: Tvergastein," in *The Ecology of Wisdom: Writings by Arne Naess*, ed. Alan Drengson and Bill Devall (Berkeley: Counterpoint, 2008), 45–64.

14. Bill Devall, *Simple in Means, Rich in Ends: Practicing Deep Ecology* (Salt Lake City: Peregrine Smith Books, 1988), 70.

15. As will be shown, some deep ecology theorists, like Warwick Fox, speak less strongly than others in favor of personally based forms of identification. Others, however, like Bill Devall, advocate it quite strongly (see *Simple in Means*, 57–58).

16. Halpenny, "Pro-Environmental Behaviours and Park Visitors," 415; Richard C. Stedman, "Toward a Social Psychology of Place: Predicting Behavior from Place-Based Cognitions, Attitude, and Identity," *Environment and Behavior* 34, no. 5 (September 2002): 561–81; Vaske and Kobrin, "Place Attachment and Environmentally Responsible Behavior," 20; Gerard Kyle et al., "Effects of Place Attachment on Users' Perceptions of Social and Environmental Conditions in a

Natural Setting," *Journal of Environmental Psychology* 24, no. 2 (2004): 221; Nathan D. Mullendore, Jessica D. Ulrich-Schadb, and Linda Stalker Prokopy, "U.S. Farmers' Sense of Place and Its Relation to Conservation Behavior," *Landscape and Urban Planning* 140 (2015): 67–75.

17. Gerard T. Kyle, James D. Absher, and Alan R. Graefe, "The Moderating Role of Place Attachment on the Relationship Between Attitudes Toward Fees and Spending Preferences," *Leisure Sciences* 25, no. 1 (2003): 33–50.

18. Tonge et al., "The Effect of Place Attachment," 730–43.

19. Kyle et al., "Effects of Place Attachment on Users' Perceptions," 221.

20. It is important to remember that place dependence and place identity are both dimensions of place attachment, and not all studies of place attachment analyze them independently. It also seems likely that bonds of dependence could facilitate or transform into bonds of identity in some cases.

21. See Arne Naess, "Identification as a Source of Deep Ecological Attitudes," in *Deep Ecology*, ed. Michael Tobias (San Diego: Avant Books, 1985), 263; Frederic L. Bender, *The Culture of Extinction: Toward a Philosophy of Deep Ecology* (Amherst: Humanity Books, 2003), 424; Bill Devall and George Sessions, *Deep Ecology: Living as if Nature Mattered* (Salt Lake City: Gibbs Smith, 1985), 67.

22. Vaske and Kobrin, "Place Attachment and Environmentally Responsible Behavior," 20.

23. Halpenny, "Pro-Environmental Behaviours and Park Visitors," 417.

24. See, for example, Patrick Devine-Wright, "Beyond NIMBYism: Towards an Integrated Framework for Understanding Public Perceptions of Wind Energy," *Wind Energy* 8 (2005): 125–39; David Uzzell et al., "Place Identification, Social Cohesion, and Environmental Sustainability," *Environment and Behavior* 34, no. 1 (January 2002): 26–53; Korpela, "Place Attachment," 157. Some of the mixed results regarding place attachment and pro-environmental behaviors may be due to the diversity of measures used to assess it, which perhaps measure different aspects, or even forms, of place attachment. Some of these issues are illustrated in a study of Hawaiian farmers, which analyzed place attachment in such a way that it seems unclear if what was being measured was attachment to the natural environment, to cultivated lands, to the sociocultural environment, or to some combination of these (see Noa Kekuewa Lincoln and Nicole M. Ardoin, "Cultivating Values: Environmental Values and Sense of Place as Correlates of Sustainable Agricultural Practices," *Agriculture and Human Values* 33 [2016]: 389–401). This point about conflicting models of place attachment is revisited below.

25. James G. Cantrill, "The Role of a Sense of Self-in-Place and Risk Amplification in Promoting the Conservation of Wildlife," *Human Dimensions of Wildlife* 16, no. 2 (2011): 78. The prior assessment of place attachment mentioned here is found in James G. Cantrill, "The Environmental Self and a Sense of Place: Communication Foundations for Regional Ecosystem Management," *Journal of Applied Communication Research* 26, no. 3 (1998): 301–18.

26. Julie Whitburn, Wayne Linklater, and Wokje Abrahamse report that social scientists currently employ at least seventeen different scales to measure this sort

of connection to nature (see "Meta-Analysis of Human Connection to Nature and Proenvironmental Behavior," *Conservation Biology* 34, no. 1 [2019]: 3). They also claim, however, that these scales are "highly correlated" and likely "measure the same underlying construct of connectedness to nature" (3).

27. For an overview of these discussions, see Clayton and Myers, *Conservation Psychology*, chapter 8; Teresa L. DeCicco and Mirella L. Stroink, "A Third Model of Self-Construal: The Metapersonal Self," *International Journal of Transpersonal Studies* 26 (2007): 82–104; Cantrill, "The Environmental Self"; Jan E. Stets and Chris F. Biga, "Bringing Identity Theory into Environmental Sociology," *Sociological Theory* 21, no. 4 (December 2003): 398–423.

28. Susan Clayton, "Environmental Identity: A Conceptual and an Operational Definition," in *Identity and the Natural Environment: The Psychological Significance of Nature*, ed. Susan Clayton and Susan Opotow (Cambridge: MIT Press, 2003), 45–46.

29. Susan D. Clayton, "Environment and Identity," in *The Oxford Handbook of Environmental and Conservation Psychology*, 172.

30. Ibid. See also Clayton and Myers, *Conservation Psychology*, 61.

31. Clayton, "Environmental Identity: A Conceptual and an Operational Definition," 46.

32. Clayton, "Environment and Identity," 170. See also Clayton and Myers, *Conservation Psychology*, 62.

33. In discussing their construct of "Nature Relatedness," Elizabeth Nisbet, John Zelenski, and Steven Murphy make this connection to deep ecological thought explicit, writing that "[n]ature relatedness is not unlike the deep ecology concept of an ecological self, the notion of a self-construal that includes the natural world. The concept of NR encompasses one's appreciation for and understanding of our interconnectedness with all other living things on the earth" ("The Nature Relatedness Scale: Linking Individuals' Connection with Nature to Environmental Concern and Behavior," *Environment and Behavior* 41, 5 [September 2009]: 718).

34. Not all assessment tools display this twin emphasis on both belonging and kinship. For example, Schultz's "Inclusion of Nature in the Self" scale is difficult to assess in these terms, as is the "Metapersonal Self Scale" developed by DeCicco and Stroink. See P. Wesley Schultz, "Inclusion with Nature: The Psychology of Human-Nature Relations," in *Psychology of Sustainable Development*, ed. Peter Schmuck and Wesley P. Schultz (New York: Springer, 2002), 61–78; DeCicco and Stroink, "A Third Model of Self-Construal."

35. F. Stephan Mayer and Cynthia McPherson Frantz, "The Connectedness to Nature Scale: A Measure of Individuals' Feeling in Community with Nature," *Journal of Environmental Psychology* 24, no. 4 (2004): 513.

36. Clayton, "Environmental Identity: A Conceptual and an Operational Definition," 61–62.

37. Fox, *Toward a Transpersonal Ecology*, chapter 8.

38. Clayton, "Environmental Identity: A Conceptual and an Operational Definition," 54–55.

39. Suzanne C. Gagnon Thompson and Michelle A. Barton, "Ecocentric and Anthropocentric Attitudes toward the Environment," *Journal of Environmental Psychology* 14, no. 2 (1994): 149.

40. Maximilian Dornhoff et al., "Nature Relatedness and Environmental Concern of Young People in Ecuador and Germany," *Frontiers in Psychology* 10 (March 2019): 1–13, https://doi: 10.3389/fpsyg.2019.00453; P. Wesley Schultz, "The Structure of Environmental Concern: Concern for Self, Other People, and the Biosphere," *Journal of Environmental Psychology* 21, no. 4 (2001): 336; Schultz, "Inclusion with Nature," 72; Mayer and Frantz, "The Connectedness to Nature Scale," 510–11.

41. Paul C. Stern and Thomas Dietz, "The Value Basis of Environmental Concern," *Journal of Social Issues* 50, no. 3 (1994): 69–70, 78.

42. Caroline M. L. Mackay and Michael T. Schmitt, "Do People Who Feel Connected to Nature Do More to Protect It? A Meta-Analysis," *Journal of Environmental Psychology* 65 (2019): 1–9, https://doi.org/10.1016/j.jenvp.201 9.101323; Marion Dresner et al., "Environmental Identity, Pro-Environmental Behaviors, and Civic Engagement of Volunteer Stewards in Portland Area Parks," *Environmental Education Research* 21, no. 7 (2015): 991–1010; P. Wesley Schultz et al., "Values and Their Relationship to Environmental Concern and Conservation Behavior," *Journal of Cross-Cultural Psychology* 36, no. 4 (July 2005): 457–75; Stets and Biga, "Bringing Identity Theory into Environmental Sociology"; Susan Clayton, "Environmental Identity: A Conceptual and an Operational Definition," 55–56.

43. Steven Arnocky, Mirella Stroink, and Teresa DeCicco, "Self-Construal Predicts Environmental Concern, Cooperation, and Conservation," *Journal of Environmental Psychology* 27, no. 4 (2007): 255–64. This essay follows previous work on the "metapersonal" self-construal, as discussed in DeCicco and Stroink, "A Third Model of Self-Construal."

44. Stets and Biga, "Bringing Identity Theory into Environmental Sociology," 413. The conception of "ecocentric environment identity" used in this study was, like Clayton's, based on the classification of ecocentric and anthropocentric views developed by Thompson and Barton (see "Ecocentric and Anthropocentric Attitudes"). When Stets and Biga assessed this type of identity, moreover, they did so using a scale very similar to Clayton's "Environmental Identity Scale" and others like it (see Stets and Biga, "Bringing Identity Theory into Environmental Sociology," 409).

45. Judith I. M. de Groot and Linda Steg, "Relationships between Value Orientations, Self-Determined Motivational Types and Pro-Environmental Behavioural Intentions," *Journal of Environmental Psychology* 30, no. 4 (2010): 368–78; Thompson and Barton, "Ecocentric and Anthropocentric Attitudes," 153.

46. Arne Naess, "Identification as a Source," 264.

47. For analyses of these limitations, see Whitburn, Linklater, and Abrahamse, "Meta-Analysis of Human Connection to Nature and Proenvironmental Behavior"; Brian Restall and Elisabeth Conrad, "A Literature Review of Connectedness to Nature and Its Potential for Environmental Management," *Journal of Environmental Management* 159 (2015): 264–78.

48. See Eric Katz, "Against the Inevitability of Anthropocentrism," in *Beneath the Surface: Critical Essays in the Philosophy of Deep Ecology*, ed. Eric Katz, Andrew

Light, and David Rothenberg (Cambridge: MIT Press, 2000), 17–42; Val Plumwood, *Feminism and the Mastery of Nature* (London: Routledge, 1993).

49. See Arne Naess, *Ecology Community and Lifestyle: Outline of an Ecosophy*, trans. and rev. David Rothenberg (Cambridge: Cambridge University Press, 1989), and Arne Naess, "Self-Realization: An Ecological Approach to Being-in-the-World," in *Deep Ecology for the Twenty-First Century: Readings on the Philosophy and Practice of the New Environmentalism*, ed. George Sessions (Boston: Shambhala, 1995), 225–39.

50. Naess, "Self-Realization," 236.

51. Warwick Fox, "Deep Ecology: A New Philosophy of Our Time?," in *Philosophical Dialogues: Arne Naess and the Progress of Ecophilosophy*, ed. Nina Witoszek and Andrew Brennan (Lanham: Rowman & Littlefield, 1999), 162.

52. Arnocky, Stroink, and DeCicco, "Self-Construal Predicts Environmental Concern," 262.

53. Mayer and Frantz, "The Connectedness to Nature Scale," 512.

54. Clayton, "Environment and Identity," 174.

55. Stern and Dietz, "The Value Basis of Environmental Concern," 70; Thompson and Barton, "Ecocentric and Anthropocentric Attitudes," 149–50.

56. Arnocky, Stroink, and DeCicco, "Self-Construal Predicts Environmental Concern," 263.

57. Clayton, "Environmental Identity: A Conceptual and an Operational Definition," 57.

58. P. Wesley Schultz et al., "Values and Their Relationship to Environmental Concern," 70–71.

59. Theodore M. Singelis et al., "Horizontal and Vertical Dimensions of Individualism and Collectivism: A Theoretical and Measurement Refinement," *Cross-Cultural Research* 29, no. 3 (August 1995): 240–75; Harry C. Triandis and Michele J. Gelfand, "Converging Measurement of Horizontal and Vertical Individualism and Collectivism," *Journal of Personality and Social Psychology* 74, no. 1 (1998): 118–28.

60. See, for example, Paul Taylor, *Respect for Nature* (Princeton: Princeton University Press, 1986). Aldo Leopold claimed that a deeply felt sense of ecological interdependence with others changes our perceived role "from conqueror of the land-community to plain member and citizen of it" (*A Sand County Almanac* [New York: Ballantine Books, 1970], 240). Likewise, Bill Devall and George Sessions assert that identification with nature leads us to "respect all human and non-human individuals in their own right as parts of the whole without feeling the need to set up hierarchies of species with humans at the top" (Bill Devall and George Sessions, *Deep Ecology: Living as if Nature Mattered* [Salt Lake City: Gibbs Smith, 1985], 68). See also Christopher Uhl, *Developing Ecological Consciousness: The End of Separation*, 2nd ed. (Lanham: Rowman & Littlefield, 2013).

61. Clayton, "Environmental Identity: A Conceptual and an Operational Definition," 54–5. See also Singelis et al., "Horizontal and Vertical Dimensions of Individualism and Collectivism."

62. See Naess, "Self-Realization," 227; Naess, "Identification as a Source," 262.

63. P. Wesley Schultz, "Empathizing With Nature: The Effects of Perspective Taking on Concern for Environmental Issues," *Journal of Social Issues* 56, no. 3 (2000): 403.

64. Clayton, "Environment and Identity," 167.

65. Patrick Devine-Wright and Susan Clayton, "Introduction to the Special Issue: Place, Identity and Environmental Behaviour," *Journal of Environmental Psychology* 30, no. 3 (2010): 268–9; Clayton and Myers, *Conservation Psychology*, 68.

66. This is primarily due to the fact that conservation and environmental psychologists seem to have focused on the relations between place attachment and pro-environmental *behaviors* more so than the possible correlations between place-specific attachments to nature and environmental *attitudes* or *values*. For some discussion of this latter topic, see Megha Budruk, Heidi Thomas, and Timothy Tyrrell, "Urban Green Spaces: A Study of Place Attachment and Environmental Attitudes in India," *Society and Natural Resources*, 22, no. 9 (2009): 824–39; Gregory Brown and Christopher Raymond, "The Relationship between Place Attachment and Landscape Values: Toward Mapping Place Attachment," *Applied Geography* 27, no. 2 (April 2007): 89–111.

67. Warwick Fox, *Toward a Transpersonal Ecology*, 255–68. Fox provides similar commentary in "The Deep Ecology-Ecofeminism Debate and Its Parallels," *Environmental Ethics* 11, no. 1 (Spring 1989): 3–25.

68. Warwick Fox, *Toward a Transpersonal Ecology*, 266–67.

69. Ibid., 267.

70. Marti Kheel, *Nature Ethics: An Ecofeminist Perspective* (Lanham: Rowman & Littlefield, 2008), 195. See also Marti Kheel, "Ecofeminism and Deep Ecology: Rethinking Identity and Difference," in *Reweaving the World: The Emergence of Ecofeminism*, ed. Irene Diamond and G. F. Orenstein (San Francisco: Sierra Club Books, 1990), 128–37.

71. Val Plumwood, *Feminism and the Mastery of Nature* (London: Routledge: 1993), 181. See also Val Plumwood, "Nature, Self and Gender: Feminism, Environmental Philosophy and the Critique of Rationalism," *Hypatia* 6, no. 1 (Spring 1991): 15.

72. Carol Gilligan, "Moral Orientation and Moral Development," in *Women and Moral Theory*, ed. Eva Feder Kittay and Diana T. Meyers (New York: Rowman & Littlefield, 1987), 24. This passage from Gilligan is cited by Plumwood in *Feminism and the Mastery of Nature*, 181.

73. Plumwood, *Feminism and the Mastery of Nature*, 182. A similar critique of Fox is found in Karen Warren's "Ecofeminist Philosophy and Deep Ecology," in *Philosophical Dialogues*, 255–69.

74. Tom Crompton and Tim Kasser, *Meeting Environmental Challenges: The Role of Human Identity* (Godalming: WWF-UK, 2009).

75. Clayton, "Environmental Identity: A Conceptual and an Operational Definition," 59.

76. Ibid., 59–60. In these remarks, Clayton is not discussing the question of whether or not environmental identity might moderate conflicts among people with more local attachments to *nature*. Rather, she talks about how environmental identity

may minimize conflicts between people with disparate *social* identities, such as national identities; the idea is that, since environmental attachments do not stop at national borders, they may encourage people with different and potentially conflicting national identities to put political differences aside and focus on environmental issues. An ability to bridge differences in social identity could, of course, be true of certain kinds of place attachment as well. The parallel that I am trying to highlight between Clayton's comments and Fox's, though, is that both portray environmental identity as an overarching sensibility that can in some sense transcend more divergent identity-forming attachments that people possess, thereby helping to ameliorate problems that may be associated with the latter. This, together with the contrast between place attachment and environmental identity that was explained earlier in this chapter, is what underlie the comments here.

77. Leila Scannell and Robert Gifford, "The Relations between Natural and Civic Place Attachment and Pro-Environmental Behavior," *Journal of Environmental Psychology* 30, no. 3 (2010): 290, 294–95.

78. Rebecca M. Niemiec et al., "Civic and Natural Place Attachment as Correlates of Resident Invasive Species Control Behavior in Hawaii," *Biological Conservation* 209 (2017): 415–22.

79. This observation might thus indicate the need for a more nuanced distinction than that of what exists between "civic" and "natural" place attachment, since attachment to nature can itself take shape in relation to different aspects of local natural environments. It is possible, that is, for people to bond with both disturbed or manipulated natural settings, as well as with more ecologically intact settings, and these different forms of place attachment seem likely to have different implications for environmental protection and conservation.

80. Some of the literature already cited regarding this issue includes Vaske and Kobrin, "Place Attachment and Environmentally Responsible Behavior"; Halpenny, "Pro-Environmental Behaviours and Park Visitors."

81. Clayton, "Environmental Identity: A Conceptual and an Operational Definition," 53, 62.

82. Arnocky, Stroink, and DeCicco, "Self-Construal Predicts Environmental Concern," 262–63; Schultz, "Empathizing With Nature," 403.

83. Frances M. Kiesling and Christie M. Manning, "How Green Is Your Thumb? Environmental Gardening Identity and Ecological Gardening Practices," *Journal of Environmental Psychology* 30, no. 3 (2010): 315–27. This article reports the results of a study of gardeners in which Kiesling and Manning employed Clayton's Environmental Identity Scale. The authors most often seem to attribute ecological gardening practices to people possessing an environmental identity, as indicated by their statement that "environmental identity does indeed provide a basis for many different expressions of environmental friendliness" (323). In places, though, they acknowledge that this relationship might be reversed, and that it could be that, through gardening practices, "environmental identity will also increase" (323). When Clayton discusses this study, she suggests that the gardening/environmental identity relationship may work in either direction: "Environmental identity," she says, "can . . . be nurtured, and socially expressed, through gardening" (Clayton, "Environment and Identity," 170).

84. Stephen Zavestoski, "Constructing and Maintaining Ecological Identities: The Strategies of Deep Ecologists," in *Identity and the Natural Environment: the Psychological Significance of Nature*, ed. Susan Clayton and Susan Opotow (Cambridge: MIT Press, 2003), 305.

85. Ibid., 304. Mitchell Thomashow reports essentially the same thing as Zavestoski in his *Ecological Identity: Becoming a Reflective Environmentalist* (Cambridge: MIT Press, 1996), 9.

86. I say "usually" here because Fox's analysis of personal identification leaves room for interpretation. Some of his remarks indicate that he believes that personal identification has many positive aspects, that it is quite closely related to transpersonal identification, and that both ought to be embraced. Other comments, however, indicate a more pessimistic view of personal identification, and thus fall more squarely in line with the critiques leveled against him by thinkers like Kheel and Plumwood. Somewhat in contrast to this, Devall is a clear proponent of place identity, and writes that "[e]cological self seems most accessible to us not by focusing on human-built places or on the organic whole or Gaea initially, but on our own bioregion" (*Simple in Means*, 57).

87. Warwick Fox, *Toward a Transpersonal Ecology*, 258.

88. Arne Naess, "Identification as a Source," 263. Plumwood, in a comment directed to Leopold, notes that this progression from close to distant could be viewed as a way of shedding the personal in favor of the abstract ("Nature, Self and Gender," 294). Michael Zimmerman cites a similar passage and indicates that this progression could be viewed as a "process of abstraction and disconnection" (*Contesting Earth's Future: Radical Ecology and Postmodernity* [Berkeley: University of California Press, 1994], 288). I cite this passage here, however, to suggest what I have argued elsewhere, which is that Naess' view of this process does not seem to privilege the abstract and universal in the way that Fox's position can be taken as doing. See Christian Diehm "Arne Naess, Val Plumwood, and Deep Ecological Subjectivity: A Contribution to the 'Deep Ecology-Ecofeminism Debate'," *Ethics and the Environment* 7, no. 1 (Spring 2002): 24–38.

89. These comments speak to a concern expressed by Mathew Humphrey, who argues that the model of ethics on which many deep ecology theorists rely is, at bottom, problematic because it is, in essence, submoral. Citing Naess and other deep ecology theorists' claims about actions done on behalf of the environment by the ecological Self being "spontaneous," "beautiful," a reflection of Self-interest or of Self-defense, Humphrey contends that these theorists ultimately root our responses to environmental problems not in a morally reasoned assessment of the relevant features of our circumstances, but in our un- or pre-reflective ideas about who we are. He then compares this approach to various problematic bases of action such as territoriality, regionalism, and nationalism. I would argue, however, that although some of Naess's comments lend themselves to this sort of interpretation, when he talks about our responses to other-than-human entities being "automatic" or "spontaneous," he is for the most part referring to the "self-motivated" character of the pro-environmental behavior engaged in by those who have identified with nature, and the

"orienting" capacity of identity just described. See Mathew Humphrey, "Ontological Determinism and Deep Ecology: Evading the Moral Questions?," in *Beneath the Surface: Critical Essays in the Philosophy of Deep* Ecology, 85–105. Replying to Humphrey, Ariel Salleh makes a very similar point in "In Defense of Deep Ecology: An Ecofeminist Response to a Liberal Critique," in *Beneath the Surface: Critical Essays in the Philosophy of Deep Ecology*, 107–24.

Chapter 3

Connection to Nature and Environmental Values

In the eyes of many activists, academics, and natural resource professionals, questions about nature's value are especially important.[1] When philosophers have addressed these questions, however, they have tended to part ways at two conceptual junctures. The first involves the distinction between anthropocentrism and nonanthropocentrism, the former being the view that nature's value is a function of how it serves human interests, the latter holding that at least some other-than-human entities ought to be valued for their own sakes.[2] The second juncture, no less important than the first, concerns the differing ideals of ethical individualism and ethical holism. Ethical individualists accord moral worth to entities with characteristics either possessed exclusively by, or discernible most clearly in, ontologically distinct individual beings.[3] Ethical holists, by contrast, contend that some kinds of collective entities (such as species and ecosystems) have equal if not greater value than the individuals that make them up, and that outlooks that fail to recognize this are inadequate to meet our most serious environmental challenges.[4]

Plotting the views of deep ecology supporters along these two major axes of environmental value theory is, in one sense at least, a fairly easy task. The first point of the deep ecology platform plainly asserts that "[t]he well-being and flourishing of human and nonhuman life on Earth have value in themselves," a value that is "independent of the usefulness of the nonhuman world for human purposes."[5] This declaration of nonanthropocentrism is obviously intended, moreover, to be understood in a broadly holistic way, as platform formulators Arne Naess and George Sessions explain that it refers to entities as diverse as "individuals, species, populations, habitat, as well as human and nonhuman cultures."[6]

Of course, theorists in the deep ecology movement regularly link this cluster of value commitments to the notions of Self-realization and identification with nature, and despite the philosophical complexities here, the most common explanation of this link is not too difficult to follow. The basic idea, as it is often repeated, is that since we usually take ourselves to have value beyond our utility to others, it follows that to include aspects of the natural world within our sense of Self results in their having moral worth of precisely the same sort.[7] Additionally, it seems only logical that in encouraging us to develop more ecologically inclusive identities, these thinkers would emphasize the value of larger relational networks of things—networks to which, as they routinely stress, we ourselves are always intimately connected.[8]

This summary explanation of deep ecological axiology has its merits, to be sure. Yet it also raises a number of questions, one of the most obvious of which concerns what many commentators contend is its overtly "Self-centered" account of ostensibly nonanthropocentric environmental values. Equally pressing, however, are the questions it raises about the relationship between identification with nature and the particular array of values Naess and Sessions mention in conjunction with the deep ecology platform, a relationship often noted but seldom examined in detail in the literature of the deep ecology movement.

In light of these lingering questions, then, and considering the import of the subject of environmental values, it seems fitting to inquire more deeply into how gaining a sense of connectedness to nature impacts how we think about its moral worth. What specific sorts of value orientations does human-nature bonding tend to foster, and why? Do different ways of connecting with nature promote different ways of caring for it? In posing these questions, we should remember what was argued in chapter 1, which is that Self-realization and identification with nature are distinct notions, such that to admit the significance of ecological identities does not commit us to Self-realization as an ultimate norm. If, therefore, we proceed in accordance with the approach outlined thus far, and bracket assumptions about the root importance of Self-realization, what remains to be said about identification with nature and environmental values?

KINSHIP WITH NATURE

In the aptly titled essay "Identification as a Source of Deep Ecological Attitudes," Naess makes two remarks that are especially illuminating of his views about how human-nature bonding shapes evaluative attitudes. The first is that identification is a "source of belief in intrinsic values."[9] The second is that people can identify with a wide variety of other-than-human entities, including "individuals, species, ecosystems and landscapes."[10] Together, these statements convey well Naess's belief that identification can facilitate precisely the sorts of sensibilities encapsulated by the first point of the deep ecology platform, sensibilities that are not only nonanthropocentric, but potentially inclusive of both individualistic and holistic ethical insights. Somewhat unexpectedly, though, when one examines Naess's comments on identification-as-*kinship*, one discovers a process that appears to incline those who undergo it away from ethical holism and toward an individualistic perspective on nature's intrinsic value.

Valuing Other-than-Human Beings Individually

To appreciate fully the axiological import of identification-as-kinship, we should first review briefly what this process entails. As explained in chapter 1, Naess often depicts identification with nature less in terms of recognizing our being *in community* with other-than-human entities than of acknowledging our having things *in common* with them. As he puts it, through identification we come to realize that there is "something of ourselves in the other creature, or something of the other creature in ourselves."[11] Naess contends, further, that such kinship-recognition is crucial for our being able to feel empathy or sympathy for others, sentiments which make it possible for us to become invested in their well-being to the point where it, too, can be counted among our own primary concerns.[12]

Given this basic structure, it seems that one way in which kinship-identification could impact our evaluative attitudes is by revealing others to have characteristics that we not only *recognize* in ourselves, but *value* therein as well. Naess mentions, for example, that identification may show other-than-human beings to be highly perceptive, socially complex, or emotionally sophisticated.[13] He suggests, in addition, that it could allow us to understand that they are intelligent, resourceful, and physically gifted.[14] It may even lead us, he speculates, to regard them as products of the same creative forces that shape ourselves, to see them as bearing within themselves "that part of God that lives in all that is living."[15] Yet surely these are not qualities to which we typically relate in value-neutral ways. Rather, we take them to be value-positive, "admirable" or "remarkable" in some sense. In a word, we regard attributes like these as "good," but if this is the case then kinship-identification would entail more than simply affirming facets of other-than-human existence that are similar to our own. It would involve, instead, a way of perceiving these others such that we simultaneously "apperceive" them as marvelous in their own right, and as "valuable in themselves."[16]

More important, however, is the way in which kinship-identification helps us to see that other-than-human beings are engaged in the same sorts of existential projects that imbue our own lives with direction, meaning, and purpose. Naess says, for instance, that identification promotes the awareness that "[a]ll living creatures try to fulfill themselves,"[17] and brings us to "regard other living creatures as genuine fellow creatures with a need for self-development."[18] Likewise, he describes identification in terms of our human capacity to "consciously perceive the urge other beings have for self-realization,"[19] and proposes that this leads us to affirm that "[e]ach living being . . . is a goal in itself."[20] Kinship-identification is thus connected to the recognition of others as active agents with characteristic potentials to unfold, teleological or intentional entities with ends at which they aim and goals toward which they strive. The enlarged perspective-taking such recognition encourages, moreover, undoubtedly gives us to understand this dimension of other-than-human existence as having an "intrinsic" or lived significance that is irreducible to whatever further meaning we might be able to assign to it. To relate to others in this way, in other words, is both to realize that they are actively engaged in their being, and to be able to appreciate such existential engagement on its own terms, or "for its own sake."

These reflections make evident, therefore, what has been asserted several times already, which is that identification-as-kinship underlies a distinctly nonanthropocentric ethical orientation. It is also revealing, however, that many of Naess's own examples portray this process as taking place with individual organisms. Indeed, the event that he refers to as a "paradigm instance" of identification occurred in relation to a single flea that he observed struggling in a chemical solution on a microscope slide.[21] Elsewhere he illustrates what identification entails with the story of people responding compassionately to an elk and a wolf after both animals were mortally wounded in a predatory clash.[22] Less dramatically, but just as illuminating, in his last major work he discusses the ease with which people usually identify with individual sentient beings, and speaks candidly of his own identification with an aging houseplant that is starting to wither and die.[23]

Beyond such anecdotal evidence Naess does, on occasion, state explicitly his belief that kinship-identification is more likely to occur with individual than with collective other-than-human entities. Perhaps most straightforwardly, in *Life's Philosophy* he mentions that "identification requires feelings," to which he adds that "it is easier for me to have positive feelings for the individual living creatures than for a species—that becomes too abstract."[24] The underlying premise of this statement, clearly, is that if an entity is experientially "abstract," or hard to encounter in our everyday interactions with others, then it also will not be something with which we can easily identify. Along with this, though, Naess is making the seemingly uncontroversial claim that entities like species are more experientially abstract than the "individual living creatures" that make them up. Generalizing from Naess's experience, then, the axiological upshot could only be that this form of human-nature bonding tends to promote individualistic sensibilities about

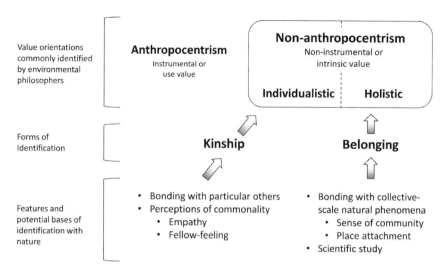

Figure 3.1 Identification with Nature and Environmental Values.
Source: Author created.

nature's intrinsic value, for the simple reason that it occurs most readily with concrete individuals of the sort we encounter directly in our lived experience of nature (figure 3.1).

Further support for this conclusion is found in Naess's statement that, while he is confident that "all living creatures have their own intrinsic value," his intuitions are different "when the matter concerns whole species of living creatures." "I do not feel," he says, "that . . . [species] have their own intrinsic worth, even if it is incontestably more important to preserve them rather than a single individual." This sharp contrast in attitudes, he informs us, is the result of his feeling that species, unlike individuals, "are abstractions and as such have no intrinsic value."[25]

In conjunction with this it is worthwhile to consider the work of Stephen Kellert, whose extensive studies of public attitudes toward nature and wildlife appear to corroborate much of what has just been said about the generally individualistic character of kinship-identification. In specific, Kellert reports that our bonding with other-than-human entities "often depends on identifying humanlike feelings and attributes" in them, and that this sort of identification typically results in our valuing them because of their "individuality and emotionally appealing qualities."[26] He even points out, as Naess does, that such affinity for particular others is especially likely to develop in relation to other-than-human animals,[27] and that it is often accompanied by a "moralistic" desire to "minimize harm to other creatures viewed as fundamentally like ourselves."[28]

Of course, to say that kinship-identification is inclined to foster individualistic ethical sentiments is not to say that it is antithetical to notions of interconnectedness, or to the idea that we and other entities are "knots in the biospherical net."[29] Quite the contrary, Naess plainly sees the perspectives that emerge from kinship-identification as being attentive to the relational character of those with whom we connect in this way. As he puts it, when we identify with others "[o]ur care continues ultimately to concern the individuals, not any collectivity. But the individual is not, and will not be isolatable, whatever exists has a gestalt character."[30] Hence even though this type of identification focuses ethical attention on individuals more so than collectives, this focus is entirely consonant with a sensitivity to the "gestalt," or relational, quality of the former, a deep appreciation for the ecological webs in which such intrinsically valuable others always exist.[31]

Kinship-Identification, Moral Extensionism, and the Assimilation of Difference

Thus far, we have argued that identification-as-kinship encourages nonanthropocentric attitudes that, while not opposed to insights into the interrelatedness of things, are nonetheless more ethically individualistic than holistic. And though the commentary leading to this conclusion suggests several issues to explore further, one of the most immediate concerns it raises has to do with whether or not this type of identification still involves an unacceptably "human-centered" perspective on the intrinsic value of other-than-human beings. Let us take a moment, then, to speak to this concern before moving on.

In order to understand the potential problem here, we might observe how Naess's views on kinship-identification and intrinsic value can be connected to the larger debates about "moral extensionism" in environmental ethics. What moral extensionists maintain, in short, is that since the intrinsic value of human beings is associated with our possession of certain characteristics (e.g., intelligence, sentience, etc.), and since at least some entities that are not human possess these same characteristics, then the only consistent position to hold is to attribute intrinsic value to these other-than-human beings as well.[32] In response to this, some critics claim that although the extensionist strategy is worthwhile in various respects, it misses the mark insofar as it does nothing to challenge our traditional ways of thinking about who or what is intrinsically valuable. It appears, that is, that instead of trying to expand our ethical sensibilities to accommodate a natural world that is in certain ways very different from ourselves, moral extensionists simply "assimilate" select other-than-human beings into our preexisting, highly restrictive categories of moral considerability and value, in essence making them honorary "persons."[33]

In light of this dispute, it looks as if critics of moral extensionism would rightly be reluctant to embrace identification-as-kinship as a wellspring of environmental attitudes. For although Naess clearly states his belief that identifying with others in this way is compatible with recognizing differences,[34] it is equally clear that he views it primarily as a matter of acknowledging various points of commonality or similarity between ourselves and other-than-human beings. Thus tying the affirmation of (other-than-human) others' value to their bearing some degree of likeness to our (human) selves, it seems plausible to say that environmental outlooks inspired by kinship-identification are every bit as "human-centered," or assimilationist, as those of moral extensionists, even if they are not, in the narrow axiological sense, anthropocentric.[35]

Before accepting this line of criticism, however, we should notice how it seems to suggest that, since the assimilation of nature is a function of our valuing it on the basis of what we have in common, avoiding assimilationism therefore requires us to relate to other-than-human entities as entirely different from, or wholly discontinuous with, ourselves. Exemplifying just such an approach, extensionist critic Emyr Vaughan Thomas argues that any authentically nonassimilationist environmental ethic will be one that "takes us away from dependency on human analogues and lets us see nature as more penetratingly set apart";[36] it must be a view that "avoids all contagion with a human-centred viewpoint"[37] and that can find ways to respect nature "without any assimilation to the human or any sense of continuity between nature and the human."[38] For Thomas, then, moving beyond assimilation requires us also to move beyond human-nature continuity, and instead find ways of relating to nature as something more radically other.

Among the most conspicuous shortcomings of this recommendation, of course, is that it reflects the same sort of separatist vision of humans and nature of which deep ecologists and other eco-theorists have long been suspicious, and not without good reason.[39] Less obvious perhaps, but equally troubling, is that it seems to require that, in our concrete dealings with other-than-human entities, we treat any extrapolations from our own situations as colonizing gestures that are, at best, irrelevant. Separated from nature in theory, we must also separate from nature in practice, which means that any forms of felt connectedness to other-than-human entities, or reliance upon our own epistemic locations in our relations with them, would have to be regarded as well-intentioned failures to respect unfathomable difference. Far from appearing as integral features of morally sensitive relationships, therefore, such modes of relating to nature could only be viewed as anthropomorphic projections of ourselves across what are, in reality, epistemically and ethically unbridgeable gaps.

But the demand for such radical epistemic dislocation goes too far, and forces us to ignore too much that is vital about caring and attentive relations with others. If, for instance, we denied all continuity between our own affective lives and those of other-than-human animals, we would eliminate the possibility of understanding what is no doubt a central feature of their ways of engaging with the world, and with that, all possibility of empathizing with their pains and pleasures.[40] In like fashion, it seems that our ability to recognize what Naess calls the "self-realizing" tendencies of other living things is to some degree contingent upon our own inside knowledge of the biological realities of desire, purpose, and striving. That we ourselves know what it is to be alive, in other words, appears to be crucial to our capacity to comprehend and appreciate the existential commitments of other living existents, the distinctive ways in which they are invested in their own diverse ways of existing.[41] Yet if all of this is correct, then to exclude from environmental ethics any reference to our own epistemic positions would not be to gain in our admiration and respect for other-than-human beings, but to lose sight of much of the reason why they command our admiration and respect in the first place.

This line of reasoning, while not explicitly articulated by Naess, clearly aligns with his thinking, particularly his claim that kinship-identification is prerequisite for empathy or sympathy for others. What is not clear, though, is if it actually bypasses the charge of moral extensionism. Sanjay Lal, for one, with specific reference to the argument for epistemic continuity sketched above, claims that "[f]or my own life experiences to be helpful for forming a proper moral attitude, those experiences cannot really be mine in any meaningfully exclusive sense"; rather, they must "underscore commonality and not difference," something that is evidenced by "our inability to select (or seriously consider) a candidate for moral consideration who is completely unlike us."[42] Lal thus concludes that because our relations with others rely on our epistemic locations like this, and because such reliance always underscores continuities and similarity, we "cannot distinguish an attitude of continuity with nature from an extensionist one."[43]

In this way Lal comes to suggest that there may indeed be a "necessary" or unavoidable element of extensionism in our relations with other-than-human entities.[44] In sharp contrast to Thomas, though, he contends that this is nothing to be regretted. Instead, it invites us to reconsider the metaphysics, and the ethics, of unity or sameness: "If reality, in essence, is one and on the surface differences are not actually real," he says, "then adopting an ethical system which perpetuates notions of separateness would not be in line with acquiring a proper metaphysical understanding."[45] Viewed in this light, he says that "[t]he inability to enable respect for differences is not so serious of a problem for an ethical approach."[46]

Lal's viewpoint is thus quite unlike Thomas's, but curiously enough, it appears to make the same assumption: that to relate to others starting from our own epistemic locations is ultimately incompatible with a genuine acknowledgment of difference. But is this assumption really warranted? To regard other animals as sentient like ourselves, for example, seems critical to understanding that they are unique individuals in perceptually unique situations, distinct subjects of experiential lives that assuredly are, to borrow Lal's phrasing, their own in a "meaningfully exclusive sense."[47] The same can be said of our ability to acknowledge the purposive or self-actualizing character of other living things, as affirming this point of human-nature continuity does not inevitably erase their differences from ourselves, but rather seems indispensable to affirming that they occupy unique biological positions with unique existential possibilities, that they are distinct "centers of life" in distinctive life-situations.[48] Even our relations with nonliving things appear to conjoin affirmations of difference with acknowledgments of commonality, as when Keekok Lee claims that abiotic other-than-human entities have their own "trajectories,"[49] or Eric Katz contends that nature can be regarded as "an ongoing subject of a history, a life process, a developmental system"[50]—concepts that clearly overlap with the human experience of the world, but which also position other-than-humans as distinct foci of autonomy, activity, or agency.

Our epistemic locations thus need not be regarded as always closing us to difference, or "centering" us on ourselves, since they can, and do, open us to what is other, effectively "de-centering" us and facing us outward toward a world that is at once both familiar and foreign. What we need in our concrete engagements with other-than-human beings, therefore, is neither to try to escape, in Thomas's words, all "contagion" with a human perspective, nor to view respect for difference as beyond our reach and, as Lal has it, "not so serious of a problem."[51] What we need, instead, is to be attentive to the ways in which our human points-of-view, or human ways of being-in-the-world, can facilitate relations with other-than-human entities in which neither similarity nor difference is necessarily distorted or marginalized.

Admittedly, Naess's writings understate the significance of these points. His project of countering human alienation from nature leads him to stress similarities between human and other-than-human beings more so than differences, and his interest in the norm of Self-realization generally focuses his attention on the Self-implicating aspects of identification more so than on those that are difference-affirming.[52] What has been argued above should thus be taken as a recommendation for a critical addendum to his thought, one that draws out a dimension of kinship-identification that he seems to have recognized but never fully developed. Nevertheless, nothing in his understanding of this sort of identification forecloses this addendum, and the notion of "kinship" upon which his thinking relies is neither excessively narrow (as it arguably is in conventional extensionist ethics), nor necessarily reductive of difference. In this it does allow for, and even invites, respect for difference of the sort we have just tried to articulate.

BELONGING TO NATURE

Kinship-identification is undoubtedly a key component of Naess's thinking about environmental values. Even so, it is not the type of human-nature bonding in which deep ecology theorists have expressed the greatest interest. More than acknowledging our *kinship* with other-than-human beings, these thinkers urge us to develop a sense of *belonging* to nature, acquiring an "ecological consciousness" that gives us to understand that we are inextricably a part of the more-than-human world.[53] Of course, as writers like Warwick Fox point out, such identification can assume not only local or place-specific forms, but also more generalized forms that include aspects of nature with which we have not had firsthand encounters.[54] Whatever form it takes, however, the process of identification-as-belonging can be shown to issue in value orientations that are noticeably more holistic than those we have considered to this point.

Valuing Other-Than-Human Entities Collectively

At the start it is important to observe that, since identification-as-belonging is often depicted as a process whereby our sense of self "expands" to include nature, so too it is often depicted as a process through which our personal sense of intrinsic worth expands to include those other-than-human entities with which we come to feel connected. Andrew Brennan, for example, writes that deep ecology theorists offer "a simple solution to the problem of value in nature. Provided I am valuable, then so is my extended self, the natural world."[55] Expressing a similar idea, Fritjof Capra says that "the recognition of value inherent in all living nature stems from the deep ecological awareness that nature and the self are one."[56] Yet while explanations such as these are consistent with various statements deep ecology theorists have made, they also make their axiological appeal to the value of our Selves rather than exploring the ways in which this type of identification might facilitate more other-oriented forms of respect for nature. But what else can be said in this latter regard?

In the first chapter it was noted that identification-as-belonging can be understood as a reversal of the tendency to minimize, or "background," the contributions the natural world makes to who and what we are. This marginalization of other-than-human activity has been a key element of Western dualistic thought, and played a central part in nature's instrumentalization: made out to be inessential, nature is dubbed inferior, and hence its appropriation is legitimized.[57] In contrast to such a dismissive outlook, however, identification-as-belonging is largely a matter of accepting our indebtedness to the wider biological and ecological realities that continually shape, support, and sustain us. In thus prompting us to reconsider the vital roles nature plays in our lives, this form of identification likewise encourages us to reconsider how we ought to assess its moral worth.

Part of the reason why developing a sense of belonging to nature has this normative function, it seems, is that it is particularly apt to provoke in us feelings of *gratitude*, feelings that several authors propose are indeed important to cultivate. Karen Bardsley, for one, refers to environmental gratitude as "the mother of all virtues," and contends that although other-than-human entities differ in key respects from our traditional notions of who or what constitutes a benefactor, it is nonetheless "appropriate to feel deeply grateful (or something like grateful) to the natural world that sustains us."[58] Reed Elizabeth Loder, too, underscores the significance of environmental gratitude, and analyzes several dimensions of the human-nature relationship in which she believes this sentiment is both fitting to express and likely to arise. One of these is "gratitude for places," wherein "affection is mixed with identity and belonging" and the feeling of gratitude can grow to become "planetary, as in the idea of earth as home."[59]

Tellingly, both Bardsley and Loder hold that although gratitude toward nature entails some focus on ourselves, its moral structure is essentially other-regarding. They maintain, that is, that while environmental gratitude involves an awareness of how we have benefitted from our relations with other-than-human entities, what characterizes it is the way in which this awareness becomes outward-facing in feelings of goodwill and respect for these others themselves. In fact, Loder argues that this can be true even in cases where gratitude originates in a frankly utilitarian admission of our dependence on what many call "ecosystem services": "Learning about the instrumental value and fragility of [environmental and ecosystemic] functions," she says, "and explicitly acknowledging gratitude for those can move human attitudes beyond entitlement towards respect and active responsibility."[60]

These remarks begin to illuminate the connections that exist between a sense of belonging, feelings of gratitude, and an attitude of *humility* toward nature, an attitude that is regularly expressed in environmental writing, and regularly associated with the phenomenon of identification.[61] In *Human Dependence on Nature*, for instance, environmental scientist Haydn Washington speaks of the "profoundly humbling experience" of coming to see that we are "only one species among many, a species that relies on the world around us to survive."[62] Echoing this, philosopher Lisa Gerber claims that "[o]ne of the most interesting aspects of humility . . . is the recognition that we are part and parcel of nature,"[63] and adds that "[a] humble person can see value in nature and acts accordingly with the proper reverence and respect."[64] Like Gerber, eco-critic Josh Weinstein contends that "if we attend to the beauty and wonder inherent in our collective and interdependent existence . . . we will intuitively and logically arrive at a feeling of humility which acknowledges not only our smallness with respect to the workings of the world . . . but also a deep sense of caring and responsibility toward the same."[65]

The axiological orientation that emerges from identification-as-belonging, then, is arguably less about our valuing nature as a part of our Selves than about our valuing nature as though we are simply one small part of it—an orientation that is neither unduly human-, nor problematically Self-, centered. But while this type of identification can thus be said to foster outlooks that are less anthropocentric than is sometimes thought, it also appears to promote views that are more holistic than those associated with identification-as-kinship, and there are several reasons for concluding that this is indeed the case.

The link between identification-as-belonging and ethical holism can be explained, first, by noticing that the experiences contributing to our having a sense of belonging to nature—including those forms of belonging social scientists refer to as "place attachment" and "environmental identity"—often involve our connecting to broader and more comprehensive units of things. The experiential basis of this type of human–nature bonding, in other words, seems not to be chiefly a matter of our bonding with individual other-than-human beings, but rather with networks of interrelated entities, all of which contribute to the total character of the places, landscapes, regions, or environments with which we identify (figure 3.1).

There are, moreover, deep ecology theorists' own frequent claims that one of identification's leading intellectual prompts is contemporary natural science, which itself is frequently associated with holistic ideas about what nature is and how it ought to be valued (figure 3.1).[66] Neatly illustrating these conceptual ties, ecologist Stan Rowe says that "ecology's chief contribution to modern thought" is that it allows us to comprehend "the vital, animated wholes of which organisms are parts,"[67] and on this basis he advocates an "ecological" or "ecospheric" ethic, the core of which is the attitude that "organisms, including humanity, are secondary in importance to the creative Earth and its geoecosystems."[68]

In connection with these observations we might also point to several studies that, taken together, provide some initial empirical indications of the correlation we are suggesting. An inquiry into the concept of "nature relatedness," for example, found that people who felt more connected to nature were more likely than others to have joined environmental organizations,[69] while a separate study examining the value orientations of members of environmental organizations discovered that they overwhelmingly "saw the unit of moral concern as being ecological collectives (species, ecosystems, etc.)."[70] Again, when researching people's sense of "connectedness to nature," Stephan Mayer and Cynthia Frantz found that college students pursuing degrees in environmental studies felt more strongly attached to the natural world than those enrolled in other academic programs.[71] Kellert's early surveys of attitudes toward wildlife, however, revealed that an interest in ecological study was correlated with what he calls "ecologistic" values,[72] or perspectives that incorporate "concern for the environment as a system, for interrelationships between wildlife species and natural habitats."[73]

Now certainly, to assert that identification-as-belonging fosters holistic values is not equivalent to asserting that it encourages callous or indifferent attitudes toward individuals. Holism can take numerous forms, and many deep ecology supporters have sought to express forms of it that ignore neither the ontological status, nor the moral worth, of particular other-than-human beings.[74] Thus, Naess says that insofar as deep ecology supporters embrace ideas of interconnectedness, "[t]heir views are compatible with many kinds and degrees of holism. But these views . . . are incompatible with the kind of holism which obliterates individuality, particularly that of persons or single specimens of any species."[75]

Belonging, Difference, and the Ontology of Connectedness

While more remains to be said about nature's value, we should not pass too quickly over the association just made between affirming the *moral* standing of individual entities, and affirming their *ontological* standing. After all, it is hard to see how having a sense of belonging to nature could allow us to admit the value of individual beings if it was somehow at odds with our admitting their existence. Nevertheless, according to some critics, the views espoused by deep ecology theorists regularly fall short in this latter regard, and thus we will do well to take this opportunity to make some more detailed remarks about connectedness to nature and on the ontology of belonging.

One way to characterize the issue at hand is to see it as a variant of the concern that identification with nature does not allow respect for difference. What commentators like Val Plumwood argue is that the sense of belonging deep ecology theorists describe ultimately denies any difference between ourselves and other-than-human entities, leading to a sense of human-nature interconnection that is better described in terms of human-nature "indistinguishability."[76] Identification of the sort advocated by deep ecology theorists, Plumwood says, involves "the obliteration of distinction"[77] between humans and other entities; it leads to a sense of Self that "rejects boundaries between self and nature"[78] and encourages us to see ourselves and all other beings as belonging to an undifferentiated, "seamless whole."[79]

This is a serious charge, to be sure. The claim that there are no boundaries between self and other is deeply problematic, and repeats a gesture of erasure which is a root problem and not a solution for environmental ethics.[80] It is true, moreover, that deep ecology theorists sometimes make statements that substantiate Plumwood's concerns. Fox, for instance, in an early and oft-cited essay, writes that the "central intuition" of deep ecology is "the idea that there is no firm ontological divide in the field of existence," by which he means that "the world simply is not divided up into independently existing subjects and objects, nor is there any bifurcation in reality between the human and nonhuman realms." "To the extent that we perceive boundaries," he writes, "we fall short of deep ecological consciousness."[81] Yet if deep ecological consciousness fails when we perceive boundaries between ourselves and others, then surely such consciousness fails to respect others' difference from ourselves.

Does identification-as-belonging necessarily involve such a difference-erasing holism? Naess, at least, is clear in his belief that it does not, and statements to this effect are evident throughout his writings.[82] At one point he says that the idea that humans are "drops in the stream of life" is "misleading if it implies that individuality of the drops is lost in the stream."[83] At another he rejects the notion that identification transforms self and other into an indistinct "mass," or "one single, integrated being."[84] On occasion, he even distances himself from the positions of other deep ecology theorists, writing of Fox, for example, that "he embraces a stronger or more radical form of holism than I do."[85]

More specific insight into the ontological status of particular existents in Naess's thought can be gained by looking briefly at his "gestalt ontology," which for present purposes has two equally important dimensions.[86] The first is that no individual things, or "parts," exist completely independently of their standing within broader relational networks, or "wholes." More critical to this discussion, however, is that no "wholes" exist in the absence of some degree of differentiation among their parts. Hence Naess says, with reference to the well-known gestaltist motto "the whole is greater than the sum of its parts," that "the whole is more than the parts, but also the parts are more than the whole, because there's nothing left if you just have the whole. You have to continue . . . to keep the most subordinate gestalt you have."[87] The reference here to individual things as "subordinate gestalts," along with the claim that "the whole is more than the parts," both serve to reinforce Naess's belief that individual things do not exist utterly discretely.[88] Yet we also see in these comments his refusal to regard parts as integrated into wholes in such a way as to lose all their particularity. Indeed, true to the tenets of gestalt theory, for Naess the absence of differentiation between parts does not leave one with a homogenous whole, but instead with nothing at all.

Applied more concretely to our analysis of connectedness to nature, what this means is that to gain a sense of belonging to nature is not to lose all sense of distinction between ourselves and the natural world, or disappear into an undifferentiated, universal "one."[89] It is rather, simply, coming to see ourselves as related to the more-than-human world in meaningful, nonaccidental ways; to understand ourselves as a part of a nature whose own distinctive character and abilities have been molded, shaped, and influenced by the distinctive characters and abilities of others. It is, in sum, to move away from the idea that we are somehow separate from or outside the natural world, and toward the understanding that we are existentially at home on planet Earth, with its wondrous diversity of places and existents.

Although this characterization of the ontology of belonging is the product of philosophical reflection and not empirical research, it does align noticeably well with the terminology social scientists tend to employ in the tools they design to measure connection to nature. While some widely used scales utilize the language of "oneness" with nature,[90] it is much more common to encounter terms consonant with Naess's emphasis on parts and wholes, community ties, and relational attachments. Hence one finds survey prompts such as "I think of myself as a part of nature, not separate from it,"[91] "I feel very connected to all living things and the earth,"[92] "I think of the natural world as a community to which I belong,"[93] and "Being at this place says a lot about who I am."[94]

Notable, too, is the way in which this account of identification-as-belonging also aligns with contemporary accounts of the attitude of humility. As one research team defines it, humility is "the understanding and experience of oneself *as one, in fact, is*—namely, as a finite and fallible being that is but an infinitesimal part of a vast universe, and so has a necessarily limited and incomplete perspective or grasp on the 'whole'," adding that "humility is the understanding and experience of oneself as only one among a host of other morally relevant beings, whose interests are foundationally as legitimate, and as worthy of attention and concern, as one's own."[95] This conceptualization neatly conveys that humility entails an awareness of both the limits of the self and the significance of others, which together are said to manifest in behaviors such as "a greater acceptance of others' beliefs, values, and ideas—even when different from one's own—and an increased desire to help and be of service to others." Humility is therefore neither self-effacing nor difference-erasing, but a way of reconfiguring relations with others that results in "an increased prioritization of their needs, interests, and benefits and increased concern for their well-being, as well as an increased appreciation for the value of others . . . and an increased sense of connectedness."[96]

NATURE'S INTRINSIC VALUE?

The discussion of environmental values to this point might be summarized by saying that whereas kinship-identification encourages individualistic environmental values that can include ideas of interconnectedness, identification-as-belonging encourages holistic values that do not necessarily exclude moral sensitivity to individuals. We have contended, though, that both types of identification promote outlooks that affirm the intrinsic value of nature, and while this contention may seem uncontroversial at this point, there are two potential objections to it that ought to be addressed, the first and most basic of which centers on the notion of intrinsic value itself.

In recent years a number of environmental thinkers, including some deep ecology theorists, have suggested that the concept of intrinsic value may be fundamentally at odds with relational conceptions of things. Frederic Bender, for instance, maintains that the language of "intrinsic" value derives from the idea that value is a quality or characteristic an entity possesses independently of its relations to any other entity. Because of this, he says, assertions of intrinsic value "obscure the fact that human and nonhuman life flourishes on Earth only because of the myriad interrelationships binding everything together."[97] Thus worried that articulating nature's moral standing in terms of intrinsic value implicitly communicates a nonrelational viewpoint, he claims that doing so ultimately "contravenes the nondualist 'relational and total-field' ontology that makes deep ecology *deep*."[98]

Remarks like these press us to consider just what it means to talk about nature's intrinsic value, and whether or not such talk is in tension with a philosophical emphasis on connectedness to nature. Upon review, however, it quickly becomes apparent that the concept of intrinsic value can legitimately be used to refer to things other than an entity's nonrelational properties. As philosophers like John O'Neill and Katie McShane have shown, it can also be employed to indicate that an entity has "non-instrumental value," or moral significance that is not limited to its usefulness to human beings.[99] When taken in this sense, McShane explains, to say that an entity has intrinsic value is not to say that value inheres in it as a property that it has independently of its relationships; it is rather to state something about "how it makes sense for us to care about the thing."[100] On this telling, to assert that an other-than-human being has intrinsic value is to assert that its worth should not be judged solely by how we *Homo sapiens* might make use of it, or that there are other facets of its existence that are equally worthy of our appreciation, concern, and respect.[101]

Interestingly, O'Neill offers the deep ecology platform as an example of such a noninstrumentalist conception of intrinsic value, citing its proclamation that the value of other-than-human entities is "independent of the usefulness these may have for narrow human purposes."[102] Eric Katz, too, says that the axiological stance of the deep ecology platform represents "a critique of anthropocentric instrumental reasoning and valuation."[103] And as McShane highlights, there is nothing in this way of understanding nature's value that conflicts with the idea that things are interconnected with other things, or that implies a dualistic outlook in which the world consists of separate entities existing in utter isolation from each other. In her words, we can readily admit that "[n]othing in our world exists in isolation and there is no reason that we should want to think of things just as isolated individuals for the purposes of ethics," while at the same time thinking that "our deeply interconnected world contains things that deserve to be intrinsically valued."[104]

Still, even if the notion of intrinsic value is not opposed to relational thinking, it might be thought that claims about such value in nature are hopelessly problematic when tied to the process of identification. This is because deep ecology theorists routinely describe identification as less a matter of logical analysis than of lived experience, and they routinely portray such experience as more spontaneous and feeling than thoughtful and deliberative.[105] This portrayal implies, perhaps correctly, that to identify with nature is to experience a shift in perspective that is, in Derek Turner's words, more akin to a religious "conversion" experience than to the development of a position "based on careful consideration of reasons and evidence."[106] Yet if belief in the intrinsic value of other-than human entities is the result of such an experiential shift, then there is not only the problem of how to justify the value claims of those who have identified with nature, but also the question of how much argumentative sway such claims could hold among those who have not.[107]

Though these are substantive concerns, it should be noted that even if identification is more experiential than deliberative, this does not mean that it wholly excludes reason and reflection. While Naess does claim that identification is "non-rational," this characterization serves mainly to highlight that human-nature bonding has centrally important affective or felt dimensions, not to assert that it is unrelated to more cognitive ones. Identification is, in his view, a "non-rational, but not irrational, process,"[108] indicating not that it excludes cognition, but rather that it is not solely, or predominantly, a cognitive phenomenon—a view that is generally in keeping with the perspectives of conservation psychologists and other social scientists.[109] Given this, it seems clear that identification should not be regarded as a discrete event, one that occurs in isolation from more reflective dimensions of human life.

Moreover, even if particular instances of identification do not involve logical analysis, this does not mean that the insights they afford cannot be reflectively examined and articulated in ways that are rationally compelling. Consider, for instance, the story told by animal ethicist Bernard Rollin of the time he was fishing and suddenly realized that the fish he was catching were struggling against him out of panic and fear, and not because they, like him, were enjoying the thrill of the competition.[110] As Rollin narrates it, this realization occurred "for no obvious reason," and he even describes it as a "gestalt shift" in his relationship to fish.[111] But it is also the sort of experience whose elements can be analyzed and formally expressed as part of a coherent argument for the moral significance of other-than-human entities, something to which Rollin's own work in this area surely attests.

What Rollin's example also illustrates, of course, is the way in which experiences of identification function as background conditions of ethical life, helping to establish the contexts within which we make sense, or non-sense, of various normative claims.[112] It is in this regard that it could be said that our varying senses of connection to nature do, in a manner of speaking, lie "behind," or "deeper," than formal argumentation. Accordingly, those who have not identified with other-than-human entities, or that have not identified with them very strongly, may very well find arguments about their intrinsic worth unconvincing. It is not likely, furthermore, that convincing such skeptics will always be a matter of appealing to reason alone. Yet this in no way discredits identification with nature as a source of evaluative attitudes, or lessens its importance to the frameworks of environmental ethics that people employ. On the contrary, these circumstances simply reflect the stubborn reality of ethical disagreements about matters of the environment, and force us to admit that logic is sometimes of limited use in resolving them, precisely because there are broader features of the evaluative logics we employ, one of which is the degree to which we do, or do not, feel connected to nature.

IDENTIFICATION AS A SOURCE OF BELIEF IN INTRINSIC VALUE

By another route, therefore, we arrive at the conclusion that ecological identity matters, not in the same way that formal argumentation does, but as one of the factors orienting our evaluations of the more-than-human world. Assuredly, identification does not stand alone in this capacity. But as deep ecology theorists argue and social scientists help us to understand, there is good reason to believe that human–nature bonding contributes substantially, albeit oftentimes subtly, to the environmental viewpoints that we hold, including our views regarding nature's value.

In taking up with the subject of environmental values, our focus has not been on every type of human-nature bonding possible, nor have we attempted to analyze the relations between identification and every type of evaluative outlook environmental philosophers have defended. Rather, we have tried to outline some of the fundamental ways in which different forms of human-nature bonding can foster different sorts of evaluative attitudes, including especially those individualistic or holistic attitudes that so frequently are at play in theoretical and practical discussions about environmental issues (figure 3.1). In doing this, we have implicitly stressed a point not often underscored in conversations about environmental ethics, which is that really comprehending environmental values requires that we also have some comprehension of the self-construals that foster and lend intelligibility to them. Our environmental values are, at least in part, expressions of our varying senses of who we are, what we feel akin to, and where we feel like we belong, which means that environmental values and environmental identity are related in ways that are at once both complementary and complex.

If, however, we have arrived at a point where the eco-philosophical significance of environmentally oriented identities is more clear, we have not for all that said much about what might promote them. What sorts of things, exactly, encourage ecologically inclusive self-construals? One response to this question that we have already heard from affiliates of the deep ecology movement is that the study of natural science, and specifically the science of ecology, might be particularly effective in this regard.[113] Yet another common reply, and not only from deep ecology supporters, is that nature experience, or time outdoors, is an important source of human-nature bonding. But does this oft-repeated claim have any merit? Is there really a link between outdoor experience and a sense of connection to nature? In the next chapter we will take up with this proposition, once again enlisting the help of social scientists, whose investigations in this area are invaluable both in helping us secure an answer to this question, and to advancing our understanding of connectedness to nature.

NOTES

1. For an overview of the concept of nature's value in conservation science circles, see John A. Vucetich, Jeremy T. Bruskotter, and Michael Paul Nelson, "Evaluating Whether Nature's Intrinsic Value Is an Axiom of or Anathema to Conservation," *Conservation Biology* 29, no. 2 (2015): 321–33.

2. These remarks are meant as a general characterization of anthropocentrism and nonanthropocentrism, and there are a number of different ways in which these perspectives can be defined. For a good overview, see Clare Palmer, "An Overview of Environmental Ethics," in *Environmental Ethics: An Anthology*, ed. Andrew Light and Holmes Rolston, III (Oxford: Blackwell, 2003), 15–37.

3. Among the best-known representatives of this perspective in environmental ethics are Peter Singer, *Practical Ethics* (Cambridge: Cambridge University Press, 1993); Tom Regan, *The Case for Animal Rights* (Berkeley: University of California Press, 1983); Paul Taylor, *Respect for Nature* (Princeton: Princeton University Press, 1986).

4. For an example of an argument of this sort, see Gregory M. Mikkelson and Colin A. Chapman, "Individualistic Environmental Ethics: A Reductio ad Exstinctum?," *Environmental Ethics* 36, no. 3 (Fall 2014): 333–38. For further

discussion of individualistic and holistic environmental ethics, see Jason Kawall, "A History of Environmental Ethics," in *The Oxford Handbook of Environmental Ethics*, ed. Stephen M. Gardner and Allen Thompson (New York: Oxford University Press, 2017), 13–26; Clare Palmer, "Contested Frameworks in Environmental Ethics," in *Linking Ecology and Ethics for a Changing World: Values, Philosophy, and Action*, ed. Ricardo Rozzi et al. (Dordrecht: Springer, 2013), 191–206.

5. Arne Naess, "The Deep Ecological Movement: Some Philosophical Aspects," *Inquiry* 8, no. 1–2 (1986): 14. Many commentators have noted, as Andrew McLaughlin puts it, that "[e]ssentially, this is a denial of anthropocentrism" (*Regarding Nature: Industrialism and Deep Ecology* [Albany: State University of New York Press, 1993], 179). See also Eric Katz's claim that deep ecology provides "a critique of anthropocentric instrumental reasoning and valuation regarding nonhuman natural life forms" ("Against the Inevitability of Anthropocentrism," in *Beneath the Surface: Critical Essays in the Philosophy of Deep Ecology*, ed. Eric Katz, Andrew Light, and David Rothenberg [Cambridge: MIT Press, 2000], 19).

6. Naess, "The Deep Ecological Movement," 14.

7. See Andrew Brennan, *Thinking About Nature: An Investigation of Nature, Value and Ecology* (Athens: University of Georgia Press, 1988), 143; Fritjof Capra, "Deep Ecology: A New Paradigm," in *Deep Ecology for the Twenty-First Century: Readings on the Philosophy and Practice of the New Environmentalism,* ed. George Sessions (Boston: Shambhala, 1995), 20.

8. As a general rule, commentators associate deep ecological thought with holistic value frameworks, though there are debates about such frameworks and their consistency, or inconsistency, with the notion of "biospherical egalitarianism" that Naess advocated. See, for example, Laslo Erdos, *Green Heroes: From Buddha to Leonardo DiCaprio* (Cham, Switzerland: Springer, 2019), 93–96; John P. Clark, "What Is Living In Deep Ecology?," *The Trumpeter* 30, no. 2 (2014): 169–74; David R. Keller, "Gleaning Lessons from Deep Ecology," *Ethics and the Environment* 2, no. 2 (Autumn 1997): 139–48; David R. Keller, "Deep Ecology," in *Encyclopedia of Environmental Ethics and Philosophy*, vol. 1, ed. J. Baird Callicott and Robert Frodeman (Detroit: Macmillan Reference USA, 2009), 206–11.

9. Arne Naess, "Identification as a Source of Deep Ecological Attitudes," in *Deep Ecology*, ed. Michael Tobias (San Diego: Avant Books, 1985), 259.

10. Ibid., 262. Elsewhere Naess makes the related comment that it is possible for us to identify with other-than-human entities not only "individually," but also "collectively or in their essence ('life itself,' ecosystems, species)" (*Ecology Community and Lifestyle: Outline of an Ecosophy*, trans. and rev. David Rothenberg [Cambridge: Cambridge University Press, 1989], 181).

11. Arne Naess with Per Ingvar Haukeland, *Life's Philosophy: Reason and Feeling in a Deeper World*, trans. Roland Huntford (Athens: University of Georgia Press, 2002), 114.

12. "It is," Naess says, "a necessary, but not sufficient condition of empathy and sympathy that one 'sees' or experiences something similar or identical with oneself" ("Identification as a Source," 262).

13. Naess with Haukeland, *Life's Philosophy*, 114–15.

14. Ibid.
15. Ibid.
16. Naess discusses "apperception" in *Ecology Community and Lifestyle*, chapter 2. For a more detailed discussion of this notion and its role in Naess's thought, see Christian Diehm, "Arne Naess and the Task of Gestalt Ontology," *Environmental Ethics* 28, no. 2 (Spring 2006): 21–35.
17. Naess with Haukeland, *Life's Philosophy*, 115.
18. Ibid.
19. Naess, *Ecology Community and Lifestyle*, 170, 166.
20. Ibid., 174.
21. Naess refers to this as a "paradigm instance" of identification in "Self-Realization: An Ecological Approach to Being-in-the-World," in *Deep Ecology for the Twenty-First Century*, 227. See also David Rothenberg, *Is It Painful to Think?: Conversations with Arne Naess* (Minneapolis: University of Minnesota Press, 1993), 178–79.
22. Naess, *Ecology Community and Lifestyle*, 198. For another account of identification in relation to individual beings, see Arne Naess, "'Here I Stand': An Interview with Arne Naess," interview by Christian Diehm, *Environmental Philosophy* 1, no. 2 (Fall 2004): 12.
23. Naess with Haukeland, *Life's Philosophy*, 114.
24. Ibid.
25. Ibid., 109. See also Arne Naess, "The Ecofeminism versus Deep Ecology Debate," where Naess says that he is "in favor of letting point one of the eight points [of the deep ecology platform] refer only to individuals" (in *Philosophical Dialogues: Arne Naess and the Progress of Ecophilosophy*, ed. N. Witoszek and A. Brennan [Lanham: Rowman & Littlefield, 1999], 272).
26. Stephen R. Kellert, *Kinship to Mastery: Biophilia in Human Evolution and Development* (Washington, DC: Island Press, 1997), 105–106.
27. Ibid., 106.
28. Stephen R. Kellert, *The Value of Life: Biological Diversity and Human Society* (Washington, DC: Island Press, 1996), 23.
29. Arne Naess, "The Shallow and the Deep, Long-Range Ecology Movements: A Summary," *Inquiry* 16, no. 1–4 (1973): 95.
30. Naess, *Ecology Community and Lifestyle*, 195.
31. The outlook we have just described is probably quite similar to that articulated by ecofeminist philosopher Marti Kheel, whose perspective is axiologically individualistic in its sense of the value of individuals, while being "praxically" holistic in recognizing that moral concern for individuals must take account of the relational networks in which they exist. See Marti Kheel, *Nature Ethics: An Ecofeminist Perspective* (Lanham: Rowman & Littlefield, 2008), and Christian Diehm, "Finding a Niche for Species in Nature Ethics," *Ethics and the Environment* 17, no. 1 (Spring 2012): 71–86.
32. For a review and discussion of the use of moral extensionism in environmental ethics, see Neil Carter, *The Politics of the Environment: Ideas, Activism, Policy*, 3rd ed. (Cambridge: Cambridge University Press, 2018).

33. See, for example, John Rodman, "Four Forms of Ecological Consciousness Reconsidered," in *Deep Ecology for the Twenty-First Century*, 121–30; Val Plumwood, *Environmental Culture: The Ecological Crisis of Reason* (London: Routledge, 2002).

34. See Naess, "Identification as a Source," 261, and *Ecology, Community and Lifestyle*, 173.

35. A charge of this sort is leveled by Katz against Freya Mathews insofar as she suggests that we relate to universe as a "self" (see Katz, "Against the Inevitability of Anthropocentrism," 34–35). For an extended treatment of this issue by Mathews, see *For Love of Matter: A Contemporary Panpsychism* (Albany: State University of New York Press, 2003).

36. Emyr Vaughan Thomas, "Rolston, Naturogenic Value and Genuine Biocentrism," *Environmental Values* 6, no. 3 (1997): 359.

37. Ibid.

38. Ibid., 357.

39. As Plumwood has explained, an orientation toward nature conceived as wholly other "retains the existential gulf [between humans and nature] of the dominant dualistic tradition in its full form" ("Comment: Self-Realization or Man Apart? The Reed-Naess Debate," in *Philosophical Dialogues*, 207).

40. See Plumwood, *Environmental Culture*, 133.

41. For an excellent discussion of this point, see Hans Jonas's *The Phenomenon of Life: Toward a Philosophical Biology* (New York: Delta Books, 1966). Discussion of how the logic being employed here might also be applied to nonliving entities can be found in Keekok Lee, "Is Nature Autonomous?" in *Recognizing the Autonomy of Nature: Theory and Practice*, ed. Thomas Heyd (New York: Columbia University Press, 2005), 54–74; Keekok Lee, "Biotic and Abiotic Nature: How Radical is Rolston's Environmental Philosophy?" in *Nature, Value, Duty: Life on Earth with Holmes Rolston, III*, ed. Christopher J. Preston and Wayne Ouderkirk (Dordrecht: Springer, 2007), 17–28.

42. Sanjay Lal, "Moral Extensionism and Nonviolence: An Essential Relation?," in *The Peace of Nature and the Nature of Peace: Essays on Ecology, Nature, Nonviolence, and Peace*, ed. Andrew Fiala (Leiden: Brill/Rodopi, 2015), 77.

43. Ibid.

44. Lal's position is much like what environmental philosophers sometimes call "perspectival anthropocentrism." This asserts that since every entity's point-of-view is shaped by its way of being-in-the-world, the views that humans have on environmental ethics will necessarily be "human-centered." In explanation of this, Tim Hayward says that since, in our attempts to value nature "the valuer is a human, the very selection of criteria of value will be limited by this fact. It is this fact which precludes the possibility of a *radically* nonanthropocentric value scheme, if by that is meant the adoption of a set of values which are supposed to be completely unrelated to any existing human values" ("Anthropocentrism: A Misunderstood Problem," *Environmental Values* 6, no. 1 [1997]: 56). The term "perspectival anthropocentrism" appears to be attributable to Frederick Ferré (see Ferré, "Personalistic Organicism: Paradox or Paradigm?," in *Philosophy and the Natural Environment*,

ed. Robin Attfield and Andrew Belsey [Cambridge: Cambridge University Press, 1994], 73). Expressions of some version of this view can be found in William Grey, "Environmental Value and Anthropocentrism," *Ethics and the Environment* 3, no. 1 (1998): 97–103; Onora O'Neill, "Environmental Values, Anthropocentrism and Speciesism," *Environmental Values* 6, no. 2 (1997): 127–42; Eugene C. Hargrove, "Weak Anthropocentric Intrinsic Value," *The Monist* 75, no. 2 (1992): 183–207. This subject is also discussed in Robin Attfield, "Beyond Anthropocentrism," *Royal Institute of Philosophy Supplement* 69 (October 2011): 29–46.

45. Lal, "Moral Extensionism and Nonviolence," 78.

46. Ibid.

47. Ibid., 77.

48. See Taylor, *Respect for Nature*, 119–29.

49. See Lee, "Is Nature Autonomous?," and "Biotic and Abiotic Nature."

50. Eric Katz, *Nature as Subject* (Lanham: Rowman & Littlefield, 1997), xvi.

51. Lal, "Moral Extensionism and Nonviolence," 78.

52. Especially noticeable in this regard is Naess's tendency to frame the process of identification in terms of "identity" with others rather than in terms of "continuity" with them. In some of my own previous work, I have highlighted this problem. See, for example, Christian Diehm "Arne Naess, Val Plumwood, and Deep Ecological Subjectivity: A Contribution to the 'Deep Ecology-Ecofeminism Debate'," *Ethics and the Environment* 7, no. 1 (Spring 2002): 24–38. This essay articulates concerns about Naess's thought similar to those articulated here, but spends less time considering the ways in which his focus on "similarity" or "commonality" may still be compatible with affirmations of difference.

53. Bill Devall and George Sessions, *Deep Ecology: Living as if Nature Mattered* (Salt Lake City: Gibbs Smith, 1985).

54. Warwick Fox, *Toward a Transpersonal Ecology: Developing New Foundations for Environmentalism* (Albany: State University of New York Press, 1995), chapter 8.

55. Brennan, *Thinking About Nature*, 143.

56. Capra, "Deep Ecology: A New Paradigm," 20.

57. See Plumwood, *Environmental Culture*, and *Feminism and the Mastery of Nature* (London: Routledge, 1993).

58. Karen Bardsley, "Mother Nature and the Mother of All Virtues: On the Rationality of Feeling Gratitude toward Nature," *Environmental Ethics* 35, no. 2 (Spring 2013): 40.

59. Reed Elizabeth Loder, "Gratitude and the Environment: Toward Individual and Collective Ecological Virtue," *The Journal Jurisprudence* 10 (2011): 411. Christopher Uhl, too, mentions gratitude in *Developing Ecological Consciousness: The End of Separation*, 2nd ed. (Lanham: Rowman & Littlefield, 2013), xiv.

60. Loder, "Gratitude and the Environment," 412–3. See also Bardsley, "Mother Nature and the Mother of All Virtues," 31. For additional commentary on gratitude and alterity, see Nathan Wood, "Gratitude and Alterity in Environmental Virtue Ethics," *Environmental Values* 29, no. 3 (2020): 1–18, https://doi.org/10.3197/0 96327119X15579936382590.

61. See Lisa Gerber, "Standing Humbly Before Nature," *Ethics and the Environment* 7, no. 1 (Spring 2002): 39–53.

62. Haydn Washington, *Human Dependence on Nature: How to Help Solve the Environmental Crisis* (New York: Routledge, 2013), 2.

63. Gerber, "Standing Humbly Before Nature," 47.

64. Ibid., 40.

65. Josh A. Weinstein, "Humility, from the Ground Up: A Radical Approach to Literature and Ecology," *Interdisciplinary Studies in Literature and Environment* 22, no. 4 (Autumn 2015): 766. In this same essay Weinstein also observes, as we are arguing, that "by arriving at an understanding of human interdependence with nature, we as humans are led to feelings of gratitude and compassion which ultimately lead to a form of humility" (769). Additional commentary on the import of environmental gratitude, as well as the gratitude-humility connection is found in Francis van den Noortgaete, "Generous Being: The Environmental Ethical Relevance of Ontological Gratitude," *Ethics and the Environment* 21, no. 2 (Fall 2016): 119–42.

66. See Devall and Sessions, *Deep Ecology*, 85–7; Fox, *Toward a Transpersonal Ecology*, 252–3; Frederic L. Bender, *The Culture of Extinction: Toward a Philosophy of Deep Ecology* (Amherst: Humanity Books, 2003), chapter 14; Michael P. Nelson, "Teaching Holism in Environmental Ethics," *Environmental Ethics* 32, no. 1 (Spring 2010): 33–49; Michael Soule, "What Is Conservation Biology?," *BioScience*, 35, no. 11 (December 1985): 727–34.

67. Stan Rowe, "The Living Earth and Its Ethical Priority," *The Trumpeter* 19, no. 2 (2003): 80.

68. Ibid., 69. In a similar vein Uhl, citing "what our best science is now revealing to us," says that nature consists of "wholes within wholes," and that this "powerful metaphor for understanding how the world is put together" not only bolsters ecological consciousness, but points to "ecocentrism," or the idea of "valuing and respecting all species and ecosystems to the same degree that we value and respect ourselves" (*Developing Ecological Consciousness*, 109). See also Clark, "What Is Living in Deep Ecology?"

69. Elizabeth K. Nisbet, John M. Zelenski, and Steven A. Murphy, "The Nature Relatedness Scale: Linking Individuals' Connection with Nature to Environmental Concern and Behavior," *Environment and Behavior* 41, no. 5 (2009): 715–40.

70. W. F. Butler and T. G. Acott, "An Inquiry Concerning the Acceptance of Intrinsic Value Theories of Nature," *Environmental Values* 16, no. 2 (2007): 158.

71. F. Stephan Mayer and Cynthia McPherson Frantz, "The Connectedness to Nature Scale: A Measure of Individuals' Feeling in Community with Nature," *Journal of Environmental Psychology* 24, no. 4 (2004): 509.

72. Stephen R. Kellert, "American Attitudes toward and Knowledge of Animals: An Update," in *Advances in Animal Welfare Science 1984/85*, ed. M. W. Fox and L. D. Mickley (Washington, DC: The Humane Society of the United States, 1984), 196.

73. Ibid., 179.

74. As the next section explains, the claim that deep ecology theorists have tended to adopt views that acknowledge individuals has been contested. In addition to the literature cited therein, relevant literature in this area includes Freya Mathews,

For Love of Matter: A Contemporary Panpsychism (Albany: State University of New York Press, 2003); George Sessions, "Ecocentrism and the Anthropocentric Detour," in *Deep Ecology for the Twenty-First Century*, 157; Marti Kheel, *Nature Ethics*; Marti Kheel "Ecofeminism and Deep Ecology: Rethinking Identity and Difference," in *Reweaving the World: The Emergence of Ecofeminism*, ed. Irene Diamond and G. F. Orenstein (San Francisco: Sierra Club Books, 1990), 128–37.

75. Naess "The Ecofeminism versus Deep Ecology Debate," 272.

76. See Plumwood, *Feminism and the Mastery of Nature*, 176–79; Val Plumwood, "Nature, Self, and Gender: Feminism, Environmental Philosophy, and the Critique of Rationalism," *Hypatia* 6, no. 1 (Spring 1991): 12–14.

77. Plumwood, *Feminism and the Mastery of Nature*, 177.

78. Ibid., 176. See also Val Plumwood, "Nature, Self, and Gender," 12.

79. Plumwood, *Feminism and the Mastery of Nature*, 176. Peter C. van Wyck echoes this critique in his *Primitives in the Wilderness: Deep Ecology and the Missing Human Subject* (Albany: SUNY Press, 1997) when he writes that the "sense of self that interests deep ecology involves a complete breakdown of the distinction between self and other" (41).

80. See Plumwood, *Feminism and the Mastery of Nature*, 176–79.

81. Warwick Fox, "Deep Ecology: A New Philosophy of Our Time?," in *Philosophical Dialogues*, 157.

82. Bender is also clear on this subject, and responds directly to Plumwood in *The Culture of Extinction*, 424–29.

83. Naess, *Ecology, Community and Lifestyle*, 165.

84. Ibid., 173.

85. Naess, "The Ecofeminism versus Deep Ecology Debate," in *Philosophical Dialogues*, 272.

86. Exposition of Naess's gestalt ontology can be found in *Ecology, Community and Lifestyle*, chapter 2; Arne Naess, "Ecosophy and Gestalt Ontology," in *Deep Ecology for the Twenty-First Century*, ed. George Sessions (Boston: Shambhala, 1995), 240–45; Diehm, "Arne Naess and the Task of Gestalt Ontology."

87. David Rothenberg, *Is it Painful to Think?: Conversations with Arne Naess* (Minneapolis: University of Minnesota Press, 1993), 159–60.

88. This is also why Naess says that the motto "The whole is greater than the sum of its parts" could be restated to read: "The part is more than a part" ("Ecosophy and Gestalt Ontology," 242).

89. Karen Warren is unambiguous on this point, claiming that Naess is clear in his desire not to "abrogate individuality" and that he avoids the indistinguishability thesis articulated by Plumwood ("Ecofeminist Philosophy and Deep Ecology," in *Philosophical Dialogues*, 265).

90. See, for example, Mayer and Frantz, "The Connectedness to Nature Scale," item #1 p. 513.

91. Susan Clayton, "Environmental Identity: A Conceptual and an Operational Definition," in *Identity and the Natural Environment: The Psychological Significance of Nature*, ed. Susan Clayton and Susan Opotow (Cambridge: MIT Press, 2003), 61.

92. Nisbet, Zelenski, and Murphy, "The Nature Relatedness Scale," 724.

93. Mayer and Frantz, "The Connectedness to Nature Scale," 513.

94. Steve Semken, "Place Attachment Inventory (ASU) 1.3," accessed November 5, 2014, http://serc.carleton.edu/NAGTWorkshops/assess/activities/semken.html. See also Daniel R. Williams and Jerry J. Vaske, "The Measurement of Place Attachment: Validity and Generalizability of a Psychometric Approach," *Forest Science* 49, no. 6 (2003): 830–40; Daniel R. Williams and Joseph W. Roggenbuck, "Measuring Place Attachment: Some Preliminary Results," paper presented at the session on Outdoor Planning and Management, NRPA Symposium on Leisure Research, San Antonio, Texas (1989).

95. Jennifer Cole Wright et al., "The Psychological Significance of Humility," *The Journal of Positive Psychology* 12, no. 1 (2017): 4–5.

96. Ibid., 5.

97. Bender, *The Culture of Extinction*, 409–10. For similar concerns about the notion of intrinsic value, see Bruce Morito, "Intrinsic Value: A Modern Albatross for the Ecological Approach," *Environmental Values* 12, no. 3 (2003): 317–36; Anthony Weston, "Beyond Intrinsic Value: Pragmatism in Environmental Ethics," *Environmental Ethics* 7, no. 4 (Winter 1985): 321–39.

98. Bender, *The Culture of Extinction*, 408.

99. John O'Neill, "The Varieties of Intrinsic Value," *The Monist* 75, no. 2 (April 1992): 119; Katie McShane, "Why Environmental Ethics Shouldn't Give Up on Intrinsic Value," *Environmental Ethics* 29, no. 1 (Spring 2007): 43–61.

100. McShane, "Why Environmental Ethics Shouldn't Give Up on Intrinsic Value," 49.

101. These comments relate to another debate about environmental values, and which concerns a category of value sometimes termed "relational." Relational value has been presented as a contrast to both instrumental and intrinsic values, and is commonly presented in terms that may seem to include precisely those values we have articulated, namely, those that emerge in relations of identity and connectedness with nature. It seems typical, however, for those who promote the notion of relational values to do so on the presumption that intrinsic value is, as we are putting it here, a "nonrelational" property of other-than-human entities, or an attribute that exists completely independently of their relations with human beings. Chan et al., for example, describe relational values as "not present in things but derivative of relationships," while at the same time characterizing intrinsic value as both "independent of humans," and "independent of human valuation" (Kai M. A. Chan et al., "Why Protect Nature?: Rethinking Values and the Environment," *Proceedings of the National Academy of Sciences* 113, no. 6 [February 9, 2016]: 1463). What we are arguing, however, is that this is not the only, or the best, way to understand intrinsic values, and that at least some of the values that emerge in the kinds of relationships we are describing—again, relationships of kinship, connectedness, and belonging—are properly regarded as forms of intrinsic value, or ways of viewing others as having moral significance in themselves.

102. O'Neill, "The Varieties of Intrinsic Value," 119. The reference to the deep ecology platform is taken from Naess, *Ecology, Community and Lifestyle*, 29.

103. Katz, "Against the Inevitability of Anthropocentrism," 19. Interestingly, this also appears to be what Bender himself asserts when he reformulates the deep ecology

platform's first principle to read: "Nonhumans do not exist for humans' sake" (*The Culture of Extinction*, 448).

104. McShane, "Why Environmental Ethics Shouldn't Give Up on Intrinsic Value," 59.

105. In Naess's words, identification is a "spontaneous, non-rational" process; it is something that can happen "without thinking at all," "without a trace of deliberation" ("Here I Stand," 12).

106. Derek D. Turner, "Monkeywrenching, Perverse Incentives and Ecodefence," *Environmental Values* 15, no. 2 (2006): 224.

107. These remarks can also be connected to Mathew Humphrey's critique of deep ecology in "Ontological Determinism and Deep Ecology: Evading the Moral Questions?," in *Beneath the Surface: Critical Essays in the Philosophy of Deep Ecology*, 85–105. See also Anne Barbeau Gardiner, "Deep Ecology and the Culture of Death," in *Life and Learning XVII: Proceedings of the Seventeenth University Faculty for Life Conference at Villanova University*, ed. Joseph W. Koterski (Washington, DC: University Faculty for Life, 2007), 179–90.

108. Naess, "Identification as a Source," 261.

109. For a brief summary of the way in which connectedness to nature is understood within the social sciences to be a multifaceted phenomenon having both cognitive and affective dimensions, see Matthew J. Zylstra et al., "Connectedness as a Core Conservation Concern: An Interdisciplinary Review of Theory and a Call for Practice," *Springer Science Reviews* 2, no. 1–2 (2014): 124.

110. Bernard Rollin, *Animal Rights and Human Morality* (Buffalo: Prometheus Books, 1992), 81.

111. Ibid.

112. Though he does not use exactly these terms, Rollin's point in *Animal Rights and Human Morality* (79–82) seems basically equivalent to that being made here.

113. Although there is anecdotal evidence for this claim, recent empirical research suggests that the relationship between ecological study and environmental identity is complex, and may in fact work in a direction opposite that which many people suppose. One study found that while French university students with majors in natural science and ecology expressed higher levels of environmental identity than students in other majors, those levels did not change significantly across classes (i.e., among freshmen, sophomores, juniors, and seniors). The study's authors thus suggest that although environmental identity may contribute to students' choice of major, their choice of major might not contribute to their environmental identity (see Anne-Caroline Prévot, Susan Clayton, and Raphael Mathevet, "The Relationship of Childhood Upbringing and University Degree Program to Environmental Identity: Experience in Nature Matters," *Environmental Education Research* 24, no. 2 [2018]: 263–79). Relatedly, a study of students in introductory environmental science courses at The Pennsylvania State University found that, in sections of the course that were focused on knowledge acquisition, students showed no increase in "nature relatedness" across their semester of enrolment. Students in sections of the course that focused specifically on cultivating increased connectedness to nature, however, showed significant increases in all dimensions of the nature relatedness scale. Interestingly, the latter students were in

a course taught by Christopher Uhl, whose pedagogical approach is patterned on his work in *Developing Ecological Consciousness* (see Greg R. Lankenau, "Fostering Connectedness to Nature in Higher Education," *Environmental Education Research* 24, no. 2 [2018]: 230–44). Additional research of this sort is reported in Erica N. Blatt, "Exploring Environmental Identity and Behavioral Change in an Environmental Science Course," *Cultural Studies of Science Education* 8, no. 2 (2013): 467–88.

Chapter 4

We Belong Outside

Connectedness to Nature and Outdoor Experience

Of all the trends conservationists have paid attention to in recent years, surely one of the most dramatic is the shift away from experiential engagement with nature. The statistics in this area are striking. One survey of American women found that while 70 percent of mothers played outdoors every day when they were young, only 31 percent of their children did the same.[1] Another study from the United States reported that, between 1997 and 2003, youth participation in outdoor activities dropped from an already low 16 percent to an even lower 10 percent. This decline, the study notes, accounts for a corresponding reduction in the average amount of time children typically spend outside each week: in 1997 it was 36 minutes, but in 2003 that number dropped to 25. Spread out across a week, that amounts to less than 4 minutes per day.[2]

To be sure, not all research in this area reports such extreme results.[3] Still, by nearly all accounts the trends regarding time outdoors are downward, and this has many people within environmental circles worried. Richard Louv, for example, famously cautions against the dangers of "nature-deficit disorder" in his celebrated book *Last Child in the Woods*.[4] Likewise, social ecologist Stephen Kellert warns about the ways in which "modern society has compromised and diminished our need for connecting with nature and living diversity."[5] Biologist and nature-writer Robert Pyle, too, decries the decline of human-nature interaction characteristic of the late twentieth and early twenty-first centuries—a phenomenon he aptly terms the "extinction of experience."[6] But why, exactly, might experiential disconnection from the natural world be so problematic? What, if anything, do we lose when we lose touch with nature?

These questions are no doubt relevant for environmental advocates of all sorts. They appear particularly significant, however, for those affiliated with the deep ecology movement. Deep ecology theorists' call for increased "identification" with nature often reads as a call for increased outdoor engagement, and many deep ecology supporters are explicit in their belief that nature experience has a role to play in their philosophical and practical agendas. As Peter Reed and David Rothenberg succinctly put it, "We don't really know what we're talking about in deep ecology unless we have some real, live experience with the *ecos* itself. . . . One does not learn ecophilosophy from books alone."[7]

Such widespread belief in the importance of experiential contact with nature urges us to examine more carefully just what the conservation significance of outdoor experience might be, and what relationship, if any, it might have to the phenomenon of identification with nature. What role does time outdoors play relative to pro-environmental outlooks? What influence might it have on people's development of a sense of connection to nature? Fortunately, researchers from multiple disciplines have investigated these questions, which enables us once again to approach our subject by drawing not only on the work of philosophers, but also social scientists. Though the findings of the latter are often presented as most relevant for environmental educators, they are equally valuable to the present inquiry, and provide insight into some of the central claims about nature experience that deep ecology theorists have made. Just as important, though, is that they extend our understanding of connectedness to nature by helping us understand its relationship to what many believe is one of its most important sources. This inquiry begins, therefore, with an extended look at what social scientists are saying about the place of outdoor experience in the contemporary environmental landscape.

SIGNIFICANT LIFE EXPERIENCES

The presumption that there is a correlation between nature experience and environmental concern was first subjected to serious academic scrutiny by Thomas Tanner in the late 1970s. An environmental educator, Tanner wanted to know what factors most contributed to the making of environmentally responsible adults. He therefore created an open-ended questionnaire to explore the backgrounds of people with demonstrated commitments to conservation, asking them to identify the "formative influences" that led them to conservation work.[8]

Hypothesizing that direct experience of the natural world would be the most common response to his inquiry, Tanner distributed his questionnaire to officers and employees of several prominent conservation organizations, including The Nature Conservancy, the National Wildlife Federation, the National Audubon Society, and the Sierra Club. When the results came in he found, as predicted, that by far the most frequently cited conservation influence was some form of outdoor experience or interaction with nature. Indeed, this was mentioned by thirty-five of the forty-five respondents (78%), with Tanner noting that if his method for coding the survey had been less conservative, the number of responses in this category could have been as high as forty-four (98%).[9] Contact with nature, it turned out, had played a role in the life-paths of nearly all of the conservationists participating in the study.

Of course, outdoor experience was not the only factor contributing to adult conservation that Tanner's investigation uncovered. The second most commonly cited influence was "parents," who were said to be instrumental either because they facilitated their children's outdoor experiences, or encouraged their nature-oriented interests. "Teachers," the majority of whom were encountered during high school and college years, comprised the third most popular category of responses, with "books" and "adults other than parents or teachers" coming in fourth and fifth, respectively. A number of people also recalled witnessing the loss of cherished places, or "habitat alteration," as being crucial to the development of their environmental concerns.[10]

In the nearly forty years since this initial foray into what is now called "significant life experiences" research, numerous studies of this sort have been conducted. A good deal of the early literature in this area focused on environmental educators, and it produced results noticeably consistent with Tanner's.[11] A survey of members of the National Association of Environmental Education in the United Kingdom, for example, found that their most commonly mentioned background influences were time outdoors (91%), education (59%), and parents or close relatives (38%).[12] Similarly, in one of the largest studies undertaken to date, a survey of over one thousand environmental educators in nine countries found that, despite certain national differences, the greatest influences on participants' environmental life choices were nature experience (55%), other people (40%), education (39%), and negative experiences with things such as pollution (38%).[13]

As one would expect, researchers have analyzed groups other than environmental educators, and they regularly present findings in keeping with those just described. A study of the formative influences of environmental professionals in El Salvador found that nearly all of the respondents mentioned experiences outdoors, with most of these occurring with family or friends.[14] When employees of Taiwanese environmental groups were asked about their life experiences, they too referenced contact with nature most often, followed by influential environmental organizations.[15] Nature experience was also the most frequently cited formative influence in a study of American and Norwegian environmentalists, for whom family and environmental organizations also proved highly significant.[16] Reporting comparable results, a survey of landowners in Indiana with conservation easements found that their most common background influences were experiences in nature, outdoor play, planned outdoor experiences, and parents or guardians.[17]

The basic response pattern apparent in most significant life experience research, then, is not too difficult to discern. As Louise Chawla writes:

> In countries as far-flung as England, Germany, Greece, Slovenia, Australia, Canada, the United States, El Salvador and South Africa, when environmental activists or environmental educators are asked the sources of their concern for the environment, from half to more than 80 percent of the respondents identify . . . experiences of nature as a significant influence. Typically, they mention family members or other role models equally often or second in importance. Smaller percentages mention organizations, education, and witnessing the destruction or pollution of a valued place.[18]

What this research indicates, in other words, is that nature experience—along with parents and other significant social relations—has thus far proven to be the most commonly cited influence on the development of people's conservationist sensibilities. These are followed by a restricted range of factors that, while nearly always mentioned by different survey populations, tend to vary in the collective importance these populations assign to them.

In conjunction with this, it is worth noting that the methodology of significant life experiences research typically allows respondents to reference multiple influences on their life choices, with most respondents citing three or four.[19] In some studies, however, participants have been asked to identify the *single* most influential factor on their conservationism, and in these cases their responses have taken a familiar form. Hence when British environmental educators were asked if they could specify one factor that most influenced their environmental focus, the majority of those who did so listed outdoor experience, with just slightly fewer mentioning parents or close relatives.[20] Nearly the same was true of Indianans with conservation easements who, when asked "What early life experience most influenced your thoughts on land conservation?" mentioned outdoor experiences most frequently, followed by family members and witnessing environmental problems.[21]

WHEN, HOW OFTEN, AND WHERE?

A great deal of life experience literature indicates that childhood outdoor experiences are more likely to influence adult environmentalism than experiences occurring at other times of life.[22] Complementing this finding is research suggesting that conservation concern sometimes develops in stages. Chawla, for one, plotted environmentalists' significant life experiences chronologically, and observed that in childhood, outdoor experience and family were most significant; in university years, education and friends dominated; and in adulthood, environmental organizations and work life came to the fore.[23] Glimpsing an analogous pattern, Shih-Jang Hsu's work revealed that nature experience and close relatives were most significant in childhood; nature experience waned and education gained in adolescence; and experience, organizations, friends, loss of special places, and fear of environmental problems dominated in adulthood.[24]

Thus, it may very well be that the conservation impact of outdoor experience varies across life stages. Such variation is less evident, however, in relation to the *kinds* of youthful nature experiences that most influence later environmental advocacy. In Hsu's study of Taiwanese environmental workers, the childhood experiences most frequently recalled were "everyday outdoor activities that were spontaneous and pleasant."[25] Chawla, too, found that while formal educational experiences were not irrelevant, it was nevertheless the case that "informal outdoor experiences and experiences of natural areas" were the most significant formative influences for American and Norwegian environmentalists.[26] Echoing these claims, James Farmer, Charles Chancellor, and Burnell Fischer close their study of Midwestern easement-holders by stating that "early life experiences in nature and free play outdoors" are among the most significant contributors to adult conservation behavior.[27]

These remarks already indicate that it is not uncommon for conservationists to recall that their formative engagement with nature involved regular contact with geographically nearby places. More than half of the respondents in Tanner's initial study claimed to have access to natural areas on a more or less daily basis, and several subsequent surveys have repeated this result.[28] It is also true, though, that many study participants report more sporadic interactions with places not regularly accessible to them.[29] It remains unclear, therefore, as to how much outdoor engagement might typically be in the backgrounds of environmentally active adults.

Other important questions raised but not clearly answered by the literature in this area concern whether or not the influence of outdoor experience is effected by the kind of environment in which it occurs, or the specific sort of activity it involves. Are some outdoor activities more likely than others to foster environmental commitment? Can nature in the built environment inspire conservation as effectively as nature in its wilder states? Though few life experience researchers address such questions directly, it is relevant here that the list of "formative outdoor experiences" one can compile from work done in this field includes things as diverse as farming, spending time in rural areas, going on family vacations, attending youth camps, participating in Scouting, gardening, and even picnicking.[30] The picture these findings paint, then, is one in which support for conservation can be encouraged by involvement with any number of places across the wild-rural-urban nature spectrum.

This conclusion notwithstanding, some studies do suggest that experiences of areas that are more evidently "natural," or less overtly influenced by human activity, exert a stronger influence on adult conservation than experiences of settings that are more obviously managed or manipulated. Tanner himself was the first to indicate something like this, noting that his outdoors-inspired respondents had interacted primarily with "natural, rural, or pristine habitats."[31] Hence he summarizes his findings by saying that, for the conservationists he surveyed, "youthful experience of the outdoors and relatively pristine environments emerges as a dominant influence in these lives."[32]

Lending further support to this observation is an oft-cited report by Nancy Wells and Kristi Lekies, which proposes that "wild nature" experiences are more strongly associated with environmentally responsible behaviors than experiences of "domesticated nature."[33] In a review of data collected on more than two thousand Americans, Wells and Lekies discovered that adults who participated in activities like hiking, playing in woods, camping, fishing, or hunting prior to age eleven were more likely to engage in pro-environmental behavior than those who had done things like gardening or tending to plants. Assuming, therefore, that the sites of the former activities are usually less manipulated than those of the latter, Wells and Lekies state that "while involvement with 'wild' and 'domesticated' natural environments both play a role [in adult environmentalism], participation with 'wild' nature before age 11 is a particularly potent pathway toward shaping both environmental attitudes and behaviors in adulthood."[34]

OUTDOOR EXPERIENCE AND HUMAN-NATURE BONDING

Despite everything said so far, it would be a mistake to conclude that extensive outdoor experience is either sufficient or necessary for the development of conservation commitment. Though it is true that many dedicated conservationists cite experience of the natural world as a formative influence, it is likewise true that not everyone who spends time outdoors dedicates themselves to conservation.[35] Nor is it the case that such experience is the only route to environmental advocacy.[36] There is recent evidence, too, that while outdoor experience may be especially relevant among people devoted to traditional conservation issues like wildlife protection and habitat preservation, it may be less influential among those concerned about problems like climate change and environmental justice.[37]

Equally mistaken would be the assumption that the association between nature engagement and pro-environmental outlooks is a simple one, or that outdoor experience by itself leads directly to concern for the protection of nature. There are, it seems, a number of factors that affect this relationship, and to understand some of these factors more fully, we must shift attention from life experience research to work that has been done in the broader field of conservation psychology.

As we saw in chapter 2, for at least the past two decades conservation psychologists have explored the significance of people's affective ties to the natural world. In doing so, they have utilized a number of related constructs to assess people's degree of comfort in, affection for, and sense of connection to the natural world. Among those not mentioned previously is "emotional affinity toward nature," which Elisabeth Kals, Daniel Schumacher, and Leo Montada define as "a positive feeling of inclination" that includes "love of nature" as well as "feeling good, free, [and] safe in nature." It also involves feelings of "oneness with nature"[38] that researchers measure with survey items asking if people "experience a close connection" to the natural world, and whether or not they perceive having "the same origin" as the beings encountered therein.[39]

The inclusion of such items in the concept of emotional affinity for nature clearly signals its overlap with the notion of identification with nature that is so vital to deep ecological thought. It also reveals a conceptual proximity to several other constructs conservation psychologists employ, including "place attachment," "connectedness to nature," and "environmental identity."[40] And this conceptual proximity is relevant here because, as studies of these related concepts have also shown, when Kals, Schumacher, and Montada surveyed German adults to test the hypothesis that emotional affinity with nature motivates people to protect it, they found that it was indeed a significant predictor of environmentally responsible behavior.[41]

But Kals, Schumacher, and Montada were interested in more than just the relationship between emotional affinity and pro-environmental behavior. Affinity for nature, they discovered, was itself correlated with multiple survey items having to do with outdoor experience, including frequency of time in nature, and frequency of time in nature accompanied by family members.[42] Thus, among their conclusions they state that "present as well as past experiences with nature are most powerful for the acquisition of emotional affinity toward nature," adding that "[t]he question with whom these experiences take place improve[s] the prediction of the emotional tie."[43]

Building on these results, Kals later collaborated on a survey of German and Lithuanian teenagers in order to determine, as the research team put it, "whether it is merely the fact that adolescents spend time outside or the more psychological attachment to nature that motivates behavior to protect nature."[44] What they found, in short, was that the teens' pro-environmental action was not simply a product of their exposure to the outdoors. Rather, their time outdoors fostered emotional affinity for nature, which in turn prompted more protective behavior.[45] With this intermediary effect of nature affinity in view, Kals and colleagues assert that "[c]ontact with nature will not directly lead to willingness for pro-environmental commitments, but only indirectly, moderated by emotional affinity toward nature."[46]

Results showing a similar relationship between nature *experience*, nature *attachment*, and pro-environmental *behavior* have been recorded by various studies focused on various forms of human-nature bonding.[47] One particularly notable project explored the notion of "connection to nature" among children in Florida public schools.[48] Utilizing a survey administered as part of the school system's environmental education programming, researchers saw a strong correlation between the amount of outdoor experience the children had and their development of this type of nature attachment. They also found a significant correlation between such attachment and the presence of accessible nature near the children's homes. Equally important, though, was their discovery that the children's sense of connection to nature was strongly related not only to their interest in pro-environmental behavior, but also their perception that their families valued nature positively.[49]

In sum, therefore, what studies like these show is what many people conclude intuitively, namely, that firsthand experience of nature, especially when it is encouraged by close social relations, tends to promote a sense of connection to it, which in turn influences more positive behavior toward it. Beyond facilitating human-nature bonding, however, further insight into why outdoor experience might incline people toward pro-environmental outlooks is offered by Robert Bixler and Joy James, who argue that a good deal of nature-based recreational activity is "serious" rather than "frivolous." In their words:

> Through participation in wild land recreation, people develop environmental competencies . . . learn about places and natural history and form affective bonds to wild lands. [While] these environmental experiences are far less focused [than], often extrinsically motivated, educational interventions, they are self determined and more likely to be valued by the participants. . . . Certainly, some participants should develop environmental concerns and think of themselves as outdoor persons.[50]

According to Bixler and James, then, outdoor engagement promotes not only emotional attachment to nature, but also learning, skill development, and feelings of environmental competency.[51] All of this, in their view, can "help explain the development of ecological identity in some persons" and, in some cases, lead to environmental activism.[52]

Perhaps not surprisingly, some of the evidence for Bixler and James's preceding claims comes from life experience research.[53] Additional support is found in work done by Bixler in collaboration with Myron Floyd and William Hammitt.[54] In two studies of middle-school children from the United States it was discovered that children who played in natural areas, in comparison to those who played in more urban or cultivated ones, had greater interest in certain outdoor activities, less aversion to living without modern comforts, less fear of various aspects of outdoor experience, and the strongest preferences for working outdoors.[55] Bixler, Floyd, and Hammitt thus conclude that nature play has measurable impacts on "environmental preferences and competencies" that could, consequently, foster pro-environmental outlooks. "Play and exploration in natural environments," they explain, "provide for novelty, challenge, control, self-determination, and positive social interactions. At least for some children, environmentalism probably begins to emerge as a function of a positive affective attachment to wild places that provided enjoyable experiences and a sense of competency."[56]

OUTDOOR EXPERIENCE IN DEEP ECOLOGICAL THOUGHT

Our commentary to this point highlights the formative role that experiential engagement with nature often plays in the development of a sense of connection to it, and how together these tend to correlate with an increase in pro-environmental behavior. We have yet to consider, however, the details of what philosophically minded deep ecology supporters have had to say regarding outdoor experience. Somewhat curiously, this is a subject about which relatively few commentators have written, despite the fact that it is discussed at length by many theorists in the deep ecology movement, including key intellectual figure Arne Naess. In what follows, therefore, we will attempt to summarize core elements of these theorists' perspectives in order to evaluate them in light of what has been said thus far.

The first and perhaps most basic explanation for deep ecology supporters' interest in outdoor experience has to do with their widespread advocacy of place-based forms of connectedness to nature. These forms of human-nature bonding, unlike more generalized ones, entail developing personal attachments to geographically specific locations, and it stands to reason that such place-connectedness would require some amount of time outdoors. As Reed and Rothenberg put it, "It is not enough that we should love our place; we have to really love it if our declarations are to have any practical consequences. This, of course, means knowing our place, and that means getting out into it."[57]

A second, overlapping reason for deep ecology theorists' emphasis on outdoor experience involves the anecdotal evidence that can be gathered from deep ecology supporters themselves. Among both theorists and practitioners, it seems, those who support the deep ecology movement often have backgrounds that include time spent in natural environments, and they tend not to think these two things are merely coincidental. Bill Devall and George Sessions, for example, list numerous outdoor activities they believe can be useful for "increasing psychological maturity and identification with all life," including "fishing, hunting, surfing, sun bathing, kayaking, canoeing, sailing, mountain climbing, hang gliding, skiing, running, bicycling and birdwatching." "There is," they say, "a very large body of literature coming from people who have participated in some of these activities . . . which attest[s] to possibilities for developing a sense of place and intuitive understanding of the connection between humans and nonhumans."[58]

It is worth pausing here for a moment to point out that although these remarks from Devall and Sessions have been noted by commentators before, what has not yet been noticed is that they mirror the approach to questions about outdoor experience taken by life experiences researchers. Indeed, the sort of literature review to which Devall and Sessions refer above is virtually identical to the way in which Tanner initiated his inquiry into the formative influences of conservationists—an inquiry that started with a review of literature on the lives of a number of influential environmental figures. One of the figures included in Tanner's initial review, moreover, was Aldo Leopold, who is not only regarded by many deep ecology theorists as an intellectual predecessor, but also widely cited by conservation psychologists.[59]

Of course, the tendency of deep ecology supporters to have nature experience in their backgrounds is not terribly hard to discern. Naess, for instance, who was himself a celebrated mountaineer, writes that

> most people in deep ecology have had the feeling—usually, but not always, in nature—that they are connected with something greater than their ego, greater than their name, their family, their special attributes as an individual—a feeling that is often called oceanic because many have had this feeling on the ocean. Without this feeling, one is not so easily drawn to become involved in deep ecology.[60]

This observation is notable for a number of reasons, one of which is its acknowledgment of the potentially diverse relations to nature experience that deep ecology affiliates might have. Perhaps most important, however, is that it repeats Devall and Sessions' central claim about the eco-philosophical significance of spending time outdoors, namely, that doing so can foster a sense of connection to, or identification with, nature. As Naess sums it up, many deep ecology supporters share the belief that some kinds of outdoor experience are "highly efficient in stimulating the sense of oneness, wholeness and in deepening identification."[61]

Beyond reiterating the widely held contention that outdoor experience promotes identification with nature, Naess also suggests that the effectiveness of outdoor experience in this regard can, and perhaps should, be enhanced by education or training. In his comments on the Scandinavian practice of outdoor life known as "*friluftsliv*," for example, he formulates "guidelines for ethically and ecologically responsible *friluftsliv*," among which is a recommendation for "education in the signs of identification." In more comprehensive sorts of outdoor education, he claims, "[c]hildren's (and adults') longing and capacity for identification with life and landscape is encouraged," and in this way people's "ability to experience deep, rich and varied interaction in and with nature is developed."[62]

In addition to these thoughts about the relationship between time in nature and identification with it, Naess further argues that the former can play a part in shaping people's broader lifestyle preferences. "Easy access to free nature," he writes, "is only one factor that can, in the early formative years, moderate . . . the quest for ever higher levels of consumption."[63] Though this idea is not developed in detail, it seems clearly related to many deep ecologists' insistence that outdoor activity itself should not be overly resource intensive, or preoccupied with the use of high-tech equipment.[64] Hence Naess proposes that "true *friluftsliv*" should be seen "as a route towards paradigm change," and the specific change he envisions is one in which time outdoors diminishes excessive consumerism and enhances people's ability to appreciate the rich ends that can be attained through simple means.[65]

As some of these remarks already indicate, there is a tendency in deep ecological thought to attach heightened importance to early life outdoor experiences, something that is manifest not only in Naess's work, but also in that of other influential theorists like Dolores LaChapelle, and Devall and Sessions.[66] In Naess's case, at least, this reflects both his own formative engagement with nature as a young boy,[67] as well as his sense of the role such engagement often plays in the lives of others.[68] He is adamant, however, that the character of this experience should be for the most part spontaneous and unconstrained. Thus in *Ecology, Community and Lifestyle* he says that certain restrictions on outdoor activities "would be considered an outrage" anywhere *friluftsliv* was taken seriously, and he singles out for criticism regulations forbidding backcountry camping, off-trail exploration, and traversal of difficult terrain.[69] Elsewhere he writes about the need for children to have easy access to natural areas where they can play without restrictions, and worries that "if there are rules of behavior laid down by neighbourhoods or parents, the feeling of freedom may be reduced."[70]

Finally, Naess also touches upon the possibility that some kinds of outdoor activity may have greater conservation value than others, noting that what are sometimes called "appreciative" outdoor activities may be more properly a part of *friluftsliv* than "consumptive" ones. The notion of *friluftsliv*, he claims, was largely a product of contemporary urban people's renewed interest in "more or less playful kinds of short excursions in nature," excursions that did "not serve to procure food" or "fit any other characterisation as work."[71] In Naess's updated version of this concept, he continually underscores the centrality of noncompetitive and nonextractive outdoor activity,[72] and thus his guidelines for *friluftsliv* state that there should be an "elimination of pleasure hunting, except for 'photographic hunting'," and he asserts that outdoor engagement should "touch the Earth lightly" in accord with what are now commonly called "leave no trace" principles.[73]

RUGGED, RURAL, AND ELITIST?

The preceding overview illuminates a number of parallels between deep ecological thought and contemporary social science on the conservation significance of outdoor experience. In particular, the stress that Naess and other deep ecology supporters place on largely unstructured childhood engagement with nature as a pathway toward more pro-environmental lifestyles, along with the contention that this pathway involves cultivating a stronger sense of connection to nature, reflects well the results lately reported by life experience researchers and conservation psychologists about the intersection of outdoor experience, human-nature bonding, and pro-environmental outlooks. But these parallels notwithstanding, deep ecology theorists have faced their share of criticism on this score, and it is to this criticism that we will now direct our attention.

Perhaps the most extended critique of deep ecological perspectives on nature experience is found in Joanna Griffiths's "The Varieties of Nature Experience." Here Griffiths explains that a "consistent theme of Deep Ecological approaches" to environmental problems is that there is a need for "a mass rediscovery of nature," one that will reacquaint people with "a crucial part of the human experience: the direct experience of the natural world."[74] Focusing on Naess's articulation of this theme, however, Griffiths finds a position fraught with difficulties, three of which are particularly important in the context of the current discussion.

Prominent among the several problems with Naess's view, Griffiths argues, is its tendency to valorize encounters with *natural* environments—or encourage the development of what she refers to as a "sense of nature"—while disparaging engagement with *built* ones.[75] "The vast majority of people have been deprived of a 'sense of nature,' as Naess understands it," she writes, "by growing up in cities and towns," and even if someone had substantial access to nature from a very young age, she says, "the 'sense of nature' to which Naess alludes can be dispelled by one's immediate surroundings and day to day immersion in the urban or non-natural."[76] Hence Griffiths detects a kind of antiurbanism within Naess's thought, one in which connectedness to nature "is a perilous quality, likely to be corroded by materialist and urban culture. Even environmentalists whose career choices are derived from a profound sense of nature-experience find their sensibilities adversely affected by an over-acquaintance with the urban."[77]

This suspicion of the built environment that Griffiths finds in Naess's work is closely connected to a second problem she sees therein, which is that it appears to privilege not only certain forms of nature experience, but also the people who are able to have them. Specifically referencing Naess's claims about the need for people to hone their abilities to perceive qualities in nature, she contends that a constant refrain in Naess's writing is the import of "the 'right' training for the nature-experiencing individual, the 'right' environment."[78] As Griffiths reads him, then, what Naess ultimately promotes is the idea that "'right' nature experience requires the presence of tutors to guide the unenlightened," which in turn means that "the Deep Ecology movement must foster an established hierarchy of individuals and of experiences." All of this, she says, "once more tends to exclusivity, and makes many strands of Deep Ecology appear rather like outward bound associations."[79]

The severity of these criticisms is only sharpened when Griffiths, in concert with the analyses of some ecofeminists, brings to the fore the potentially masculinist or gender-biased character of the ideal of outdoor engagement promoted in the literature of the deep ecology movement.[80] As she puts it, there is a "strength-testing notion of nature" that emerges when deep ecology supporters emphasize—as some of them surely do—fairly rugged, time-intensive types of backcountry or wilderness travel, and she worries that the fact that such a notion "might more generally be congenial to men appears to have escaped the notice of many deep ecologists."[81]

Now, stepping back a bit, it should be admitted in regards to this last point that Griffiths is correct to point out that conversations among environmentalists about outdoor experience can, and often do, take on an elitist, macho tone in which intensive engagement with physically demanding environments functions as a litmus test not only for people's love of nature, but also their commitment to conservation causes. That being acknowledged, however, it also seems that Naess's remarks about experiential engagement with nature need not be interpreted as contributing to this potentially exclusionary and elitist discourse in the way Griffiths suggests, and this is so for a cluster of related reasons.

To begin, it is true that Naess's writing sometimes conveys the view that urban lifestyles are experientially nature-poor in certain respects. In his discussions of *friluftsliv*, however, he surely does not villainize urban residents, nor does he say that urban life necessarily disconnects people and nature. In fact, his view is quite the opposite: he clearly believes that urbanites have as much fondness for and interest in engaging with nature as anyone else, and straightforwardly claims that "[c]ontrary to expectation, urbanised life has not killed human fascination with free nature, but only made access more difficult and promoted mass tourism."[82] In this comment, then, his central complaint is not that too many urbanites have too little interest in time outdoors. It is rather that city planners have done too poor a job of providing urban populations with green space sufficient to accommodate their genuine interest in nature. This failure is, moreover, one that Naess associates with some all-too-familiar forms of elitism, privilege, and promotion of consumer culture: the "easily accessible free areas" of nature near urban centers, he says, "have proven to be insufficient, and quickly assumed an urban façade" issuing in the "fatal curtailment of freedom of movement, [and] luxury residences and luxurious living rather than simple *life*."[83]

With these ideas in view, therefore, we can begin to understand why Naess places such emphasis on the protection of what he calls "free nature," or parts of the natural world that are, as he says, "not dominated by humans."[84] Of course, such areas can include extensive tracts of wilderness of the sort so often associated with the agenda of the deep ecology movement. But Naess also takes them to include those less celebrated areas nearby urban spaces to which people, and especially young children, have easy access.[85] In Naess's estimation the latter types of places play absolutely vital roles, one of the most essential of which is providing people a source of connection to nature in an increasingly urbanized world. This is why, in the short essay "Access to Free Nature," he claims that the loss of such areas "should be looked upon as a calamity," and he argues that people in wealthy nations have a pressing moral obligation to protect what remains of them.[86]

To be sure, Naess, like some other deep ecology theorists, does encourage people occasionally to spend longer periods of time in more expansive natural environments. One of the reasons for this recommendation, of course, is his belief that extended time in less manipulated environments is especially conducive to promoting environmentally friendly attitudes—a belief that echoes the claims of some of the social scientists previously cited. Yet Naess does not contend that urbanites are unable, or unwilling, to participate in this activity,[87] and his emphasis on self-reliance in such places is less a matter of celebrating a form of hypermasculine individualism than it is a matter of discouraging the commodification of nature experience. Corporations, he observes, place substantial "outfitting pressure" on people's time outdoors, in which "new so-called improvements appear and are marketed continuously, and norms about equipment replacement are impressed upon and accepted by large sections of the population."[88] Expressing particular concern for the *friluftsliv* tradition, he says that "[e]xtremely powerful forces are attempting to replace *friluftsliv* with mechanized, competitive, and environmentally destructive intrusions into nature,"[89] something that in Naess's view not only puts nature at risk from outdoor recreationists, but also threatens to diminish the truly transformative potential of what they are doing—the power of outdoor experience to impact people's sense of who they are, how much they believe they need, and what kinds of lives they think are really worth leading.

Relatedly, just as Naess does not habitually cast outdoor recreationists as rugged conquerors of nature, his claims about mentors do not necessarily valorize a class of outdoor elites. Many of his remarks appear, instead, to acknowledge the efficacy of certain types of outdoor education, and to anticipate research findings about the roles of teachers, mentors, and close social relations in the life-courses of adult environmentalists. In a 2001 interview, for example, he describes a time in New Mexico when he was camping with a group of graduate students, and urged them to contemplate their surroundings in silence for an hour.[90] Earlier in the same interview, he gives the example of a man directing children's attention toward some small plants on the ground, saying that while part of the man's activity could be to "tell them a bit" about the plants, "the most important thing" is for him to "bend all the way down, so the children get the impression that this must be something very important."[91] In these scenarios, the role of the mentor is not to initiate intense physical activity or risk-taking, but to promote attentive reflection and a sense of wonder, largely through the use of bodily gestures and nonverbal cues.[92] Such mentor-encouraged responses to nature are far from "strength-testing" and, as Naess might quickly add, are every bit as possible in urban-accessible free nature as they are in remote corners of the wilderness.

OUTDOOR EXPERIENCE AS A SOURCE OF DEEP ECOLOGICAL ATTITUDES

What one finds in deep ecological thought, therefore, and perhaps especially in the work of Naess, seems considerably less problematic than Griffiths suggests. Rather than ideals of nature engagement as the province of antiurban, hypermasculine elites, what emerges here is instead an agenda for a diverse array of people to engage with outdoor environments across the urban-rural-wild spectrum, and that issues related calls for more and better urban green space along with increasingly connection-focused environmental education. In articulating this agenda, deep ecological thought aligns itself with the findings of contemporary social scientists and environmental educators as it highlights the potential for time outdoors to foster feelings of connectedness and care for nature, along with the pro-environmental practices that tend to accompany them.

It is helpful to reiterate, however, that although outdoor experience does, as a general rule, tend to influence an array of pro-environmental variables, it is not the case that it always results in a commitment to conservation. Nor does all commitment to conservation originate in outdoor experience. What can be said is that, among the many people who interact with the outdoors, those who do so in childhood with social encouragement, and who develop environmental preferences and high levels of connectedness to nature, are likely also to develop pro-environmental attitudes and to engage in some kinds of environmentally friendly behaviors. Considering that outdoor experience itself tends to promote such preferences and attachments, it is not surprising that so many dedicated conservationists cite it as an influence. Still, not everyone who experiences the outdoors will become a conservation advocate, and there certainly are committed conservationists and environmentalists who are not much influenced by outdoor experience at all.

Nevertheless, evidence for a link between outdoor experience and pro-environmental outlooks exists, and recognizing this goes a long way toward vindicating an area of deep ecological thought that twenty-first-century readers could easily view as outdated. It is easy to imagine, that is, that as lifestyles become less and less directly engaged with natural environments, the promotion of such engagement by deep ecology theorists would come more and more to be seen as an antiquated appeal to "get outside," or get "back to nature." In light of everything just discussed, however, it seems better to interpret deep ecological thought on this subject as a considered position that gives environmentally inclusive identities their due, and that takes seriously the ways in which these can be, and routinely are, nurtured by experiential engagement with the natural world. Philosophical perspectives calling for outdoor experience, therefore, need not be looked upon as expressing some romantic nostalgia for a bygone rural past. They can, instead, be seen as expressing ideas consistent with what the best available evidence shows us, and as articulating a practical agenda that is as appropriate to our current situation as any other.

Certainly, deep ecological philosophy is not the only area of environmental thinking that expresses an interest in outdoor experience. Advocates of the notion of "biophilia" do so as well, and their views have numerous points of intersection with those of deep ecology theorists. In the next chapter, then, we will examine the notion of biophilia as it is articulated in the work of Stephen Kellert, with an eye to determining what it adds to an understanding of deep ecological thought, what deep ecological thought can contribute to it in return, and how together these two intellectual streams can enhance our understanding and appreciation of connection to nature.

NOTES

1. Rhonda Clements, "An Investigation of the Status of Outdoor Play," *Contemporary Issues in Early Childhood* 5, no. 1 (2004): 68–80. It was also learned that the majority of mothers who had played outdoors did so for at least 3 hours at a time, but the same was true for less than a quarter of their children.

2. Sandra L. Hofferth, "Changes in American Children's Time—1997 to 2003," *Electronic International Journal of Time Use Research* 6, no. 1 (2009): 26–47.

3. See, for example, V. Cleland, et. Al, "Predictors of Time Spent Outdoors among Children: 5-Year Longitudinal Findings," *Journal of Epidemiology and Community Health* 64, no. 5 (May 2010): 400–406. This study found that although there were noticeable declines in time spent outside among Australian children from 2001 to 2006, they still spent an average of about an hour outside per day. A similar result for Britons, based on time of year, is reported in B. L. Diffey, "An Overview Analysis of the Time People Spend Outdoors," *British Journal of Dermatology* 164, no. 4 (April 2011): 848–54.

4. Richard Louv, *Last Child in the Woods: Saving Our Children from Nature-Deficit Disorder* (Chapel Hill: Algonquin Books, 2006).

5. Stephen R. Kellert, *Kinship to Mastery: Biophilia in Human Evolution and Development* (Washington, DC: Island Press, 1997), 164.

6. Robert Pyle, *The Thunder Tree: Lessons from an Urban Wildland* (New York: The Lyons Press, 1993).

7. Peter Reed and David Rothenberg, eds., *Wisdom in the Open Air: The Norwegian Roots of Deep Ecology* (Minneapolis: University of Minnesota Press, 1993), 155.

8. Thomas Tanner, "Significant Life Experiences: A New Research Area in Environmental Education," *Journal of Environmental Education* 11, no. 4 (1980): 20–24. Specifically, Tanner asked respondents to identify (a) "the formative influences which led her or him to choose conservation work," (b) the approximate age at which those influences occurred, and (c) a summary of their conservation activities (21).

9. Ibid., 21, 23.

10. Ibid., 22.

11. Among the earliest of these studies is Nancy J. Peterson, "Developmental Variables Affecting Environmental Sensitivity in Professional Environmental Educators," MA thesis (Southern Illinois University at Carbondale, 1982), cited in Louise Chawla, "Significant Life Experiences Revisited: A Review of Research on Sources of Environmental Sensitivity," *Environmental Education Research* 4, no. 4 (1998): 369–82. Environmental educators have also been studied by Peter B. Corcoran, "Formative Influences in the Lives of Environmental Educators in the United States," *Environmental Education Research*, 5, no. 2 (1999): 207–20.

See also Chawla's review of literature in "Significant Life Experiences Revisited," 375–76.

12. Joy A. Palmer, "Development of Concern for the Environment and Formative Experiences of Educators," *Journal of Environmental Education* 24, no. 3 (1993): 28.

13. Joy A. Palmer et al., "An Overview of Significant Influences and Formative Experiences on the Development of Adults' Environmental Awareness in Nine Countries," *Environmental Education Research* 4, no. 4 (1998): 453.

14. Leesa L. Sward, "Significant Life Experiences Affecting the Environmental Sensitivity of El Salvadoran Environmental Professionals," *Environmental Education Research* 5, no. 2 (1999): 201–206.

15. Shih-Jang Hsu, "Significant Life Experiences Affect Environmental Action: A Confirmation Study in Eastern Taiwan," *Environmental Education Research* 15, no. 4 (2009): 497–517.

16. Louise Chawla, "Life Paths into Effective Environmental Action," *The Journal of Environmental Education* 31, no. 1 (1999): 15–26.

17. James R. Farmer, Charles Chancellor, and Burnell C. Fischer, "Space to Romp and Roam and How It May Promote Land Conservation," *Natural Areas Journal* 31, no. 4 (2011): 343–45. Similar results are reported in a study of employees of animal-themed education facilities (including Carolina Tiger Rescue, the Duke Lemur Center, and the North Carolina Aquarium), which found that "influential people" and "outdoor experiences" were their most widely cited formative influences (Susan Caplow and Jennifer Thomsen, "Significant Life Experiences and Animal-Themed Education," in *Animals in Environmental Education: Interdisciplinary Approaches to Curriculum and Pedagogy*, ed. Teresa Lloro-Bidart and Valerie S. Banschbach [Cham, Switzerland: Palgrave-Macmillan, 2019], 237–57).

18. Louise Chawla, "Childhood Experiences Associated with Care for the Natural World: A Theoretical Framework for Empirical Results," *Children, Youth and Environments* 17, 4 (2007): 145.

19. Chawla, "Life Paths," 17.

20. Palmer, "Development of Concern for the Environment," 29.

21. Farmer, Chancellor, and Fischer, "Space to Romp and Roam," 344–45.

22. Among American and Norwegian environmentalists, for example, nearly every respondent who claimed to have formative nature experiences identified childhood as the time of their occurrence (Chawla, "Life Paths," 19). Childhood was also a critical time for nature experience in Palmer's study of British environmental educators, which concludes by saying that "childhood experience of the outdoors is the single most important factor in developing personal concern for the environment" (Palmer, "Development of Concern for the Environment," 29–30). See also Tanner, "Significant Life Experiences," 22; Hsu, "Significant Life Experiences," 506.

23. Chawla, "Life Paths," 21.

24. Hsu "Significant Life Experiences," 508. See also Palmer, "Development of Concern for the Environment," 30. These developmental models of the sources of conservation concern receive some further support from research targeting populations younger than those that are often the focus of this research. In initial interviews with environmentally active high school students in Wisconsin, the most commonly

cited sources of students' environmental sensitivity were "role models" (teachers, followed by parents, relatives, and friends) and "environmental influences" (access to the outdoors, followed by in-depth learning or programmatic involvement in nature, and experiences with animals) (Daniel J. Sivek, "Environmental Sensitivity among Wisconsin High School Students," *Environmental Education Research* 8, no. 2 [2002]: 155–70). Similarly, teen-aged Canadian environmental leaders cited parents equally as often as outdoor experience among their influences (Heather E. Arnold, Fay G. Cohen, and Alan Warner, "Youth and Environmental Action: Perspectives of Young Environmental Leaders on Their Formative Influences," *The Journal of Environmental Education* 40, no. 3 [2009]: 27–36). A pattern in which the import of nature experience seemed to wane in adolescence also appears in Nicolette L. Cagle, "Changes in Experiences with Nature through the Lives of Environmentally Committed University Faculty," *Environmental Education Research*, 24, no. 6 (2018): 889–98.

25. Hsu, "Significant Life Experiences," 506.

26. Chawla, "Life Paths," 25.

27. Farmer, Chancellor, and Fischer, "Space to Romp and Roam," 345.

28. Tanner, "Significant Life Experiences," 23; Chawla, "Life Paths," 19; Peterson, "Developmental Variables Affecting Environmental Sensitivity," in Chawla, 371–72; Sivek, "Environmental Sensitivity," 161.

29. In several studies, for example, people have cited family vacations in outdoor areas or with outdoor components as formative influences. See Peterson, "Developmental Variables Affecting Environmental Sensitivity," in Chawla, 371–72; Palmer, "Development of Concern for the Environment," 28.

30. Peterson, "Developmental Variables Affecting Environmental Sensitivity," in Chawla, 371; Palmer, "Development of Concern for the Environment," 28; Corcoran, "Formative Influences," 212; Sward, "Significant Life Experiences," 204–205; Sivek, "Environmental Sensitivity," 162; Arnold, Cohen, and Warner, "Youth and Environmental Action," 32; Hsu, "Significant Life Experiences," 506; Farmer, Chancellor, and Fischer, "Space to Romp and Roam," 343; Shinichi Furihata et al., "Potentials and Challenges of Research on 'Significant Life Experiences' in Japan," *Children, Youth and Environments* 17, no. 4 (2007): 220–22.

31. Tanner, "Significant Life Experiences," 21.

32. Ibid., 23.

33. Nancy M. Wells and Kristi S. Lekies, "Nature and the Life Course: Pathways from Childhood Nature Experiences to Adult Environmentalism," *Children, Youth and Environments* 16, no. 1 (2006): 1–24. As the commentary on this study should make clear, its use of the terms "wild" and "domesticated" is not based on assessment of the *locations* of respondents' activities; it is based on assessment of the *activities* in which people engaged (7).

34. Wells and Lekies, "Nature and the Life Course," 13. Wells and Lekies also found that youthful participation in formal outdoor education programs was not correlated with adult environmentalism (14).

35. Significant life experience researchers often note the paucity of comparative data in this field. The few studies that have compared conservationists to less

environmentally active people have found that although nature experience does tend to have some influence on environmental advocacy, it is not the most prominent influence that emerges. Hsu, for example, found that whereas childhood nature experience was the most cited formative influence of dedicated conservationists, in a comparison study it ranked thirteenth among life experience items that distinguished people who were environmentally active from those who were environmentally apathetic. When Hsu's comparison group was considered in its entirety, nature experience was not a significant predictor of environmental action at all ("Significant Life Experiences," 509, 510). Similarly, Danqing Li and Jin Chen found that early life nature experience was one of two influences most commonly mentioned by environmentally active Chinese college students. A study of the general population of students, however, found that "life principles" and "college education" were more significant predictors of environmental action than nature experience in college or nature experience in youth, which ranked third and fifth, respectively ("Significant Life Experiences on the Formation of Environmental Action among Chinese College Students," *Environmental Education Research* 21, no. 4 [2015]: 612–630). The takeaway from these findings, then, is that while conservationists may tend to have more nature experience than is typical of other populations, these other populations clearly do not lack nature experience entirely. What distinguishes these groups appears to be a cluster of factors, some of which contribute to the increased significance that nature experience often takes on among people dedicated to conservation.

36. See Chawla, "Life Paths."

37. See, for example, Rachel A. Howell and Simon Allen, "Significant Life Experiences, Motivations and Values of Climate Change Educators," *Environmental Education Research* 25, no. 6 (2019): 813–831; Rachel Howell and Simon Allen, "People and Planet: Values, Motivations and Formative Influences of Individuals Acting to Mitigate Climate Change," *Environmental Values* 26, no. 2 (2017): 131–55; Scott R. Fisher, "Life Trajectories of Youth Committing to Climate Activism," *Environmental Education Research* 22, no. 2 (2016): 229–47. Relatedly, work done by Donovon Ceaser suggests that the significant life experiences of environmental justice advocates also tend to differ from those of more traditional conservationists, and not to emphasize positive experiences of the outdoors. See Donovon Ceaser, "Significant Life Experiences and Environmental Justice: Positionality and the Significance of Negative Social/Environmental Experiences," *Environmental Education Research* 21, no. 2 (2015): 205–20; Donovon Ceaser, "Why I Came to the OSBG: The SLEs of Environmental Justice Youth at Our School at Blair Grocery," *Race, Gender and Class; New Orleans* 25, no. 1–2 (2018): 147–65.

38. Elisabeth Kals, Daniel Schumacher, and Leo Montada, "Emotional Affinity Toward Nature as a Motivational Basis to Protect Nature," *Environment and Behavior* 31, no. 2 (1999): 182. See also Markus Muller, Elisabeth Kals, and Ramune Pansa, "Adolescents' Emotional Affinity toward Nature: A Cross-Societal Study," *Journal of Developmental Processes* 4, no. 1 (2009): 60.

39. In "Emotional Affinity toward Nature as a Motivational Basis to Protect Nature," Kals, Schumacher, and Montada do not provide their emotional affinity scale. The scale is provided in Muller, Kals, and Pansa's "Adolescents' Emotional

Affinity toward Nature," 69. Interestingly, and in keeping with our claims in chapter 3, while the idea of "oneness" is conceptually related to the emotional affinity construct, the term "oneness" does not appear in the survey instrument used to measure it.

40. For an overview of these concepts, see Susan Clayton, "Environment and Identity," in *The Oxford Handbook of Environmental and Conservation Psychology*, ed. Susan Clayton (New York: Oxford, 2012), 164–80.

41. Kals, Schumacher, and Montada, "Emotional Affinity toward Nature," 191.

42. Ibid., 191–93.

43. Ibid., 193. A similar correlation between time outdoors and "nature relatedness" was found among Australians by Anne Cleary et al., "Predictors of Nature Connection Among Urban Residents: Assessing the Role of Childhood and Adult Nature Experiences," *Environment and Behavior* 52, no. 6 (2020): 579–610.

44. Muller, Kals, and Pansa, "Adolescents' Emotional Affinity toward Nature," 62.

45. Ibid., 60.

46. Ibid., 63. Further analysis of the relation between affinity for nature and environmental identity can be found in Joe Hinds and Paul Sparks, "Engaging with the Natural Environment: The Role of Affective Connection and Identity," *Journal of Environmental Psychology*, 28, no. 2 (2008): 109–20.

47. In addition to the studies cited below, see Ian Alcocka et al., "Associations between Pro-Environmental Behaviour and Neighbourhood Nature, Nature Visit Frequency and Nature Appreciation: Evidence from a Nationally Representative Survey in England," *Environment International* 136 (2020): 1–10, https://doi.org/10.1016/j.envint.2019.105441; Weizhe Zhang, Eben Goodale, and Jin Chen, "How Contact with Nature Affects Children's Biophilia, Biophobia and Conservation Attitude in China," *Biological Conservation* 177 (2014): 109–16.

48. Judith Chen-Hsuan Cheng and Martha C. Monroe, "Connection to Nature: Children's Affective Attitude toward Nature," *Environment and Behavior* 44, no. 1 (2012): 40.

49. Ibid., 44–5. See also Silvia Collado, Henk Staats, and José Corraliza, "Experiencing Nature in Children's Summer Camps: Affective, Cognitive and Behavioural Consequences," *Journal of Environmental Psychology* 33 (2013): 37–44; Gary W. Evans, Siegmar Otto, and Florian G. Kaiser, "Childhood Origins of Young Adult Environmental Behavior," *Psychological Science* 29, no. 5 (2018): 679–87.

50. Robert D. Bixler and J. Joy James, "Environmental Socialization: The Critical Peripheral?," in *Handbook of Sustainability Research*, ed. Walter Leal Filho (Peter Lang: Frankfurt, 2005), 23.

51. Ibid., 22.

52. Ibid., 24, 15.

53. Ibid., 18–19; Chawla, "Childhood Experiences," 145–8. See also Louv, *Last Child in the Woods*, chapter 12, "Where Will Future Stewards of Nature Come From?"

54. Robert D. Bixler, Myron F. Floyd, and William E. Hammitt, "Environmental Socialization: Quantitative Tests of the Childhood Play Hypothesis," *Environment and Behavior* 34, no. 6 (2002): 795–818.

55. Ibid., 807–12. The children in this study were divided into three categories: "wildland adventurers" who usually played near ponds, farms, fields, or woods; "urban adventurers" who played most frequently in streets, alleys, playgrounds, and yards; and "yard adventurers" who usually spent time in their own or others' yards (802). The differences just cited, then, were those found between "wildland adventurers" and both "yard" and "urban adventurers."

56. Ibid., 800. In these authors' estimation, "[d]eeply committed environmentalists, at least those focusing on land conservation, are probably a subpopulation of the WA [wildland adventurers] group" (814).

57. Reed and Rothenberg, *Wisdom in the Open Air*, 155. Another fairly common way in which these ideas are conveyed can be seen in Bill Devall's *Simple in Means, Rich in Ends: Practicing Deep Ecology* (Salt Lake City: Peregrine Smith Books, 1988), where he suggests that people might gain a "sense-of-place" (66) by engaging in an "exercise in bioregional studies," one that contains multiple outdoor-experiential components (71–2).

58. Bill Devall and George Sessions, *Deep Ecology: Living as if Nature Mattered* (Salt Lake City: Gibbs Smith, 1985), 187–8. See also Dolores LaChapelle, *Earth Wisdom* (Los Angeles: The Guild of Tutors Press, 1978), chapter 19. Although Devall and Sessions did not intend these remarks to refer to what are today commonly called "extreme sports" participants, their list does overlap to some extent with this category of activity, and there is some evidence that participation in the latter fosters connection to nature. See Eric Brymer, Greg Downey, and Tonia Gray, "Extreme Sports as a Precursor to Environmental Sustainability," *Journal of Sport and Tourism* 14, no. 2–3 (2009): 193–204. For further discussion specifically of surfing and its relationship to deep ecology, nature connectedness, and spirituality, see Bron Taylor, *Dark Green Religion: Nature Spirituality and the Planetary Future* (Berkeley: University of California Press, 2010), chapter 5.

59. Tanner, "Significant Life Experiences," 21.

60. Arne Naess, "Simple in Means, Rich in Ends: An Interview with Arne Naess," interview by Stephan Bodian, in *Deep Ecology for the Twenty-First Century: Readings on the Philosophy and Practice of the New Environmentalism,* ed. George Sessions (Boston: Shambhala, 1995), 30.

61. Arne Naess, *Ecology Community and Lifestyle*: *Outline of an Ecosophy*, trans. and rev. David Rothenberg (Cambridge: Cambridge University Press, 1989), 177.

62. Naess, *Ecology, Community and Lifestyle*, 179. Further analysis of *friluftsliv* can be found in Nils Faarlund, "A Way Home," *Wisdom in the Open Air*, 157–69; Hans Gelter, "*Friluftsliv*: The Scandinavian Philosophy of Outdoor Life," *Canadian Journal of Environmental Education* 5, no. 1 (2000): 77–92.

63. Arne Naess, "Access to Free Nature," *The Trumpeter* 21, no. 2 (2005): 49.

64. For an interesting treatment of the relation between technology, outdoor (wilderness) recreation, and a critique of "front-country" consumerism, see Sarah Pohl, "Technology and the Wilderness Experience," *Environmental Ethics* 28, no. 2 (Summer 2006): 147–63. Though Pohl does not self-identify as a deep ecology supporter, her analysis seems broadly consonant with the positions of Naess and other deep ecology theorists.

65. Naess, *Ecology, Community and Lifestyle*, 179.

66. See, for instance, LaChapelle. *Earth Wisdom*; Devall and Sessions, *Deep Ecology*, 189.

67. David Rothenberg, *Is It Painful to Think?: Conversations with Arne Naess* (Minneapolis: University of Minnesota Press, 1993), chapter 1.

68. Naess, "Access to Free Nature," 48.

69. Naess, *Ecology, Community and Lifestyle*, 180.

70. Naess, "Access to Free Nature," 48. In *Earth Wisdom* LaChapelle, like Naess, has a fairly extensive discussion of human development that includes an emphasis on contact with nature, especially in childhood where she emphasizes the role of play.

71. Naess, *Ecology, Community and Lifestyle*, 178.

72. Ibid., 179–81. These pages show further that Naess's emphasis on the non-competitive character of outdoor activity is related to his belief that such activity also should not be overly laden with gear and gadgets. The link here is that Naess regards competition as one of the factors driving the desire for better and more sophisticated equipment.

73. Ibid., 178–9.

74. Joanna Griffiths, "The Varieties of Nature Experience," *Worldviews* 6, no. 3 (2002): 254. This claim is, arguably, something of an overstatement, particularly if taken as a claim about the works of philosophical theorists in the deep ecology movement. While most of these thinkers do, as we have argued, place some importance on outdoor experience, it could be asserted that they do not stress it to the degree that Griffiths here implies.

75. See also Kirsti Pedersen Gurholt, "Joy of Nature, *Friluftsliv* Education and Self: Combining Narrative and Cultural-Ecological Approaches to Environmental Sustainability," *Journal of Adventure Education and Outdoor Learning* 14, no. 3 (2014): 233–246.

76. Griffiths, "The Varieties of Nature Experience," 267.

77. Ibid., 266.

78. Ibid., 268–69.

79. Ibid., 272.

80. See, for example, Marti Kheel, "License to Kill: An Ecofeminist Critique of Hunters' Discourse," in *Animals and Women: Feminist Theoretical Explorations*, ed. Carol J. Adams and Josephine Donovan (Durham: Duke University Press, 1995), 85–125.

81. Griffiths, "The Varieties of Nature Experience," 272.

82. Naess, *Ecology, Community and Lifestyle*, 177.

83. Ibid., 180, emphasis in original.

84. Arne Naess, "Interview with Norwegian Philosopher Arne Naess," interview by Jan van Boeckel, accessed September 10, 2018, http://www.naturearteducation.org/Interview_Arne_Naess_1995.pdf.

85. Naess, "Access to Free Nature," 48.

86. Ibid., 49.

87. Naess, *Ecology, Community and Lifestyle*, 179.

88. Ibid., 180.

89. Ibid.

90. Arne Naess, "'Here I Stand': An Interview with Arne Naess," interview by Christian Diehm, *Environmental Philosophy* 1, no. 2 (Fall 2004): 11.

91. Ibid., 10.

92. For an extended commentary on this example, see Carol Bigwood, "Standing and Stooping to Tiny Flowers: An Ecofemnomenological Response to Arne Naess," *Environmental Philosophy* 1, no. 2 (Fall 2004): 28–45. Naess's comments also seem to reflect the sort of sensibility articulated by Devall and Sessions in *Deep Ecology*, chapter 7.

Chapter 5

Loving More-than-Human Life
Connectedness to Nature, Deep Ecology, and Biophilia

The term "biophilia" was first used in 1964 by psychologist Erich Fromm to describe the "passionate love of life and of all that is alive" that he believed was a key feature of human psychology.[1] Roughly two decades later, biologist Edward O. Wilson began utilizing the same terminology, as he independently began to develop a similar idea about our human psychological makeup. In his 1984 text *Biophilia: The Human Bond with Other Species*, Wilson presented what quickly became known as the "biophilia hypothesis," speculating that the long course of human evolution had left us with an inherent fascination with living things, an evolutionarily endowed "tendency to focus on life and life-like processes."[2] Subsequent to this early formulation, and across numerous theoretical developments, biophilia has become a truly pervasive idea, influencing contemporary thought on everything from wilderness protection and species conservation to urban planning and the design of the built environment.

Though Wilson is rightly credited with popularizing the notion of biophilia as most people understand it today, its influence in so many spheres is due in good part to the efforts of Stephen R. Kellert. Not only did Kellert develop a theoretically distinctive version of the biophilia hypothesis, but he also pushed its application in novel directions, with much of his late-career focus being on interior and architectural design.[3] Yet despite Kellert's significant contributions in this area, and the current widespread interest in biophilic thought, environmental philosophers have not yet paid much detailed attention to his work, including his attempts to use biophilic theory to contribute to the field of environmental ethics.

This general lack of extended analysis of Kellert's writing by philosophers represents a missed opportunity, especially for deep ecology theorists, since there is indeed an intriguing initial similarity between the biophilic postulate that relationships to and interest in the natural world are core features of human existence, and deep ecological ideas about identification with nature, or "ecological identity." But what, precisely, is the relationship between these two schools of thought? And what, if anything, might biophilic and deep ecological theories have to contribute to one another?

In this concluding chapter we will take up with these questions, focusing on the biophilia hypothesis as Kellert has articulated it. Exploring his understanding of biophilia and biophilic environmental ethics reveals not only key points of convergence with the writings of deep ecology theorists, but also some points of rather sharp divergence from them. By examining these areas of similarity and difference, and paying special attention to Kellert's preference for anthropocentric ethical approaches, we will come to see not only how biophilic theory can deepen our appreciation of the extent of human connectedness to nature, but also how our analyses of deep ecological thought can help move the conversation about biophilia in more inclusive, less human-centered directions.

BIOPHILIA IN THE WORK OF STEPHEN KELLERT

At the root of Kellert's work on the biophilia hypothesis is his well-known typology of values (table 5.1). Developed early in his career in conjunction with research he was doing for the U.S. Fish and Wildlife Service, Kellert's first iteration of the typology sought to encapsulate American attitudes toward animals.[4] This initial focus quickly expanded, however, as Kellert continued to catalog public perspectives on a wide array of environmental and natural resource-related issues, including predator control, habitat preservation, and the value of endangered species.[5] The cumulative result of these efforts, then, was a typology providing researchers and resource managers with a concise inventory of American environmental attitudes, an instructive glimpse into the ways Americans viewed, and valued, nature and wildlife (table 5.1, columns 1 and 2).

As his work continued, however, Kellert was increasingly impressed by the diverse arenas in which the attitudes included in the typology were proving to be operative. They appeared in studies of public perceptions of a variety of animals and taxa, as well as in research conducted in different geographic regions of the United States. They could be found among diverse environmental stakeholders and interest groups, and also in Western attitudes toward nature across historical periods. There were even indications of their presence in other cultures, as similar research was being conducted in Germany, Botswana, and Japan.[6] These findings prompted Kellert to consider the possibility that his typology might represent something more

Table 5.1 Kellert's Typology of Biophilic Values

Value	Definition/Attitudinal Orientation	Proposed Function
Utilitarian	Material and physical utility of nature	Physical sustenance, material productivity, survival skills
Dominionistic	Mastery and control over nature	Physical prowess, confidence, mastery skills
Negativistic	Fear of and aversion to nature	Safety, protection, awe
Humanistic	Emotional bonding with nature	Bonding, cooperation, companionship
Moralistic	Moral and spiritual relation to nature	Curiosity, exploration, discovery
Naturalistic	Exploration and discovery of nature	Order, meaning, connection
Scientific-Ecologistic	Systematic/empirical study of nature	Knowledge, understanding, critical thinking
Aesthetic	Physical attraction and appeal of nature	Harmony, security, creativity
Symbolic	Nature in language and expressive thought	Communication, mental development, analytical skills

Source: Adapted by the author from Stephen R. Kellert, "A Biocultural Basis for an Ethic toward the Natural Environment," in *Foundations of Environmental Sustainability: The Evolution of Science and Policy*, ed. Larry L. Rockwood, Ronald E. Stewart, and Thomas Dietz (Oxford: Oxford University Press, 2008), 325. Copyright © 2008 by Oxford University Press, Inc. Reproduced with permission of the Licensor through PLSclear.

than just the snapshot of American values that he initially took it to be. What Kellert began to think, that is, was that even though the typology was originally intended simply as "a convenient shorthand for describing varying perspectives of nature,"[7] it might actually be touching upon "universal dispositions toward nature somewhat independent of group affiliation, history, and culture."[8]

Fortuitously, it was around this same time that Kellert encountered Wilson's emerging work on biophilia.[9] The core of Wilson's idea, as we saw at the outset, is that humans have an evolved inclination to affiliate with living things, and although the dispositions in which Kellert was interested were not solely oriented toward life, nor exclusively associated with "philic" feelings of positive affection, the notion of biophilia remained attractive, since it seemed to provide a way to account for the widespread expression of the attitudes his research had uncovered. As Kellert saw it, then, the question to be investigated was essentially one of evolutionary psychology: could the attitudes in his typology have been adaptive for *Homo sapiens* such that, in the course of evolutionarily history, they became inherent features of humans' psychological character?

Kellert took up with this question in numerous places throughout his career, including his last major work, *Birthright*. His most detailed early treatment of the subject, however, comes in *Kinship to Mastery: Biophilia in Human Evolution and Development*. Here Kellert isolates the typological dispositions in order to detail the evolutionary advantages that could accrue to humans who possessed them, discussing everything from the way in which negativistic responses to predators or insects can result in increased safety,[10] to how scientific curiosity about the natural world can provide practical benefits and stimulate cognitive development (table 5.1, column 3).[11] With such possibilities in view, Kellert concludes that it is indeed reasonable to believe that we "evolved these values of nature because they enhanced our capacity to survive and prosper physically, emotionally, and intellectually."[12] The categories of the typology, he writes elsewhere, can be understood "to represent a basic human relationship and dependence on nature indicating some measure of adaptational value in the struggle to survive."[13]

Thus, Kellert arrived at a unique version of the biophilia hypothesis, one that is distinctive for its incorporation of the typology of values, but still like others in claiming that the inclinations to affiliate with nature it represents have an "inherent and evolutionary basis."[14] This latter claim, of course, is the subject of much of the scientific and critical discussion about the biophilia hypothesis, which likely explains why Kellert so regularly qualifies his understanding of it.[15] His contention, in short, is that while humans' biophilic inclinations are in fact innate and thus "characteristic of all people independent of culture and history,"[16] they are nevertheless "weak dispositions" open to significant cultural influence and individual variation.[17] In a word, then, Kellert believes that our biophilic tendencies have a "biocultural" character,[18] meaning that although they are biologically based, it is still the case that "culture modifies their form, content, and occurrence."[19]

Considered in the larger context of Kellert's thought, this last point is surely one of the most important, since it gets to the heart of a dilemma that animates much of his practical philosophy. The fact that the biophilic dispositions are dependent on situational factors for their development indicates, on the one hand, that they can be expressed in individually and culturally distinctive ways. On the other hand, it also opens the possibility that our personal and cultural settings might inhibit or skew their development, resulting in their taking distorted and unhealthy forms.[20] Lack of exposure to natural environments, for example, may stunt our aesthetic appreciation of nature, or issue in excessive fear of the natural world and a lack of appreciation for its material value.[21] Similarly, inadequate opportunities for outdoor engagement may frustrate our drives for exploration and mastery, and curb the development of the physical skills, creativity, and self-esteem such opportunities provide.[22] The overarching problem, therefore, as Kellert himself explains, is that if the biophilic dispositions are "insufficiently stimulated and nurtured," they will almost certainly end up "latent, atrophied, and dysfunctional,"[23] with such outcomes "resulting in emotional and intellectual deficits" for those who suffer them.[24]

BIOPHILIA, DEEP ECOLOGY, AND ENVIRONMENTAL ETHICS

Without doubt, the central claim that emerges from Kellert's writing is that humans are adapted to natural environments both physically and psychologically, which means that we depend on such environments for much more than just our material welfare.[25] People have, he explains, "a fundamental physical, emotional, and intellectual dependence on nature and living diversity," and thus the degradation of natural environments poses "considerable risk to humans materially, affectively, cognitively, and even spiritually."[26] For biophilic humans, therefore, to damage the natural world and cut ourselves off from engagement with it—as many of us surely have tended to do—threatens not just the obvious sorts of material harms, but it also "reduces the human potential for achieving meaningful and satisfying lives physically, emotionally, and intellectually."[27]

Of course, as Kellert is well aware, claims like these are to a considerable extent empirically testable, and there is an increasingly compelling body of empirical evidence that exists to support them. Numerous studies have found, for instance, that spending time in natural environments—or even well-designed interior ones—can reduce stress, promote intellectual functioning, and aid in recovery from illness. Others show that engaging with nature can boost critical thinking, decrease rumination, and elevate the moods of people struggling with depression.[28] The psychological benefits of interacting with nature are so significant, in fact, that a recent study based on data about national park visitation in Australia calculates that, per year, protected natural areas provide Australians with mental health services worth 100 billion U.S. dollars. The same study makes a conservative estimate that, when calculated at a global scale, the value of these services increases to roughly six trillion.[29]

References to such far-reaching cognitive and therapeutic benefits of nature contact are fairly common in the literature on the biophilia hypothesis. They are less common, however, in the literature of the deep ecology movement, where detailed treatments of the notion of biophilia are difficult to find. Still, even in the absence of fine-grained analyses, it is not difficult to discern points of convergence between Kellert's perspective and those of deep ecology theorists, the first and most fundamental of which is their mutual insistence on human connectedness to nature.

For Kellert's part, it is nearly impossible not to be struck by the regularity with which his writing reminds us that we are inhabitants of a natural world that has been, and continues to be, formative of what and who we are. As he puts it in *Birthright*:

> Humanity is the product of its evolved relationship to nature, countless yesterdays of ongoing interaction and experience of the natural world. Our senses, our emotions, our intellect, and even our culture developed in association with, and adaptive response to, the nonhuman world. Moreover, our physical and mental health, productivity, and well-being continue to rely on our connections to nature, even as our world becomes increasingly fabricated and constructed.[30]

Immediately following this remark, Kellert observes that his vision of humanity "defies what many have come to believe is the foundation of human progress and the hallmark of contemporary civilization: the conquest and transformation of nature and seeming triumph over our biology as just another animal species."[31] Summarizing these thoughts a few lines later, he concludes that "[w]e will never be truly healthy, satisfied, or fulfilled if we live apart and alienated from the environment from which we evolved."[32]

Considering the extent to which deep ecology theorists also decry alienation from nature and stress human-nature interconnectedness, it is not startling that, on those occasions when they do reference the biophilia hypothesis, they typically flag this point of conceptual overlap. George Sessions, for instance, contends that Wilson's understanding of biophilia contrasts with Western "mastery over Nature" views since it acknowledges the importance of experiential and psychological bonding with nature.[33] Arne Naess, too, in a review of Wilson's 1998 text *Consilience*, picks up on the theme of human-nature connectedness when he asks rhetorically: "Do you think that your status as a human being is reduced when someone describes you as one link in a causal chain that leads back to animals resembling today's great apes—and even all the way back to complex molecules?" In response to his own prompt, and alluding to Wilson, Naess replies that "[s]ome, like myself, are proud to have an ancestry spanning millions of years."[34]

Another area of convergence between deep ecological and biophilic thought has to do with their common emphasis on the import of outdoor experience. Both perspectives, that is, routinely assert the need for people to spend time in nature, and both regard such engagement as truly a need rather than a mere amenity.[35] A crucial difference quickly appears, though, when we consider what motivates this area of emphasis in each intellectual stream.

What most interests deep ecology theorists about nature experience is its ability to heighten people's sense of connection to nature and, with that, increase their respect for the more-than-human world. Kellert, on the other hand, restricts his account of the role of outdoor experience to the restorative and therapeutic benefits it provides for people. Such benefits are, as we have just seen, considerable, and biophilic thought's promotion of research in this area is surely one of its most significant contributions to contemporary environmental discourse. Nevertheless, such an exclusive focus on the ability of outdoor experience to foster human well-being points to a deeper theoretical fissure between Kellert's perspective and those of deep ecology theorists, one that, to all appearances, separates them decisively.

For deep ecology supporters, as chapter 3 explained, identification with nature is linked to a broad cluster of noninstrumental values, values that they present not only as components of their individual ecosophies, but also as the first principle of the deep ecology platform. Thus, their commitment to promoting connectedness to nature—as well as the outdoor experiences that can foster it—is tied to an equally strong commitment to nonanthropocentric environmental ethics. Kellert, by contrast, explicitly rejects nonanthropocentrism and advocates an "instrumental" or "utilitarian" ethic that begins by acknowledging the tremendous range of human interests dependent on the natural world for their satisfaction.[36] In his view, recognizing the extent of our connectedness to nature is crucial mainly insofar as it helps us recognize just how extensively we rely upon it, which in turn serves not only as the practical impetus for getting outdoors, but more generally as "the self-interested basis for an ethic of care and concern for biological diversity."[37] For Kellert, therefore, "preserving natural diversity represents less an act of kindness or compassion than a profound expression of self-interest,"[38] and his variant of biophilic environmental ethics rests squarely on an "expanded concept of personal and social self-interest."[39]

ANTHROPOCENTRISM AND BIOPHILIC ANTHROPOCENTRISM

Considering the prominent role that the anthropocentrism/nonanthropocentrism distinction often plays in debates about environmental ethics, it is not surprising that deep ecological and biophilic theories would part along this line. It is worth noticing here, though, that Kellert regards his biophilically informed anthropocentrism as an alternative not only to nonanthropocentric outlooks of the sort held by deep ecologists, but also to more traditional forms of anthropocentrism. His remarks about the deficiencies of the latter, however, raise some critical questions about the adequacy of his own view, and force us to ask if biophilic anthropocentrism really surmounts the problems that Kellert intends it to overcome.

Kellert's primary objection to traditional forms of human-centered ethics is that they afford too few environmental protections, since the only worth they attribute to nature is economic and material. To be sure, Kellert does not deny that nature is valuable in these ways, but he does contend that this narrow utilitarian framework is inadequate for environmental ethics, mainly because, as he puts it, "[m]ost creatures and habitats will never result in tangible benefits to people and society."[40] He worries, additionally, that even for those aspects of the natural world that do provide such benefits, strictly economic or materialistic evaluations can just as readily call for their exploitation as their preservation.[41] What Kellert believes, in other words, is that while many things in nature are materially important to humans, a great many others are not, and in neither case is such importance a guarantee of protection. This outlook is thus said to contain the "seeds of self-destruction,"[42] since it "extends practical value to only a portion of life and declares, by implication, the rest expendable."[43]

Beyond these more pragmatic objections, Kellert also questions the logic of approaching environmental problems from a standpoint that is, to all appearances, one of their leading ideological causes. "Is it wise," he asks, "to place confidence in a materialistic ethic that contributed so much to our environmental crisis in the first place?"[44] Predictably, his own answer to this question is no. Thus, rather than relying on values whose record in matters of the environment is at best suspect, Kellert argues for an ethic that accounts for the full range of benefits humans derive from nature—benefits that include our physical and material well-being, but also go well beyond them to embrace a wide variety of experiential, recreational, aesthetic, and even symbolic values.[45]

Now it seems undeniable that environmentalists of every sort—including deep ecologists—would do well to take seriously Kellert's convincing account of human biophilic needs. On the surface of it, moreover, it appears reasonable to conclude that such a broad understanding of the human need for nature would support a wider range of environmental protections than is typical of more conventional anthropocentric views. Still, the unique brand of anthropocentrism Kellert advocates is more limited in its protective scope than he seems to realize, and to see why this is the case we can consider just one of the challenges it runs up against: "the substitution problem."[46]

The substitution problem, briefly stated, is that if some part of nature is preserved for human benefit, but a substitute exists that can provide that benefit without requiring the same protective measures, then the protective measures may be dropped.[47] This problem exists for all varieties of human-centered environmental ethics, but becomes an issue for Kellert specifically when he insists, first, that the "quality and intimacy" of our engagement with nature "can occur in nearly any location,"[48] including places like backyard ditches or abandoned city lots that are significantly ecologically disturbed.[49] Yet if it is true that artifacted and degraded environments can serve biophilic interests nearly as well as environments that are more ecologically intact, then one has to question just how much protective power environmental advocates stand to gain from acknowledging these interests' existence.

Additionally, there is Kellert's frequent contention that people can benefit from "indirect" experiences of nature, or experiences mediated by "art, language, story, video, and more."[50] Now certainly, to say that such indirect experiences are beneficial in some cases is not the same as saying that they can substitute completely for firsthand engagement with nature. Kellert does claim, furthermore, that "[n]ature in the zoo, or on the television set, or in the fantasy world of virtual reality will remain a vicarious fraud."[51] Nevertheless, his comments about the potential benefits of indirect experiences of nature do require us to ask exactly what "nature" humans require to meet biophilic needs, and to speculate that at least some of those needs can be met in ways that do not involve the protection of species and habitats.[52]

Although this last point might seem far-fetched, it is arguably more pressing than some biophilia theorists would be comfortable admitting, particularly in light of recent research into the therapeutic benefits of nature-simulating environments and artifacts. Several studies conducted by Peter Kahn, for example, found that while technological means did not fully replicate nature's restorative ends, it was still the case that at least some of the benefits of interaction with nature could be gained via interaction with technological devices. Curiously enough, included among the devices Kahn studied were high-definition television "windows," virtual "telegardens," and even robotic dogs.[53]

Such research leaves open the question of whether or not future technological developments might increase the therapeutic value of simulated nature, and indeed, such developments may already be underway.[54] A study of virtual versus actual biophilic office spaces, for instance, found that people's physiological and cognitive responses to the virtual offices were comparable to their responses to the real ones. The authors of the study thus point to "the possibility of reducing stress and improving cognition by using virtual reality to provide exposures to natural elements in a variety of indoor settings where access to nature may not be possible."[55] Another group of researchers draws a similar conclusion, stating that "[o]nce the research has been conducted and appropriate software written, the provision of artificial environments is likely to become readily affordable and of widespread use to our health services." This development, the authors add, "could also reinforce the trend for spending less and less time outdoors," a result they concede would be "precisely the opposite of the intention of most health care professionals and environmental scientists."[56]

To highlight these issues in relation to Kellert's work is in no way to suggest that his position is wholly problematic. It is intended, rather, to point out that even though he recognizes certain shortcomings of anthropocentric ethics, he also believes that the problem ultimately lies with the particular form that people's anthropocentrism has taken, and not with human-centered thinking more generally. But while recognizing biophilic needs almost certainly would contribute to greater *human* well-being, it is not so certain that it vastly expands the rationale for protecting *nature*, precisely because it continues to frame nature's protection as auxiliary to human well-being rather than something worthwhile in itself.

BIOPHILIA BEYOND ANTHROPOCENTRISM

The obvious implication of the preceding observation is, of course, that biophilic environmental ethics would benefit from moving away from the idea that nature's protection must always be viewed as a matter of safeguarding human interests. And fortunately, not only is Kellert's thought exceptionally well positioned to make such a move, but our discussions of deep ecology provide insight into just how it could be accomplished.

One of the most curious aspects of Kellert's defense of anthropocentric environmental ethics is that it is noticeably at odds with his typology of values. That is, when one examines the evaluative attitudes that Kellert counts as biophilic dispositions, one quickly discovers that several of them are not at all expressions of self-interest. Among the clearest examples of this is the "humanistic" attitude, which Kellert takes to describe our tendency to form caring, empathic bonds with other-than-human beings, commonly coming to regard them as "companions and intimates not unlike other people."[57] Bonds of kinship likewise characterize the "moralistic" attitude, which is associated with a strong sense of "right and wrong conduct toward the nonhuman world."[58] The moralistic attitude is linked, moreover, to what Kellert calls "existence value," or the idea that other-than-human entities have "inherent rights" not derived from their utility to people.[59] Both of these attitudes, therefore, involve feelings of fondness, caring, and emotional attachment to entities in nature, along with the sense that their worth is not reducible to how they serve human interests.[60] Both attitudes, in other words, have distinctly "other-regarding" structures, and thus differ significantly from the self- or human-centered models of valuing endemic to anthropocentric outlooks.

A similar case can be made for the "naturalistic" and "scientific-ecologistic" attitudes, both of which are characterized by self-transcending feelings of awe, wonder, and appreciation for the natural world. The naturalistic attitude, Kellert says, "involves an especially refined capacity for experiencing fascination, wonder and diversity," and is accompanied by "a related tendency . . . to place value on all creation."[61] The scientific-ecologistic attitude, too, brings with it "awe of nature's complexity and diversity,"[62] and as Katie McShane has argued, to view others through the lens of such feelings is "precisely to see the world as valuable in ways other than serving our interests."[63]

On the whole, then, Kellert's typology shows clearly that people are by no means limited to valuing other-than-human beings self-interestedly, but can and do express a considerable array of noninstrumental environmental attitudes. Indeed, this inclusive aspect of Kellert's typology may be one of its strongest features, as John Simaika and Michael Samways suggest when they say that an advantage of his position is that "it includes utilitarian ... values and moralistic (intrinsic value theory) values on an equal footing with other values."[64] Even Kellert himself seems to concede this interpretation, writing at one point that some of the attitudes his typology contains are "often associated with a rights-based or biocentric position."[65]

In light of all of this, and especially considering this last remark, it seems odd that Kellert would deliberately exclude noninstrumental values from his discussions of ethics, or neglect to mention them in his extensive critique of anthropocentrism. How could biophilic *anthropocentrism* be derived from such a careful account of the diversity of people's *non*instrumental evaluative attitudes? Interestingly, at least part of the answer seems to be that Kellert follows an interpretive path much like that which was mapped in our previous discussions of deep ecology.

Critics of deep ecology, as well as deep ecology theorists themselves, often argue *from* the fact that identification with nature leads us to feel impacted by the fates of others, *to* the idea that what moves us to act on their behalf is concern for ourselves. What this interpretive move does, in essence, is to focus on the self-implicating *effects* or *results* of certain ways of relating to nature, rather than the *content* or *character* of those relations themselves—relations that often have other-oriented dimensions, and that therefore are not best described as being driven by self-interest. A similar interpretive shift occurs in Kellert's thinking when he stresses the beneficial *outcomes* of engaging with other-than-human entities, and claims that making appeals to those outcomes is the best that environmental ethics can do, even as his typology illustrates that our *concrete engagements* with the world often involve valuing nature for reasons other than our own benefit.

Clear evidence that such interpretive maneuvering is operative in Kellert's thinking can be found in the essay "A Biocultural Basis for an Ethic toward the Natural Environment," where he situates his views on environmental ethics among other positions in the field:

> I want to suggest that a broad utilitarian-based ethic can encompass many of the arguments traditionally advanced to rationalize and support a biocentric ethic, such as nature defended as a source of affection, love, beauty, and spiritual

inspiration. I will thus offer an environmental ethic based on an understanding of human biology and culture that connects human physical and mental well-being not only to material and commodity advantage, but to a host of equally compelling benefits people derive from their inclination to value nature for its aesthetic, emotional, intellectual, moral, and other qualities.[66]

Kellert's use of the term "biocentric" here is synonymous with "non-anthropocentric," and his references to "affection" and "love" for nature, as well as the "inclination to value nature" for "emotional" or "moral" reasons, all indicate some of the noninstrumental ways that people sometimes value nature. Yet simultaneous with this enumeration of noninstrumental values, Kellert announces his intent to "encompass" them in an instrumental framework, presenting the case for conservation in terms of the "compelling benefits people derive" from their expression.

The appropriate response to this interpretive shifting is, I believe, more or less self-evident, and once again, our analyses of deep ecology indicate the route to be taken. Throughout the previous chapters we have continually insisted that nothing about bonds of identification with nature necessitates self-oriented interpretations of the behaviors of those who form them, much like we are insisting here that there is nothing in Kellert's work to suggest that environmental ethics must make the case for nature's preservation solely in terms of human benefit. Hence, just as we have argued that conversations about the ecological Self can and should go beyond notions of "Self-protectiveness" or "Self-defense"—and that indeed these conversations are far more productive when we do so—similarly it is the case that the conversation about biophilic ethics can and should be expanded beyond the highly arbitrary, human-centered limit that Kellert imposes on it. Not only does his account of environmental attitudes invite such an expansion, but doing so would be practically advantageous, helping his biophilic ethic avoid the problem of substitution that potentially restricts its protective scope. The result of this repositioning, then, would ultimately be a biophilic ethic that is much better situated to articulate in the widest possible terms the many reasons there are for protecting and advocating for the natural world.[67]

LOVING MORE-THAN-HUMAN LIFE

If at this point it has been established that Kellert would have done well to move biophilic ethics in the noninstrumental directions illuminated by his typology, it remains unclear why he himself never travelled this particular interpretive path. Why, given what we have just argued, would Kellert not try to advance some form of biophilic *non*-anthropocentrism? Why, given his clear interest in upholding and expanding environmental protections, would he not have embraced the full array of values people are capable of expressing in defense of the environment?

One possible answer to this question is simply that Kellert's writing reflects a tendency—not uncommon in some areas of environmental thought—to characterize every human-nature relationship instrumentally, even when this category of valuation seems inappropriate or difficult to apply. The literature on "ecosystem services," for example, is inclined to frame every point of human-nature interaction in terms of the "services" nature provides, even when nature appears as something more than a means to human ends.[68] This approach, and others like it, remolds the values appearing in human-nature relations to fit human-centered frameworks, rather than remolding our conceptual frameworks to accommodate the noninstrumental ways that people sometimes actually value nature.

It would be too hasty, however, to claim that adopting an anthropocentric framework is, for Kellert, merely an expression of unexamined bias. For him it is, rather, very clearly a considered move, guided by his belief that nonanthropocentric views have the potential neither to be widely adopted, nor to be pragmatically effective. A noninstrumentalist ethic, he says, "convinces few and is politically unrealistic and untenable"—both of which, in his estimation, make nonanthropocentrism a nonstarter.[69] As we bring this commentary to a close, therefore, let us say a few words about these concerns as we offer some final thoughts on biophilia, nonanthropocentrism, and the fundamental importance of connectedness to nature.

The apprehensiveness about nonanthropocentrism that Kellert voices is not uncommon, and it is undoubtedly true that his empirical research puts him in an excellent position to discuss the typical extent, or lack thereof, of people's moral regard for nature. But just as his work enables him to describe some of the limits of noninstrumentalist environmental values, it also puts him in a better position than most to underscore our potential for cultivating them. Many of his own case studies, for instance, track the historical increase of nonanthropocentric attitudes in North America, and some contemporary research documents similar attitudinal change over the past few decades.[70] People's evaluative attitudes are not set in stone, and Kellert's work, as much as anyone else's, gives us both reasons to seek moral growth in our regard for the more-than-human world, along with the confidence that such growth is possible.[71]

That Kellert's work is so well positioned in this respect, it should be stressed, is to a considerable extent a product of its explicit and implicit promotion of connectedness to nature. To highlight the fact that we are so intimately a part of nature that its presence or absence in our lives affects not only our physical health but our intellectual functioning and mental well-being, surely indicates a degree of connection to the natural world far beyond what many of us would imagine. Advancing this sweeping understanding of human belonging to and kinship with nature, biophilic thinking not only helps us better understand the countless ways in which we continue to need nature, but fosters exactly the sorts of noninstrumentalist attitudes that some of its advocates disavow.

This last point is worth emphasizing, as it gets to the heart of what biophilic anthropocentrists like Kellert seem to overlook in their rush to embrace human-centered ethics. What we have been so keen to show throughout these pages is that to encourage people to connect deeply to nature both ideologically and experientially, as Kellert and other biophilia theorists surely do, is to encourage precisely the sorts of ideological and experiential transformations most likely to foster noninstrumentalist attitudes and values—what social scientists describe as "biospheric," "biocentric," or "ecocentric" outlooks, or what Kellert so carefully details in his discussions of the "moralistic," "naturalistic," and "humanistic" values. To promote connectedness to nature is, at the same time, to discourage strictly human-centered modes of value and belief, which means that biophilic theory's foundational view of human beings stands in tension with its advocacy of human-centered ethics, even if such advocacy is only pragmatic.[72]

Happily, while the need to encourage connectedness to nature remains, there is no evidence to suggest that this awareness is beyond our reach, or that the nonanthropocentric attitudes it tends to promote are pragmatically ineffective. Quite the opposite, the growing body of literature emerging from the social sciences clearly indicates that nature-oriented evaluative attitudes are at least as relevant to concrete conservation practice as any others. A survey of attendees at the International Congress of Conservation Biologists, for example, revealed that many on-the-ground conservationists agreed with the goal of "[c]onserving nature for nature's sake," and expressed a "distinctly biocentric" rationale for their efforts.[73] Another cluster of studies comparing egoistic, altruistic, and "biospheric" values found that the latter correlated most strongly with several pro-environmental lifestyle choices, including lower energy consumption, reduced water use, and support for restaurants serving organic food.[74] Related research has found these same values to be most strongly correlated with intentions to donate to environmental organizations, as well as general concern for the environment.[75]

The upshot, then, is that while it may be that we have yet to develop a full appreciation of the human need for nature, it seems that we also have yet to develop fully our capacities to care for nature for its own sake, or to appreciate the pragmatic efficacy of attitudes rooted in respect, concern, and love for the more-than-human world.[76] Surely the widest realization of such love, and the widest realization of our capacities for wonder, awe, and caring attention to nature, are things for which environmental advocates of every sort ought also to be aiming.

Of course, accomplishing these objectives requires, among other things, an understanding of what both biophilic and deep ecological thought emphasize, and that we have been arguing throughout: namely that, in multiple and varied ways, connectedness to nature matters, in no small degree because it encourages our nature-regarding attitudes and, with them, a wide array of environmentally friendly behaviors. There simply is no reason to fail to promote these attitudes, and the ecological identities that underlie them, as effective pathways to the protection of the natural world. In the end, getting it right with nature is at least partly a matter of getting it right about ourselves, and it is no doubt time that we embrace our potential to do both.

NOTES

1. Fromm's first use of "biophilia" appears in *The Heart of Man: Its Genius for Good and Evil* (New York: Harper & Row, 1964). The quote cited here is from Fromm's *The Anatomy of Human Destructiveness* (New York: Fawcett Crest, 1973), 406. Though Fromm's conception of biophilia is similar in various ways to more contemporary ones, it is also distinctive. For discussion of this subject, see Ryan Gunderson, "Erich Fromm's Ecological Messianism: The First Biophilia Hypothesis as Humanistic Social Theory," *Humanity & Society* 38, no. 2 (2014): 182–204.

2. Edward O. Wilson, *Biophilia: The Human Bond with Other Species* (Cambridge: Harvard University Press, 1984), 1.

3. See Stephen R. Kellert, *Building for Life: Designing and Understanding the Human-Nature Connection* (Washington, DC: Island Press, 2005), and Stephen R. Kellert, Judith H. Heerwagen, and Martin L. Mador, eds., *Biophilic Design: The Theory, Science and Practice of Bringing Buildings to Life* (Hoboken: John Wiley and Sons, 2008).

4. Stephen R. Kellert, "American Attitudes toward and Knowledge of Animals: An Update," in *Advances in Animal Welfare Science 1984/85*, ed. M. W. Fox and L. D. Mickley (Washington, DC: The Humane Society of the United States, 1984), 177. See also Stephen R. Kellert, *The Value of Life: Biological Diversity and Human Society* (Washington, DC: Island Press, 1996), 6; Stephen R. Kellert, "The Biological Basis for Human Values of Nature," in *The Biophilia Hypothesis*, ed. Stephen R. Kellert and Edward O. Wilson (Washington, DC: Island Press, 1993), 43.

5. Kellert, "American Attitudes toward and Knowledge of Animals," 177–8. See also United States Department of the Interior Fish and Wildlife Service, *Public Attitudes Toward Critical Wildlife and Habitat Issues*, Phase I of *American Attitudes, Knowledge and Behaviors Toward Wildlife and Natural Habitats*, by Stephen R. Kellert with Joyce K. Berry (Washington, DC: U.S. Government Printing Office, 1979), and United States Department of the Interior Fish and Wildlife Service, *Activities of the American Public Relating to Animals*, Phase II of *American Attitudes,*

Knowledge and Behaviors Toward Wildlife and Natural Habitats, by Stephen R. Kellert with Joyce K. Berry (Washington, DC: U.S. Government Printing Office, 1980).

6. Kellert, "The Biological Basis for Human Values of Nature," 43–44.

7. Ibid., 44.

8. Kellert, *The Value of Life*, 6. See also Stephen R. Kellert, *Birthright: People and Nature in the Modern World* (New Haven: Yale University Press, 2012), 2–3, where he writes: "If these widely held perspectives are universal across culture and history, they may be regarded as reflections of our biology and thus our evolution as a species."

9. Kellert, *The Value of Life*, 6.

10. Stephen R. Kellert, *Kinship to Mastery: Biophilia in Human Evolution and Development* (Washington, DC: Island Press, 1997), 156–57.

11. Ibid., 60–68.

12. Ibid., 6.

13. Kellert, "The Biological Basis for Human Values of Nature," 58–59.

14. Kellert, *The Value of Life*, 132.

15. For commentary emphasizing evolutionary-scientific questions as part of a broad analysis of the biophilia hypothesis, see Yannick Joye and Andreas De Block, "'Nature and I are Two': A Critical Examination of the Biophilia Hypothesis," *Environmental Values* 20, no. 2 (2011): 189–215. For additional critical commentary on the biophilia hypothesis, see Michael E. Soulé, "Biophilia: Unanswered Questions," in *The Biophilia Hypothesis*, 441–55; Sanford S. Levy, "The Biophilia Hypothesis and Anthropocentric Environmentalism," *Environmental Ethics* 25, no. 3 (Fall 2003): 227–46; Peter H. Kahn, Jr., "Developmental Psychology and the Biophilia Hypothesis: Children's Affiliation with Nature," *Developmental Review* 17 (1997): 1–61; Andrew Johnson, "Love of Life," review of *The Biophilia Hypothesis* by Stephen R. Kellert and Edward O. Wilson, *Bioscience* 44, no. 5 (May 1994): 363–64.

16. Kellert, *The Value of Life*, 132.

17. Kellert, *Kinship to Mastery*, 6. See also Kellert, *The Value of Life*, 26, and Stephen R. Kellert, "Biodiversity, Quality of Life, and Evolutionary Psychology," in *Biodiversity Change and Human Health: From Ecosystem Services to Spread of Disease*, ed. Osvaldo E. Sala, Laura A. Meyerson, and Camille Parmesan (Washington, DC: Island Press, 2009), 100.

18. Kellert, "Biodiversity, Quality of Life, and Evolutionary Psychology," 114.

19. Kellert, *The Value of Life*, 132.

20. Kellert, "Biodiversity, Quality of Life, and Evolutionary Psychology," 114.

21. See Kellert, *Kinship to Mastery*, 49; *The Value of Life*, 58–59.

22. See Kellert, *Kinship to Mastery*, 104, 131–32.

23. Stephen R. Kellert, "Dimensions, Elements, and Attributes of Biophilic Design," in *Biophilic Design*, 4.

24. Kellert, "Biodiversity, Quality of Life, and Evolutionary Psychology," 114.

25. Human well-being, Kellert says, "remains highly contingent on contact with the natural environment, which is a necessity rather than a luxury for achieving

lives of fitness and satisfaction even in our modern urban society" ("Dimensions, Elements, and Attributes of Biophilic Design," 4).

26. Kellert, *The Value of Life*, 7.

27. Kellert, *Kinship to Mastery*, 214.

28. There has been a veritable explosion of research in this area in recent years, including several well-known texts, some of which did not appear in Kellert's professional lifetime. These include Florence Williams, *The Nature Fix: Why Nature Makes Us Happier, Healthier, and More Creative* (New York: W. W. Norton and Company, 2017); Richard Louv, *Vitamin N: The Essential Guide to a Nature-Rich Life* (Chapel Hill: Algonquin Books, 2016); Wallace J. Nichols, *Blue Mind* (New York: Little, Brown and Company, 2014); Gregory N. Bratman et al., "Nature Experience Reduces Rumination and Subgenual Prefrontal Cortex Activation," *Proceedings of the National Academy of Sciences* 112, no. 28 (July 14, 2015): 8567–72; Marc G. Berman et al., "Interacting with Nature Improves Cognition and Affect for Individuals with Depression," *Journal of Affective Disorders* 140, no. 3 (November 2012): 300–305; Deborah Franklin, "How Hospital Gardens Help Patients Heal: Hospital Gardens Turn Out to Have Medical Benefits," *Scientific American* 306, no. 3 (March 2012): 24–25. In Kellert's own writing, similar findings are cited in "Biodiversity, Quality of Life, and Evolutionary Psychology," and "Dimensions, Elements, and Attributes of Biophilic Design," 4.

29. Ralf Buckley et al., "Economic Value of Protected Areas via Visitor Mental Health," *Nature Communications* 10 (2019), https://doi.org/10.1038/s41467-019-12631-6. Such empirical research is interesting for many reasons, one of which is that it indicates the possibility that Kellert's conclusions about *ethics* could be reached independently of any appeal to the innate or evolved character of biophilic tendencies. Steven J. Bissell succinctly expresses this idea, writing that "It is important to emphasize . . . whether or not one accepts the contention that these [biophilic dispositions] are inborn tendencies or feels that . . . [they] can only be acquired, that Kellert shows that there are values which contribute to the quality of life for individuals and society and can be used as the basis for the construction of environmentally sound life styles" (review of *The Value of Life* and *Kinship to Mastery*, by Stephen R. Kellert, *Environmental Ethics* 21, no. 2 [Summer 1999]: 216).

30. Kellert, *Birthright*, ix.

31. Ibid.

32. Ibid., x.

33. George Sessions, "Deep Ecology, New Conservation, and the Anthropocene Worldview," *The Trumpeter* 30, no. 2 (2014): 113.

34. Arne Naess, "All Together Now," review of *Consilience* by Edward O. Wilson, *New Scientist* 2148 (August 22, 1998): 42. Harold Glasser also mentions briefly the idea of a fundamental compatibility between deep ecological and biophilic thought in "Deep Ecology Clarified: A Few Fallacies and Misconceptions," *The Trumpeter* 12, no. 3 (1995): 8.

35. Naess, "Self-Realization: An Ecological Approach to Being-in-the-World," in *Deep Ecology for the Twenty-First Century: Readings on the Philosophy and*

Practice of the New Environmentalism, ed. George Sessions (Boston: Shambhala, 1995), 232.

36. Kellert, "A Biocultural Basis," 322.

37. Kellert, *Kinship to Mastery*, 214.

38. Ibid., 9.

39. Kellert, *The Value of Life*, 214.

40. Kellert, *Kinship to Mastery*, 206. See also Kellert, "A Biocultural Basis," 322 and *The Value of Life*, 216.

41. Kellert, *Kinship to Mastery*, 206. See also Kellert, "A Biocultural Basis," 322–23.

42. Kellert, *The Value of Life*, 216.

43. Kellert, *Kinship to Mastery*, 206.

44. Ibid., 206.

45. See Kellert, "A Biocultural Basis," 323.

46. For analysis of some of the other challenges to Kellert's anthropocentrism, see Christian Diehm, "Biophilia and Biodiversity," *Environmental Ethics* 34, no. 2 (Spring 2012): 51–66.

47. Martin Gorke, *The Death of Our Planet's Species: A Challenge to Ecology and Ethics*, trans. Patricia Nevers (Washington, DC: Island Press, 2003), 171.

48. Kellert, *Kinship to Mastery*, 7.

49. Claims of this sort can be found in Kellert, *The Value of Life*, 28; *Kinship to Mastery*, 7, 185; *Birthright*, 205–206.

50. Kellert, "Biodiversity, Quality of Life, and Evolutionary Psychology," 99.

51. Kellert, *Kinship to Mastery*, 208.

52. O. Gene Myers raises this same question about the import of the notion of biophilia for environmental ethics, saying that "[i]t is not at all clear what normative obligations (to humans) derive from needs so flexibly met. Perhaps some minimum is indicated, but do we need rain forests? Or do New Guineans need rain forests while 'we' only need city parks—or worse, virtual parks and 'social' computers?" (Review of *The Biophilia Hypothesis*, edited by Stephen R. Kellert and Edward O. Wilson, *Environmental Ethics* 18, 3 [Fall 1996]: 329). See also Levy, "The Biophilia Hypothesis and Anthropocentric Environmentalism," 235.

53. Peter H. Kahn, Jr., *Technological Nature: Adaptation and the Future of Human Life* (Cambridge: MIT Press, 2011), xvi.

54. For comments by Kahn that speak to this question, see *Technological Nature*, 63–64, 150, 161.

55. Jie Yina et al., "Physiological and Cognitive Performance of Exposure to Biophilic Indoor Environment," *Building and Environment* 132 (2018): 255.

56. M. H. Depledge, R. J. Stone, and W. J. Bird, "Can Natural and Virtual Environments Be Used to Promote Improved Human Health and Wellbeing?," *Environmental Science and Technology* 45 (April 2011): 4664. See also Y. A. W. de Kort et al., "What's Wrong with Virtual Trees?: Restoring from Stress in a Mediated Environment," *Journal of Environmental Psychology* 26, no. 4 (December 2006): 309–20. This study found that technology providing more "immersive" experiences

of nature films had more therapeutic benefits than technology providing less immersive ones.

57. Kellert, *The Value of Life*, 21.

58. Ibid., 23.

59. Kellert, "American Attitudes Toward and Knowledge of Animals," 177–213; Stephen R. Kellert, "Social and Perceptual Factors in Endangered Species Management," *The Journal of Wildlife Management* 49, no. 2 (April 1985): 529.

60. See Kellert, "Biodiversity, Quality of Life, and Evolutionary Psychology," 117, and *The Value of Life*, 21.

61. Stephen R. Kellert, "The Biophilia Hypothesis: Aristotelian Echoes of 'The Good Life'," in *Nature and Humankind in the Age of Environmental Crisis*, ed. Shuntaro Ito and Yoshinori Yasuda (Kyoto: International Research Center for Japanese Studies, 1995), 201–21.

62. Ibid., 205.

63. Katie McShane, "Anthropocentrism vs. Nonanthropocentrism: Why Should We Care?," *Environmental Values* 16 (2007): 176. Writing specifically of awe, McShane says elsewhere that "to be in awe of something is in part to treat it as having a kind of greatness in its own right" ("Why Environmental Ethics Shouldn't Give Up on Intrinsic Value," *Environmental Ethics* 29, no. 1 [Spring 2007]: 53).

64. John P. Simaika and Michael J. Samways, "Biophilia as a Universal Ethic for Conserving Biodiversity," *Conservation Biology* 24, no. 3 (2010): 905.

65. Kellert, "A Biocultural Basis," 325.

66. Ibid., 323.

67. John O'Neill, "Life Beyond Capital," Centre for the Understanding of Sustainable Prosperity Essay Series on the Morality of Sustainable Prosperity, no. 6 (October 2017), https://www.cusp.ac.uk/themes/m/m1-6/. For additional commentary on the problem of substitution in Kellert's work, see Diehm, "Biophilia and Biodiversity."

68. Something similar occurs in Kellert's thinking when he narrows his focus to emphasize the benefits that human–nature relations have for people, even as he acknowledges that some of these relations are characterized by other-oriented concern and a sense of nature's intrinsic value. For further commentary on the limitations of the ecosystem services framework, even within human-centered value systems, see Simon P. James, "Ecosystem Services and the Value of Places," *Ethical Theory and Moral Practice* 19, no. 1 (2016): 101–13; Simon P. James, "Cultural Ecosystem Services: A Critical Assessment," *Ethics, Policy and Environment* 18, no. 3 (2015): 338–50.

69. Kellert, "A Biocultural Basis," 323.

70. Kelly A. George et al., "Changes in Attitudes toward Animals in the United States from 1978 to 2014," *Biological Conservation* 201 (2016): 237–42; Michael J. Manfredo, *Who Cares About Wildlife?: Social Science Concepts for Exploring Human-Wildlife Relationships and Conservation Issues* (New York: Springer-Verlag, 2008); Michael Manfredo, Tara Teel, and Alan Bright, "Why Are Public Values Toward Wildlife Changing?," *Human Dimensions of Wildlife* 8, no. 4 (2003): 287–306.

71. For another positive indication of the potential for developing noninstrumentalist attitudes, see Eugene C. Hargrove, "Teaching Intrinsic Value to Children," *Environmental Ethics* 32, no. 3 (Fall 2010): 227–28.

72. See Christian Diehm, "Staying True to Trees: A Specific Look at Anthropocentrism and Non-Anthropocentrism," *Environmental Philosophy* 5, no. 2 (2008): 3–16.

73. George Holmes, Chris Sandbrook, and Janet A. Fisher, "Understanding Conservationists' Perspectives on the New-Conservation Debate," *Conservation Biology* 31, no. 2 (2017): 359.

74. Judith I. M. de Groot and Linda Steg, "Value Orientations to Explain Beliefs Related to Environmental Significant Behavior: How to Measure Egoistic, Altruistic, and Biospheric Value Orientations," *Environment and Behavior* 40, no. 3 (2008): 330–54.

75. Ibid. See also Judith I. M. de Groot and Linda Steg, "Mean or Green: Which Values Can Promote Stable Pro-Environmental Behavior?" *Conservation Letters* 2 (2009): 61–66. For further discussion of these ideas, see Chelsea Batavia and Michael Paul Nelson, "For Goodness Sake! What Is Intrinsic Value and Why Should We Care?" *Biological Conservation* 209 (2017): 366–76.

76. Not surprisingly, an appreciation of just this latter sort was voiced by Naess more than three decades ago, who wrote: "Conservation strategy will be more eagerly implemented by people who love what they are conserving, and who are convinced that what they love is intrinsically lovable. Such lovers will not want to hide their attitudes and values, but rather will increasingly give voice to them in public. They have a genuine ethics of conservation, not merely a tactically useful instrument for social and political ends" ("The Deep Ecological Movement: Some Philosophical Aspects," *Inquiry* 8, no. 1–2 [1986]: 13).

Bibliography

Alcocka, Ian, Mathew P. White, Sabine Pahl, Raquel Duarte-Davidson, and Lora E. Fleming. "Associations between Pro-Environmental Behaviour and Neighbourhood Nature, Nature Visit Frequency and Nature Appreciation: Evidence from a Nationally Representative Survey in England." *Environment International* 136 (2020): 1–10. https://doi.org/10.1016/j.envint.2019.105441.

Arnocky, Steven, Mirella Stroink, and Teresa DeCicco. "Self-Construal Predicts Environmental Concern, Cooperation, and Conservation." *Journal of Environmental Psychology* 27, no. 4 (2007): 255–64.

Arnold, Heather E., Fay G. Cohen, and Alan Warner. "Youth and Environmental Action: Perspectives of Young Environmental Leaders on Their Formative Influences." *The Journal of Environmental Education* 40, no. 3 (2009): 27–36.

Attfield, Robin. "Beyond Anthropocentrism." *Royal Institute of Philosophy Supplement* 69 (October 2011): 29–46.

Bardsley, Karen. "Mother Nature and the Mother of All Virtues: On the Rationality of Feeling Gratitude toward Nature." *Environmental Ethics* 35, no. 2 (Spring 2013): 27–40.

Barnhill, David Landis, and Roger S. Gottlieb, eds. *Deep Ecology and World Religions: New Essays on Sacred Ground*. Albany: State University of New York Press, 2001.

Batavia, Chelsea, and Michael Paul Nelson. "For Goodness Sake! What Is Intrinsic Value and Why Should We Care?" *Biological Conservation* 209 (2017): 366–76.

Bender, Frederic L. *The Culture of Extinction: Toward a Philosophy of Deep Ecology*. Amherst: Humanity Books, 2003.

Bennett, Nathan J., and Robin Roth, eds. *The Conservation Social Sciences: What?, How? and Why?* Vancouver, BC: Canadian Wildlife Federation and Institute for Resources, Environment and Sustainability, University of British Columbia, 2015.

Berman, Marc G., Ethan Kross, Katherine M. Krpan, Mary K. Askren, Aleah Burson, Patricia J. Deldin, Stephen Kaplan, Lindsey Sherdell, Ian H. Gotlib, and John Jonides. "Interacting with Nature Improves Cognition and Affect for Individuals with Depression." *Journal of Affective Disorders* 140, no. 3 (November 2012): 300–5.

Bhardwaj, Richa. "Deep Ecology: Origins, Influences and Relevance." *Writers Editors Critics* 9, no. 1 (March 2019): 65–71.

Bigwood, Carol. "Standing and Stooping to Tiny Flowers: An Ecofemnomenological Response to Arne Naess." *Environmental Philosophy* 1, no. 2 (Fall 2004): 28–45.

Birkeland, Janice. "Ecofeminism: Linking Theory and Practice." In *Ecofeminism: Women, Animals, Nature*, edited by Greta Gaard, 13–59. Philadelphia: Temple University Press, 1993.

Bissell, Steven J. Review of *The Value of Life* and *Kinship to Mastery*, by Stephen R. Kellert. *Environmental Ethics* 21, no. 2 (Summer 1999): 213–16.

Bixler, Robert D., and J. Joy James. "Environmental Socialization: The Critical Peripheral?" In *Handbook of Sustainability Research*, edited by Walter Leal Filho, 15–39. Peter Lang: Frankfurt, 2005.

Bixler, Robert D., Myron F. Floyd, and William E. Hammitt. "Environmental Socialization: Quantitative Tests of the Childhood Play Hypothesis." *Environment and Behavior* 34, no. 6 (2002): 795–818.

Blatt, Erica N. "Exploring Environmental Identity and Behavioral Change in an Environmental Science Course." *Cultural Studies of Science Education* 8, no. 2 (2013): 467–88.

Booth, Kate. "Deep Ecology." In *Encyclopedia of Global Environmental Governance and Politics*, edited by Philipp H. Pattberg and Fariborz Zelli, 88–95. Northampton, MA: Edward Elgar Publishing, 2015.

Bott, Suzanne, James G. Cantrill, and Olin Eugene Myers, Jr. "Place and the Promise of Conservation Psychology." *Human Ecology Review* 10, no. 2 (2003): 100–12.

Bragg, Elizabeth Ann. "Towards Ecological Self: Deep Ecology Meets Constructionist Self-Theory." *Journal of Environmental Psychology* 16, no. 2 (1996): 93–108.

Bratman, Gregory N., J. Paul Hamilton, Kevin S. Hahn, Gretchen C. Daily, and James J. Gross. "Nature Experience Reduces Rumination and Subgenual Prefrontal Cortex Activation." *Proceedings of the National Academy of Sciences* 112, no. 28 (July 14, 2015): 8567–72.

Brennan, Andrew. *Thinking About Nature: An Investigation of Nature, Value and Ecology*. Athens: University of Georgia Press, 1988.

Brown, David Jay, ed. *MAPS Bulletin* 19, 1 (2009). Accessed October 15, 2017. https://maps.org/news-letters/v19n1/v19n1-maps_bulletin_spring_2009.pdf.

Brown, Gregory, and Christopher Raymond. "The Relationship between Place Attachment and Landscape Values: Toward Mapping Place Attachment." *Applied Geography* 27, no. 2 (April 2007): 89–111.

Brymer, Eric, Greg Downey, and Tonia Gray. "Extreme Sports as a Precursor to Environmental Sustainability." *Journal of Sport and Tourism* 14, no. 2–3 (2009): 193–204.

Buckley, Ralf, Paula Brough, Leah Hague, Alienor Chauvenet, Chris Fleming, Elisha Roche, Ernesta Sofija, and Neil Harris. "Economic Value of Protected Areas via Visitor Mental Health." *Nature Communications* 10 (2019). https://doi.org/10.1038/s41467-019-12631-6.

Budruk, Megha, Heidi Thomas, and Timothy Tyrrell. "Urban Green Spaces: A Study of Place Attachment and Environmental Attitudes in India." *Society and Natural Resources*, 22, no. 9 (2009): 824–39.

Butler, W. F., and T. G. Acott. "An Inquiry Concerning the Acceptance of Intrinsic Value Theories of Nature." *Environmental Values* 16, no. 2 (2007): 149–68.

Cagle, Nicolette L. "Changes in Experiences with Nature through the Lives of Environmentally Committed University Faculty." *Environmental Education Research*, 24, no. 6 (2018): 889–98.

Callicott, J. Baird. "The Metaphysical Implications of Ecology." In *In Defense of the Land Ethic: Essays in Environmental Philosophy*, 101–14. Albany: SUNY Press, 1989.

Cantrill, James G. "The Role of a Sense of Self-in-Place and Risk Amplification in Promoting the Conservation of Wildlife." *Human Dimensions of Wildlife* 16, no. 2 (2011): 73–86.

Cantrill, James G. "The Environmental Self and a Sense of Place: Communication Foundations for Regional Ecosystem Management." *Journal of Applied Communication Research* 26, no. 3 (1998): 301–18.

Caplow, Susan, and Jennifer Thomsen. "Significant Life Experiences and Animal-Themed Education." In *Animals in Environmental Education: Interdisciplinary Approaches to Curriculum and Pedagogy*, edited by Teresa Lloro-Bidart and Valerie S. Banschbach, 237–57. Cham, Switzerland: Palgrave-Macmillan, 2019.

Capra, Fritjof. "Deep Ecology: A New Paradigm." In *Deep Ecology for the Twenty-First Century: Readings on the Philosophy and Practice of the New Environmentalism*, edited by George Sessions, 19–25. Boston: Shambhala, 1995.

Carter, Neil. *The Politics of the Environment: Ideas, Activism, Policy*, 3rd ed. Cambridge: Cambridge University Press, 2018.

Ceaser, Donovon. "Significant Life Experiences and Environmental Justice: Positionality and the Significance of Negative Social/Environmental Experiences." *Environmental Education Research* 21, no. 2 (2015): 205–20.

Ceaser, Donovon. "Why I Came to the OSBG: The SLEs of Environmental Justice Youth at Our School at Blair Grocery." *Race, Gender and Class; New Orleans* 25, no. 1–2 (2018): 147–65.

Chan, Kai M. A., Patricia Balvanera, Karina Benessaiah, Mollie Chapman, Sandra Díaz, Erik Gómez-Baggethune, Rachelle Gould et al. "Why Protect Nature?: Rethinking Values and the Environment." *Proceedings of the National Academy of Sciences* 113, no. 6 (February 9, 2016): 1462–65.

Chawla, Louise. "Childhood Experiences Associated with Care for the Natural World: A Theoretical Framework for Empirical Results." *Children, Youth and Environments* 17, no. 4 (2007): 144–70.

Chawla, Louise. "Significant Life Experiences Revisited: A Review of Research on Sources of Environmental Sensitivity." *Environmental Education Research* 4, no. 4 (1998): 369–82.

Chawla, Louise. "Life Paths into Effective Environmental Action." *The Journal of Environmental Education* 31, no. 1 (1999): 15–26.

Cheney, Jim. "Eco-Feminism and Deep Ecology." *Environmental Ethics* 9, no. 2 (Summer 1987): 115–45.

Cheng, Judith Chen-Hsuan, and Martha C. Monroe. "Connection to Nature: Children's Affective Attitude toward Nature." *Environment and Behavior* 44, no. 1 (2012): 31–49.

Clark, John P. "What Is Living In Deep Ecology?" *The Trumpeter* 30, no. 2 (2014): 169–74.

Clayton, Susan and Gene Meyers. *Conservation Psychology: Understanding and Promoting Human Care for Nature.* West Sussex: Wiley-Blackwell, 2009.

Clayton, Susan D. "Environment and Identity." In *The Oxford Handbook of Environmental and Conservation Psychology*, edited by Susan D. Clayton, 164–80. Oxford: Oxford UP, 2012.

Clayton, Susan D. "Environmental Identity: A Conceptual and an Operational Definition." In *Identity and the Natural Environment: The Psychological Significance of Nature*, edited by Susan Clayton and Susan Opotow, 45–65. Cambridge: MIT Press, 2003.

Clayton, Susan D., and Carol D. Saunders. "Environmental and Conservation Psychology." Introduction to *The Oxford Handbook of Environmental and Conservation Psychology*, 1–7.

Cleary, Anne, Kelly S. Fielding, Zoe Murray, and Anne Roiko. "Predictors of Nature Connection Among Urban Residents: Assessing the Role of Childhood and Adult Nature Experiences." *Environment and Behavior* 52, no. 6 (2020): 579–610.

Cleland, V., A. Timperio, J. Salmon, C. Hume, L. A. Baur, and D. Crawford. "Predictors of Time Spent Outdoors Among Children: 5-Year Longitudinal Findings." *Journal of Epidemiology and Community Health* 64, no. 5 (May 2010): 400–406.

Clements, Rhonda. "An Investigation of the Status of Outdoor Play." *Contemporary Issues in Early Childhood* 5, no. 1 (2004): 68–80.

Collado, Silvia, Henk Staats, and José Corraliza. "Experiencing Nature in Children's Summer Camps: Affective, Cognitive and Behavioural Consequences." *Journal of Environmental Psychology* 33 (2013): 37–44.

Corcoran, Peter B. "Formative Influences in the Lives of Environmental Educators in the United States." *Environmental Education Research*, 5, no. 2 (1999): 207–20.

Crompton, Tom, and Tim Kasser. *Meeting Environmental Challenges: The Role of Human Identity.* Godalming: WWF-UK, 2009.

DeCicco, Teresa L., and Mirella L. Stroink. "A Third Model of Self-Construal: The Metapersonal Self." *International Journal of Transpersonal Studies* 26 (2007): 82–104.

de Groot, Judith I. M., and Linda Steg. "Mean or Green: Which Values Can Promote Stable Pro-Environmental Behavior?" *Conservation Letters* 2 (2009): 61–66.

de Groot, Judith I. M., and Linda Steg. "Relationships Between Value Orientations, Self-Determined Motivational Types and Pro-Environmental Behavioural Intentions." *Journal of Environmental Psychology* 30, no. 4 (2010): 368–78.

de Groot, Judith I. M., and Linda Steg. "Value Orientations to Explain Beliefs Related to Environmental Significant Behavior: How to Measure Egoistic, Altruistic, and Biospheric Value Orientations." *Environment and Behavior* 40, no. 3 (2008): 330–54.

de Jonge, Eccy. *Spinoza and Deep Ecology: Challenging Traditional Approaches to Environmentalism*. London: Routledge, 2016.

de Kort, Y. A. W., A. L. Meijnders, A. A. G. Sponselee, and W. A. IJsselsteijn. "What's Wrong with Virtual Trees?: Restoring from Stress in a Mediated Environment." *Journal of Environmental Psychology* 26, no. 4 (December 2006): 309–20.

Depledge, M. H., R. J. Stone, and W. J. Bird. "Can Natural and Virtual Environments Be Used To Promote Improved Human Health and Wellbeing?" *Environmental Science and Technology* 45 (April 2011): 4660–65.

Devall, Bill. *Simple in Means, Rich in Ends: Practicing Deep Ecology*. Salt Lake City: Peregrine Smith Books, 1988.

Devall, Bill, and George Sessions. *Deep Ecology: Living as if Nature Mattered*. Salt Lake City: Gibbs Smith, 1985.

Devine-Wright, Patrick. "Beyond NIMBYism: Towards an Integrated Framework for Understanding Public Perceptions of Wind Energy." *Wind Energy* 8 (2005): 125–39.

Devine-Wright, Patrick, and Susan Clayton. "Introduction to the Special Issue: Place, Identity and Environmental Behaviour." *Journal of Environmental Psychology* 30, no. 3 (2010): 267–70.

Diehm, Christian. "Arne Naess and the Task of Gestalt Ontology." *Environmental Ethics* 28, no. 2 (Spring 2006): 21–35.

Diehm, Christian. "Arne Naess, Val Plumwood, and Deep Ecological Subjectivity: A Contribution to the 'Deep Ecology-Ecofeminism Debate'." *Ethics and the Environment* 7, no. 1 (Spring 2002): 24–38.

Diehm, Christian. "Biophilia and Biodiversity." *Environmental Ethics* 34, no. 2 (Spring 2012): 51–66.

Diehm, Christian. "Finding a Niche for Species in Nature Ethics." *Ethics and the Environment* 17, no. 1 (Spring 2012): 71–86.

Diehm, Christian. "Identification with Nature: What It Is and Why It Matters." *Ethics and the Environment* 12, no. 2 (Autumn 2007): 1–22.

Diehm, Christian. "Staying True to Trees: A Specific Look at Anthropocentrism and Non-Anthropocentrism." *Environmental Philosophy* 5, no. 2 (2008): 3–16.

Diffey, B. L. "An Overview Analysis of the Time People Spend Outdoors." *British Journal of Dermatology* 164, no. 4 (April 2011): 848–54.

Dobson, Andrew. "Deep Ecology: A Study in the Philosophy of the Green Movement . . . But Philosophy Is Not Enough." *Cogito* 3, no. 1 (Spring 1989): 41–46.

Donovan, Josephine, and Carol J. Adams, eds. *Beyond Animal Rights: A Feminist Caring Ethic for the Treatment of Animals*. New York: Continuum, 1996.

Dornhoff, Maximilian, Jan-Niklas Sothmann, Florian Fiebelkorn, and Susanne Menzel. "Nature Relatedness and Environmental Concern of Young People in Ecuador and Germany." *Frontiers in Psychology* 10 (March 2019): 1–13. https://doi:10.3389/fpsyg.2019.00453.

Drengson, Alan. "The Life and Works of Arne Naess: An Appreciative Overview." Introduction to *The Ecology of Wisdom: Writings by Arne Naess*, edited by Alan Drengson and Bill Devall, 3–41. Berkeley: Counterpoint, 2008.

Drengson, Alan, and Yuichi Inoue. Introduction to *The Deep Ecology Movement: An Introductory Anthology*, edited by Alan Drengson and Yuichi Inoue, xvii–xxviii. Berkeley: North Atlantic Books, 1995.

Dresner, Marion, Corinne Handelman, Steven Braun, and Gretchen Rollwagen-Bollens. "Environmental Identity, Pro-Environmental Behaviors, and Civic Engagement of Volunteer Stewards in Portland Area Parks." *Environmental Education Research* 21, no. 7 (2015): 991–1010.

Erdos, Laslo. *Green Heroes: From Buddha to Leonardo DiCaprio*. Cham, Switzerland: Springer, 2019.

Evans, Gary W., Siegmar Otto, and Florian G. Kaiser. "Childhood Origins of Young Adult Environmental Behavior." *Psychological Science* 29, no. 5 (2018): 679–87.

Faarlund, Nils. "A Way Home." In *Wisdom in the Open Air: The Norwegian Roots of Deep Ecology*, edited by Peter Reed and David Rothenberg, 157–69. Minneapolis: University of Minnesota Press, 1993.

Farmer, James R., Charles Chancellor, and Burnell C. Fischer, "Space to Romp and Roam and How It May Promote Land Conservation." *Natural Areas Journal* 31, no. 4 (2011): 340–48.

Ferré, Frederick. "Personalistic Organicism: Paradox or Paradigm?" In *Philosophy and the Natural Environment*, edited by Robin Attfield and Andrew Belsey, 59–73. Cambridge: Cambridge University Press, 1994.

Fisher, Scott R. "Life Trajectories of Youth Committing to Climate Activism." *Environmental Education Research* 22, no. 2 (2016): 229–47.

Fox, Warwick. "Deep Ecology: A New Philosophy of Our Time?" In *Philosophical Dialogues: Arne Naess and the Progress of Ecophilosophy*, edited by Nina Witoszek and Andrew Brennan, 153–65. Lanham: Rowman & Littlefield, 1999.

Fox, Warwick. "The Deep Ecology-Ecofeminism Debate and Its Parallels." *Environmental Ethics* 11, no. 1 (Spring 1989): 3–25.

Fox, Warwick. *Toward a Transpersonal Ecology: Developing New Foundations for Environmentalism*. Albany: State University of New York Press, 1995.

Franklin, Deborah. "How Hospital Gardens Help Patients Heal: Hospital Gardens Turn Out to Have Medical Benefits." *Scientific American* 306, no. 3 (March 2012): 24–5.

Fromm, Erich. *The Anatomy of Human Destructiveness*. New York: Fawcett Crest, 1973.

Fromm, Erich. *The Heart of Man: Its Genius for Good and Evil*. New York: Harper & Row, 1964.

Furihata, Shinichi, Takayoshi Ishizaka, Mei Hatakeyama, Mamiyo Hitsumoto and Seiichi Ito. "Potentials and Challenges of Research on 'Significant Life Experiences' in Japan." *Children, Youth and Environments* 17, no. 4 (2007): 207–26.

Gardiner, Anne Barbeau. "Deep Ecology and the Culture of Death." In *Life and Learning XVII: Proceedings of the Seventeenth University Faculty for Life Conference at Villanova University*, edited by Joseph W. Koterski, 179–90. Washington, DC: University Faculty for Life, 2007.

Gelter, Hans. "*Friluftsliv*: The Scandinavian Philosophy of Outdoor Life." *Canadian Journal of Environmental Education* 5, no. 1 (2000): 77–92.

George, Kelly A., Kristina M. Slagle, Robyn S. Wilson, Steven J. Moeller, and Jeremy T. Bruskotter. "Changes in Attitudes toward Animals in the United States from 1978 to 2014." *Biological Conservation* 201 (2016): 237–42.

Gerber, Lisa. "Standing Humbly Before Nature." *Ethics and the Environment* 7, no. 1 (Spring 2002): 39–53.

Gilligan, Carol. "Moral Orientation and Moral Development." In *Women and Moral Theory*, edited by Eva Feder Kittay and Diana T. Meyers, 19–33. New York: Rowman & Littlefield, 1987.

Glasser, Harold. "Deep Ecology Clarified: A Few Fallacies and Misconceptions." *The Trumpeter* 12, no. 3 (1995): 2–12.

Glasser, Harold. "On Warwick Fox's Assessment of Deep Ecology." *Environmental Ethics* 19, no. 1 (Spring 1997): 69–85.

Gorke, Martin. *The Death of Our Planet's Species: A Challenge to Ecology and Ethics*. Translated by Patricia Nevers. Washington, DC: Island Press, 2003.

Gough, Annette, and William Smith. "Deep Ecology as a Framework for Student Eco-Philosophical Thinking." *Journal of Philosophy in Schools* 2, no. 1 (2015): 38–55.

Gräntzdörffer, Ansgar Johannes, Angela James, and Doris Elster. "Exploring Human-Nature Relationships amongst Young People: Findings of a Quantitative Survey between Germany and South Africa." *International Journal of Environmental and Science Education* 14, no. 7 (2019): 417–24.

Grey, William. "Environmental Value and Anthropocentrism." *Ethics and the Environment* 3, no. 1 (1998): 97–103.

Griffiths, Joanna. "The Varieties of Nature Experience." *Worldviews* 6, no. 3 (2002): 253–75.

Gunderson, Ryan. "Erich Fromm's Ecological Messianism: The First Biophilia Hypothesis as Humanistic Social Theory." *Humanity & Society* 38, no. 2 (2014): 182–204.

Gurholt, Kirsti Pedersen. "Joy of Nature, *Friluftsliv* Education and Self: Combining Narrative and Cultural-Ecological Approaches to Environmental Sustainability." *Journal of Adventure Education and Outdoor Learning* 14, no. 3 (2014): 233–46.

Halpenny, Elizabeth A. "Pro-Environmental Behaviours and Park Visitors: The Effect of Place Attachment." *Journal of Environmental Psychology* 30, no. 4 (2010): 409–21.

Hargrove, Eugene C. "Teaching Intrinsic Value to Children." *Environmental Ethics* 32, no. 3 (Fall 2010): 227–28.

Hargrove, Eugene C. "Weak Anthropocentric Intrinsic Value." *The Monist* 75, no. 2 (1992): 183–207.

Hayward, Tim. "Anthropocentrism: A Misunderstood Problem." *Environmental Values* 6, no. 1 (1997): 49–63.

Hill, Thomas E. Jr. "Ideals of Human Excellence and Preserving Natural Environments." *Environmental Ethics* 5, no. 3 (Fall 1983): 211–24.

Hinds, Joe, and Paul Sparks. "Engaging with the Natural Environment: The Role of Affective Connection and Identity." *Journal of Environmental Psychology*, 28, no. 2 (2008): 109–20.

Hofferth, Sandra L. "Changes in American Children's Time—1997 to 2003." *Electronic International Journal of Time Use Research* 6, no. 1 (2009): 26–47.

Holmes, George, Chris Sandbrook, and Janet A. Fisher. "Understanding Conservationists' Perspectives on the New-Conservation Debate." *Conservation Biology* 31, no. 2 (2017): 353–63.

Howell, Rachel, and Simon Allen. "People and Planet: Values, Motivations and Formative Influences of Individuals Acting to Mitigate Climate Change." *Environmental Values* 26, no. 2 (2017): 131–55.

Howell, Rachel A., and Simon Allen. "Significant Life Experiences, Motivations and Values of Climate Change Educators." *Environmental Education Research* 25, no. 6 (2019): 813–31.

Hsu, Shih-Jang. "Significant Life Experiences Affect Environmental Action: A Confirmation Study in Eastern Taiwan." *Environmental Education Research* 15, no. 4 (2009): 497–517.

Humphrey, Mathew. "Ontological Determinism and Deep Ecology: Evading the Moral Questions?" In *Beneath the Surface: Critical Essays in the Philosophy of Deep Ecology*, edited by Eric Katz, Andrew Light, and David Rothenberg, 85–105. Cambridge, MA: MIT Press, 2000.

Ims, Knut J. "Quality of Life in a Deep Ecological Perspective: The Need for a Transformation of the Western Mindset?" *Society and Economy* 40, no. 4 (2018): 531–52.

International Society for Environmental Ethics. "CFP—Whatever Happened to Deep Ecology?" Accessed December 2, 2019. https://enviroethics.org/2014/03/28/cfp-whatever-happened-to-deep-ecology/.

Ives, Christopher D., David J. Abson, Henrik von Wehrden, Christian Dorninger, Kathleen Klaniecki, and Joern Fischer, "Reconnecting with Nature for Sustainability." *Sustainability Science* 13, no. 5 (2018): 1389–97.

James, Simon P. "Cultural Ecosystem Services: A Critical Assessment." *Ethics, Policy and Environment* 18, no. 3 (2015): 338–50.

James, Simon P. "Ecosystem Services and the Value of Places." *Ethical Theory and Moral Practice* 19, no. 1 (2016): 101–13.

Johnson, Andrew. "Love of Life." Review of *The Biophilia Hypothesis*, edited by Stephen R. Kellert and Edward O. Wilson. *Bioscience* 44, no. 5 (May 1994): 363–4.

Jonas, Hans. *The Phenomenon of Life: Toward a Philosophical Biology*. New York: Delta Books, 1966.

Joye, Yannick, and Andreas De Block. "'Nature and I are Two': A Critical Examination of the Biophilia Hypothesis." *Environmental Values* 20, no. 2 (2011): 189–215.

Kahn, Peter H. Jr. "Developmental Psychology and the Biophilia Hypothesis: Children's Affiliation with Nature." *Developmental Review* 17 (1997): 1–61.

Kahn, Peter H. Jr. *Technological Nature: Adaptation and the Future of Human Life*. Cambridge: MIT Press, 2011.

Kahn, Peter H. Jr. "The Next Phase for Ecopsychology: Ideas and Directions." *Ecopsychology* 5, no. 3 (September 2013): 163–66.

Kals, Elisabeth, Daniel Schumacher, and Leo Montada. "Emotional Affinity Toward Nature as a Motivational Basis to Protect Nature." *Environment and Behavior* 31, no. 2 (1999): 178–202.

Katz, Eric. "Against the Inevitability of Anthropocentrism." In *Beneath the Surface: Critical Essays in the Philosophy of Deep Ecology*, edited by Eric Katz, Andrew Light, and David Rothenberg, 17–42. Cambridge, Mass.: MIT Press, 2000.

Katz, Eric. *Nature as Subject*. Lanham: Rowman & Littlefield, 1997.

Katz, Eric, Andrew Light, and David Rothenberg. "Deep Ecology as Philosophy." Introduction to *Beneath the Surface: Critical Essays in the Philosophy of Deep Ecology*, edited by Eric Katz, Andrew Light, and David Rothenberg, ix–xxiv. Cambridge, Mass.: MIT Press, 2000.

Kawall, Jason. "A History of Environmental Ethics." In *The Oxford Handbook of Environmental Ethics*, edited by Stephen M. Gardner and Allen Thompson, 13–26. New York: Oxford University Press, 2017.

Keller, David R. "Gleaning Lessons from Deep Ecology." *Ethics and the Environment* 2, no. 2 (Autumn 1997): 139–48.

Keller, David. "Deep Ecology." In *Encyclopedia of Environmental Ethics and Philosophy*, vol. 1, edited by J. Baird Callicott and Robert Frodeman, 206–11. Detroit: Macmillan Reference USA, 2009.

Kellert, Stephen R. "American Attitudes toward and Knowledge of Animals: An Update." In *Advances in Animal Welfare Science 1984/85*, edited by M. W. Fox and L. D. Mickley, 177–213. Washington, DC: The Humane Society of the United States, 1984.

Kellert, Stephen R. "A Biocultural Basis for an Ethic toward the Natural Environment." In *Foundations of Environmental Sustainability: The Evolution of Science and Policy*, edited by Larry L. Rockwood, Ronald E. Stewart, and Thomas Dietz, 321–32. Oxford: Oxford University Press, 2008.

Kellert, Stephen R. "Biodiversity, Quality of Life, and Evolutionary Psychology." In *Biodiversity Change and Human Health: From Ecosystem Services to Spread of Disease*, edited by Osvaldo E. Sala, Laura A. Meyerson, and Camille Parmesan, 99–127. Washington, DC: Island Press, 2009.

Kellert, Stephen R. "The Biological Basis for Human Values of Nature." In *The Biophilia Hypothesis*, edited by Stephen R. Kellert and Edward O. Wilson, 42–69. Washington, DC: Island Press, 1993.

Kellert, Stephen R., Judith H. Heerwagen, and Martin L. Mador, eds. *Biophilic Design: The Theory, Science and Practice of Bringing Buildings to Life*. Hoboken: John Wiley and Sons, 2008.

Kellert, Stephen R. "The Biophilia Hypothesis: Aristotelian Echoes of 'The Good Life'." In *Nature and Humankind in the Age of Environmental Crisis*, edited by Shuntaro Ito and Yoshinori Yasuda, 201–21. Kyoto: International Research Center for Japanese Studies, 1995.

Kellert, Stephen R. *Birthright: People and Nature in the Modern World*. New Haven: Yale University Press, 2012.

Kellert, Stephen R. *Building for Life: Designing and Understanding the Human-Nature Connection*. Washington, DC: Island Press, 2005.

Kellert, Stephen R. "Dimensions, Elements, and Attributes of Biophilic Design." In *Biophilic Design: The Theory, Science and Practice of Bringing Buildings to Life*, edited by Stephen R. Kellert, Judith H. Heerwagen, and Martin L. Mador, 3–19. Hoboken: John Wiley and Sons, 2008.

Kellert, Stephen R. *Kinship to Mastery: Biophilia in Human Evolution and Development*. Washington, DC: Island Press, 1997.

Kellert, Stephen R. "Social and Perceptual Factors in Endangered Species Management." *The Journal of Wildlife Management* 49, no. 2 (April 1985): 528–36.

Kellert, Stephen R. *The Value of Life: Biological Diversity and Human Society*. Washington, DC: Island Press, 1996.

Kettner, Hannes, Sam Gandy, Eline C. H. M. Haijen, and Robin L. Carhart-Harris. "From Egoism to Ecoism: Psychedelics Increase Nature Relatedness in a State-Mediated and Context-Dependent Manner." *International Journal of Environmental Research and Public Health* 16, no. 24 (2019). https://doi.org/10.3390/ijerph16245147.

Kheel, Marti. *Nature Ethics: An Ecofeminist Perspective*. Lanham: Rowman & Littlefield, 2008.

Kheel, Marti. "Ecofeminism and Deep Ecology: Rethinking Identity and Difference." In *Reweaving the World: The Emergence of Ecofeminism*, edited by Irene Diamond and G. F. Orenstein, 128–37. San Francisco: Sierra Club Books, 1990.

Kheel, Marti. "From Heroic to Holistic Ethics: The Ecofeminist Challenge." In *Ecofeminism: Women, Animals, Nature*, 243–67.

Kheel, Marti. "License to Kill: An Ecofeminist Critique of Hunters' Discourse." In *Animals and Women: Feminist Theoretical Explorations*, edited by Carol J. Adams and Josephine Donovan, 85–125. Durham: Duke University Press, 1995.

Kiesling, Frances M., and Christie M. Manning. "How Green Is Your Thumb? Environmental Gardening Identity and Ecological Gardening Practices." *Journal of Environmental Psychology* 30 (2010): 315–27.

Klemmer, Cary L., and Kathleen A. McNamara. "Deep Ecology and Ecofeminism: Social Work to Address Global Environmental Crisis." *Affilia: Journal of Women and Social Work* (2019): 1–13. https://doi.org/10.1177/0886109919894650.

Kopnina, Helen, and Brett Cherniakdoi. "Cultivating a Value for Non-Human Interests through the Convergence of Animal Welfare, Animal Rights, and Deep Ecology in Environmental Education." *Education Sciences* 5 (2015): 363–79. https://doi.org/10.3390/educsci5040363.

Korpela, Kalevi M. "Place Attachment." In *The Oxford Handbook of Environmental and Conservation Psychology*, edited by Susan D. Clayton, 148–63. Oxford: Oxford UP, 2012.

Kortetmäki, Teea. "Is Broad the New Deep in Environmental Ethics?: A Comparison of Broad Ecological Justice and Deep Ecology." *Ethics and the Environment* 21, no. 1 (Spring 2016): 89–108.

Kowalsky, Nathan. "Whatever Happened to Deep Ecology?" *The Trumpeter* 30, no. 2 (2014): 95–100.

Kyle, Gerard T., James D. Absher, and Alan R. Graefe. "The Moderating Role of Place Attachment on the Relationship Between Attitudes Toward Fees and Spending Preferences." *Leisure Sciences* 25 (2003): 33–50.

Kyle, Gerard, Alan Graefe, Robert Manning, and James Bacon. "Effects of Place Attachment on Users' Perceptions of Social and Environmental Conditions in a Natural Setting." *Journal of Environmental Psychology* 24 (2004): 213–25.

LaChapelle, Dolores. *Earth Wisdom*. Los Angeles: The Guild of Tutors Press, 1978.

Lal, Sanjay. "Moral Extensionism and Nonviolence: An Essential Relation?" In *The Peace of Nature and the Nature of Peace: Essays on Ecology, Nature, Nonviolence, and Peace*, edited by Andrew Fiala, 71–80. Leiden: Brill/Rodopi, 2015.

Lankenau, Greg R. "Fostering Connectedness to Nature in Higher Education." *Environmental Education Research* 24, no. 2 (2018): 230–44.

Lee, Keekok. "Biotic and Abiotic Nature: How Radical is Rolston's Environmental Philosophy?" In *Nature, Value, Duty: Life on Earth with Holmes Rolston, III*, edited by Christopher J. Preston and Wayne Ouderkirk, 17–28. Dordrecht: Springer, 2007.

Lee, Keekok. "Is Nature Autonomous?" In *Recognizing the Autonomy of Nature: Theory and Practice*, edited by Thomas Heyd, 54–74. New York: Columbia University Press, 2005.

Leopold, Aldo. *A Sand County Almanac with Essays on Conservation from Round River*. New York: Ballantine Books, 1970.

Levy, Sanford S. "The Biophilia Hypothesis and Anthropocentric Environmentalism." *Environmental Ethics* 25, no. 3 (Fall 2003): 227–46.

Li, Danqing, and Jin Chen. "Significant Life Experiences on the Formation of Environmental Action Among Chinese College Students." *Environmental Education Research* 21, no. 4 (2015): 612–30.

Lima, Nathan Willig, and Cristiano Moura. "Stop Teaching Science: A Philosophical Framework to Depart from Science Education into Deep Ecological Education." In *Re-Introducing Science: Sculpting the Image of Science for Education and Media in Its Historical and Philosophical Background*, edited by Fanny Seroglou and Vassilis Koulountzos, 3–9. Proceedings of the 15th International History, Philosophy and Science Teaching Conference, July 15–19, 2019.

Lincoln, Noa Kekuewa, and Nicole M. Ardoin, "Cultivating Values: Environmental Values and Sense of Place as Correlates of Sustainable Agricultural Practices." *Agriculture and Human Values* 33 (2016): 389–401.

Livingston, John A. *The John A. Livingston Reader*. Toronto: McClelland and Stewart, 2007.

Loder, Reed Elizabeth. "Gratitude and the Environment: Toward Individual and Collective Ecological Virtue." *The Journal Jurisprudence* 10 (2011): 383–435.

Louv, Richard. *Last Child in the Woods: Saving Our Children from Nature-Deficit Disorder*. Chapel Hill: Algonquin Books, 2006.

Louv, Richard. *Vitamin N: The Essential Guide to a Nature-Rich Life*. Chapel Hill: Algonquin Books, 2016.

Lynch, Tony, and Stephen Norris. "On the Enduring Importance of Deep Ecology." *Environmental Ethics* 38, no. 2 (Spring 2016): 63–75.

Mackay, Caroline M. L., and Michael T. Schmitt. "Do People Who Feel Connected to Nature Do More to Protect It? A Meta-Analysis." *Journal of Environmental Psychology* 65 (2019): 1–9. https://doi.org/10.1016/j.jenvp.2019.101323.

Macy, Joanna, and Pat Fleming. "Guidelines for a Council of All Beings Workshop." In John Seed, Joanna Macy, Pat Fleming, and Arne Naess, *Thinking Like a Mountain: Towards a Council of All Beings*, 97–116. Gabriola Island, BC: New Society Publishers, 1988.

Macy, Joanna, and Molly Young Brown. *Coming Back to Life: The Updated Guide to the Work That Reconnects*. Gabriola Island, BC: New Society Publishers, 2014.

Manfredo, Michael J. *Who Cares About Wildlife?: Social Science Concepts for Exploring Human-Wildlife Relationships and Conservation Issues*. New York: Springer-Verlag, 2008.

Manfredo, Michael, Tara Teel, and Alan Bright. "Why Are Public Values Toward Wildlife Changing?" *Human Dimensions of Wildlife* 8, no. 4 (2003): 287–306.

Mathews, Freya. "Conservation and Self-Realization: A Deep Ecology Perspective." *Environmental Ethics* 10, no. 4 (Winter 1988): 347–55.

Mathews, Freya. *For Love of Matter: A Contemporary Panpsychism*. Albany: State University of New York Press, 2003.

Mayer, F. Stephan, and Cynthia McPherson Frantz. "The Connectedness to Nature Scale: A Measure of Individuals' Feeling in Community with Nature." *Journal of Environmental Psychology* 24, no. 4 (2004): 503–15.

McLaughlin, Andrew. "The Heart of Deep Ecology." In *Deep Ecology for the Twenty-First Century: Readings on the Philosophy and Practice of the New Environmentalism*, edited by George Sessions, 85–93. Boston: Shambhala, 1995.

McLaughlin, Andrew. *Regarding Nature: Industrialism and Deep Ecology*. Albany: State University of New York Press, 1993.

McShane, Katie. "Anthropocentrism vs. Nonanthropocentrism: Why Should We Care?" *Environmental Values* 16, no. 2 (2007): 169–85.

McShane, Katie. "Why Environmental Ethics Shouldn't Give Up on Intrinsic Value." *Environmental Ethics* 29, no. 1 (Spring 2007): 43–61.

Merchant, Carolyn. *The Death of Nature: Women, Ecology and the Scientific Revolution*. San Francisco: Harper, 1983.

Mikkelson, Gregory M., and Colin A. Chapman. "Individualistic Environmental Ethics: A Reductio ad Exstinctum?" *Environmental Ethics* 36, no. 3 (Fall 2014): 333–38.

Miller, James R. "Biodiversity Conservation and the Extinction of Experience." *Trends in Ecology and Evolution* 20, no. 8 (August 2005): 430–34.

Moore, Roger L., and Alan R. Graefe. "Attachments to Recreation Settings: The Case of Rail-Trail Users." *Leisure Sciences* 16, no. 1 (1994): 17–31.

Morito, Bruce. "Intrinsic Value: A Modern Albatross for the Ecological Approach." *Environmental Values* 12, no. 3 (2003): 317–36.

Mullendore, Nathan D., Jessica D. Ulrich-Schadb, and Linda Stalker Prokopy. "U.S. Farmers' Sense of Place and Its Relation to Conservation Behavior." *Landscape and Urban Planning* 140 (2015): 67–75.

Muller, Markus, Elisabeth Kals, and Ramune Pansa. "Adolescents' Emotional Affinity toward Nature: A Cross-Societal Study." *Journal of Developmental Processes* 4, no. 1 (2009): 59–69.

Myers, O. Gene. Review of *The Biophilia Hypothesis*, edited by Stephen R. Kellert and Edward O. Wilson. *Environmental Ethics* 18, no. 3 (Fall 1996): 327–30.

Naess, Arne. "Access to Free Nature." *The Trumpeter* 21, no. 2 (2005): 48–50.

Naess, Arne. "All Together Now." Review of *Consilience* by Edward O. Wilson. *New Scientist* 2148 (August 22, 1998): 42–3.

Naess, Arne. "The Deep Ecological Movement: Some Philosophical Aspects." *Inquiry* 8, no. 1–2 (1986): 10–31.

Naess, Arne. "The Ecofeminism versus Deep Ecology Debate." In *Philosophical Dialogues: Arne Naess and the Progress of Ecophilosophy*, edited by Nina Witoszek and Andrew Brennan, 270–3. Lanham: Rowman & Littlefield, 1999.

Naess, Arne. *Ecology, Community and Lifestyle: Outline of an Ecosophy*. Translated and revised by David Rothenberg. Cambridge: Cambridge University Press, 1989.

Naess, Arne. "Ecosophy and Gestalt Ontology." In *Deep Ecology for the Twenty-First Century*, 240–45.

Naess, Arne. "Ecosophy and Gestalt Ontology." In *Deep Ecology for the Twenty-First Century: Readings on the Philosophy and Practice of the New Environmentalism*, edited by George Sessions, 240–45. Boston: Shambhala, 1995.

Naess, Arne. "An Example of a Place: Tvergastein." In *The Ecology of Wisdom: Writings by Arne Naess*, edited by Alan Drengson and Bill Devall, 45–64. Berkeley: Counterpoint, 2008.

Naess, Arne. *Gandhi and Group Conflict: An Exploration of Satyagraha*. Oslo: Universitetsforlaget, 1974.

Naess, Arne. "'Here I Stand': An Interview with Arne Naess." Interview by Christian Diehm. *Environmental Philosophy* 1, no. 2 (Fall 2004): 6–19.

Naess, Arne. "Identification as a Source of Deep Ecological Attitudes." In *Deep Ecology*, edited by Michael Tobias, 256–70. San Diego: Avant Books, 1985.

Naess, Arne. "Interview with Norwegian Philosopher Arne Naess." Interview by Jan van Boeckel. Accessed September 10, 2018. http://www.naturearteducation.org/Interview_Arne_Naess_1995.pdf.

Naess, Arne. "Self-Realization: An Ecological Approach to Being-in-the-World." In *Deep Ecology for the Twenty-First Century: Readings on the Philosophy and Practice of the New Environmentalism*, edited by George Sessions, 225–39. Boston: Shambhala, 1995.

Naess, Arne. "The Shallow and the Deep, Long-Range Ecology Movement. A Summary." *Inquiry* 16, no. 1–4 (1973): 95–100.

Naess, Arne. "Simple in Means, Rich in Ends: An Interview with Arne Naess." Interview by Stephan Bodian. In *Deep Ecology for the Twenty-First Century: Readings on the Philosophy and Practice of the New Environmentalism*, edited by George Sessions, 26–36. Boston: Shambhala, 1995.

Naess, Arne. "Spinoza and the Deep Ecology Movement." In *The Ecology of Wisdom: Writings by Arne Naess*, edited by Alan Drengson and Bill Devall, 230–51. Berkeley: Counterpoint, 2008.

Naess, Arne. "Spinoza and Ecology." *Philosophia* 7, no. 1 (1977): 45–54.

Naess, Arne, Alfred Ayer, and Fons Elders. "The Glass Is on the Table: The Empiricist versus Total View." In *Philosophical Dialogues: Arne Naess and the Progress of Ecophilosophy*, edited by Nina Witoszek and Andrew Brennan, 10–28. Lanham: Rowman & Littlefield, 1999.

Naess, Arne, with Per Ingvar Haukeland. *Life's Philosophy: Reason and Feeling in a Deeper World*. Translated by Roland Huntford. Athens: University of Georgia Press, 2002.

Nelson, Michael P. "Teaching Holism in Environmental Ethics." *Environmental Ethics* 32, no. 1 (Spring 2010): 33–49.

Nichols, Wallace J. *Blue Mind*. New York: Little, Brown and Company, 2014.

Niemiec, Rebecca M., Nicole M. Ardoin, Candace B. Wharton, and Frances Kinslow Brewer. "Civic and Natural Place Attachment as Correlates of Resident Invasive Species Control Behavior in Hawaii." *Biological Conservation* 209 (2017): 415–22.

Nisbet, Elizabeth K., John M. Zelenski, and Steven A. Murphy. "The Nature Relatedness Scale: Linking Individuals' Connection with Nature to Environmental Concern and Behavior." *Environment and Behavior* 41, no. 5 (2009): 715–40.

Nolt, John. *Environmental Ethics for the Long Term: An Introduction.* New York: Routledge, 2015.

O'Neill, John. "Life Beyond Capital." Centre for the Understanding of Sustainable Prosperity essay series on the Morality of Sustainable Prosperity, no. 6 (October 2017). https://www.cusp.ac.uk/themes/m/m1-6/.

O'Neill, John. "The Varieties of Intrinsic Value." *The Monist* 75, no. 2 (April 1992): 119–37.

O'Neill, Onora. "Environmental Values, Anthropocentrism and Speciesism." *Environmental Values* 6, no. 2 (1997): 127–42.

Palmer, Clare. "An Overview of Environmental Ethics." In *Environmental Ethics,* edited by Andrew Light and Holmes Rolston, III, 15–37. Oxford: Blackwell, 2003.

Palmer, Clare. "Contested Frameworks in Environmental Ethics." In *Linking Ecology and Ethics for a Changing World: Values, Philosophy, and Action,* edited by Ricardo Rozzi, S.T.A. Pickett, Clare Palmer, Juan J. Armesto, and J. Baird Callicott, 191–206. Dordrecht: Springer, 2013.

Palmer, Joy A. "Development of Concern for the Environment and Formative Experiences of Educators." *Journal of Environmental Education* 24, no. 3 (1993): 26–30.

Palmer, Joy A., Jennifer Suggate, Barbara Bajd, Paul Hart, Roger K. P. Ho, J. K. W. Ofwono-Orecho, Marjorie Peries, Ian Robottom, Elissavet Tsaliki, and Christie Van Staden. "An Overview of Significant Influences and Formative Experiences on the Development of Adults' Environmental Awareness in Nine Countries." *Environmental Education Research* 4, no. 4 (1998): 445–64.

Peterson, Nancy J. "Developmental Variables Affecting Environmental Sensitivity in Professional Environmental Educators." M.A. thesis (Southern Illinois University at Carbondale, 1982). Cited in Louise Chawla, "Significant Life Experiences Revisited," 369–82.

Plumwood, Val. "Comment: Self-Realization or Man Apart? The Reed-Naess Debate." In *Philosophical Dialogues: Arne Naess and the Progress of Ecophilosophy,* edited by Nina Witoszek and Andrew Brennan, 206–10. Lanham: Rowman & Littlefield, 1999.

Plumwood, Val. *Environmental Culture: The Ecological Crisis of Reason.* London: Routledge, 2002.

Plumwood, Val. *Feminism and the Mastery of Nature.* London: Routledge, 1993.

Plumwood, Val. "Nature, Self, and Gender: Feminism, Environmental Philosophy, and the Critique of Rationalism." *Hypatia* 6, no. 1 (Spring 1991): 3–27.

Pohl, Sarah. "Technology and the Wilderness Experience." *Environmental Ethics* 28, no. 2 (Summer 2006): 147–63.

Prévot, Anne-Caroline, Susan Clayton, and Raphael Mathevet. "The Relationship of Childhood Upbringing and University Degree Program to Environmental Identity: Experience in Nature Matters." *Environmental Education Research* 24, no. 2 (2018): 263–79.

Proshansky, Harold M. "The City and Self-Identity." *Environment and Behavior* 10, no. 2 (1978): 147–69.

Proshansky, Harold M., Abbe K. Fabian, and Robert Kaminoff. "Place-Identity: Physical World Socialization of the Self." *Journal of Environmental Psychology* 3, no. 1 (1983): 57–83.

Pyle, Robert. *The Thunder Tree: Lessons from an Urban Wildland*. New York: The Lyons Press, 1993.

Reed, Peter. "Man Apart: An Alternative to the Self-Realization Approach." In *Philosophical Dialogues: Arne Naess and the Progress of Ecophilosophy*, edited by Nina Witoszek and Andrew Brennan, 181–97. Lanham: Rowman & Littlefield, 1999.

Reed, Peter, and David Rothenberg, eds. *Wisdom in the Open Air: The Norwegian Roots of Deep Ecology*. Minneapolis: University of Minnesota Press, 1993.

Regan, Tom. *The Case for Animal Rights*. Berkeley: University of California Press, 1983.

Restall, Brian, and Elisabeth Conrad. "A Literature Review of Connectedness to Nature and Its Potential for Environmental Management." *Journal of Environmental Management* 159 (2015): 264–78.

Rodman, John. "Four Forms of Ecological Consciousness Reconsidered." In *Deep Ecology for the Twenty-First Century: Readings on the Philosophy and Practice of the New Environmentalism*, edited by George Sessions, 121–30. Boston: Shambhala, 1995.

Rollin, Bernard. *Animal Rights and Human Morality*. Buffalo: Prometheus Books, 1992.

Rothenberg, David. "Ecosophy T: From Intuition to System." Introduction to Ecology, Community and Lifestyle: Outline of an Ecosophy, Arne Naess, 1–22. Cambridge: Cambridge University Press, 1989.

Rothenberg, David. *Is It Painful to Think?: Conversations with Arne Naess*. Minneapolis: University of Minnesota Press, 1993.

Rowe, Stan. "The Living Earth and Its Ethical Priority." *The Trumpeter* 19, no. 2 (2003): 69–82.

Salleh, Ariel. "In Defense of Deep Ecology: An Ecofeminist Response to a Liberal Critique." In *Beneath the Surface: Critical Essays in the Philosophy of Deep Ecology*, edited by Eric Katz, Andrew Light, and David Rothenberg, 107–24. Cambridge, Mass.: MIT Press, 2000.

Saunders, Carol D. "The Emerging Field of Conservation Psychology." *Human Ecology Review* 10, no. 2 (2003): 138–9.

Scannell, Leila, and Robert Gifford. "Defining Place Attachment: A Tripartite Organizing Framework." *Journal of Environmental Psychology* 30, no. 1 (2010): 1–10.

Scannell, Leila, and Robert Gifford. "The Relations between Natural and Civic Place Attachment and Pro-Environmental Behavior." *Journal of Environmental Psychology* 30 (2010): 289–97.

Schultz, P. Wesley. "Empathizing With Nature: The Effects of Perspective Taking on Concern for Environmental Issues." *Journal of Social Issues* 56, no. 3 (2000): 391–406.

Schultz, P. Wesley. "Inclusion with Nature: The Psychology of Human-Nature Relations." In *Psychology of Sustainable Development*, edited by Peter Schmuck and Wesley P. Schultz, 61–78. New York: Springer, 2002.

Schultz, P. Wesley. "The Structure of Environmental Concern: Concern for Self, Other People, and the Biosphere." *Journal of Environmental Psychology* 21, no. 4 (2001): 327–39.

Schultz, P. Wesley, Valdiney V. Gouveia, Linda D. Cameron, Geetika Tankha, Peter Schmuck, and Marek Franek. "Values and Their Relationship to Environmental Concern and Conservation Behavior." *Journal of Cross-Cultural Psychology* 36, no. 4 (July 2005): 457–75.

Seed, John. "To Hear Within Ourselves the Sound of the Earth Crying." In *Introduction to Thinking Like a Mountain*, edited by John Seed, Joanna Macy, Pat Fleming, and Arne Naess, 5–17. Gabriola Island, B.C.: New Society Publishers, 1988.

Semken, Steve. "Place Attachment Inventory (ASU) 1.3." Accessed November 5, 2014. http://serc.carleton.edu/NAGTWorkshops/assess/activities/semken.html.

Sessions, George. "Basic Principles of Deep Ecology." *Ecophilosophy* VI (May 1984): 3–7.

Sessions, George. "Deep Ecology, New Conservation, and the Anthropocene Worldview." *The Trumpeter* 30, no. 2 (2014): 106–14.

Sessions, George. "Ecocentrism and the Anthropocentric Detour." In *Deep Ecology for the Twenty-First Century: Readings on the Philosophy and Practice of the New Environmentalism*, edited by George Sessions, 156–83. Boston: Shambhala, 1995.

Simaika, John P., and Michael J. Samways. "Biophilia as a Universal Ethic for Conserving Biodiversity." *Conservation Biology* 24, no. 3 (2010): 903–6.

Singelis, Theodore M., Harry C. Triandis, Dharm P. S. Bhawuk, and Michele J. Gelfand. "Horizontal and Vertical Dimensions of Individualism and Collectivism: A Theoretical and Measurement Refinement." *Cross-Cultural Research* 29, no. 3 (August 1995): 240–75.

Singer, Peter. *Practical Ethics*. Cambridge: Cambridge University Press, 1993.

Sivek, Daniel J. "Environmental Sensitivity among Wisconsin High School Students." *Environmental Education Research* 8, no. 2 (2002): 155–70.

Soulé, Michael E. "Biophilia: Unanswered Questions." In *The Biophilia Hypothesis*, edited by Stephen R. Kellert and Edward O. Wilson, 441–55. Washington, D.C.: Island Press, 1993.

Soulé, Michael E. "What Is Conservation Biology?" *BioScience*, 35, no. 11 (December 1985): 727–34.

Stedman, Richard C. "Toward a Social Psychology of Place: Predicting Behavior from Place-Based Cognitions, Attitude, and Identity." *Environment and Behavior* 34, no. 5 (2002): 561–81.

Stern, Paul C., and Thomas Dietz. "The Value Basis of Environmental Concern." *Journal of Social Issues* 50, no. 3 (1994): 65–84.

Stets, Jan E., and Chris F. Biga. "Bringing Identity Theory into Environmental Sociology." *Sociological Theory* 21, no. 4 (December 2003): 398–423.

Sward, Leesa L. "Significant Life Experiences Affecting the Environmental Sensitivity of El Salvadoran Environmental Professionals." *Environmental Education Research* 5, no. 2 (1999): 201–6.

Talukder, Md. Munir Hossain. *Nature and Life: Essays on Deep Ecology and Applied Ethics*. Newcastle upon Tyne, UK: Cambridge Scholars Publishing, 2018.

Tanner, Thomas. "Significant Life Experiences: A New Research Area in Environmental Education." *Journal of Environmental Education* 11, no. 4 (1980): 20–24.

Taylor, Bron. *Dark Green Religion: Nature Spirituality and the Planetary Future*. Berkeley: University of California Press, 2010.

Taylor, Paul. *Respect for Nature*. Princeton: Princeton University Press, 1986.
Thomas, Emyr Vaughan. "Rolston, Naturogenic Value and Genuine Biocentrism." *Environmental Values* 6, no. 3 (1997): 355–60.
Thomashow, Mitchell. *Ecological Identity: Becoming a Reflective Environmentalist*. Cambridge: MIT Press, 1996.
Thompson, Suzanne C. Gagnon, and Michelle A. Barton. "Ecocentric and Anthropocentric Attitudes toward the Environment." *Journal of Environmental Psychology* 14 (1994): 149–57.
Tonge, Joanna, Maria M. Ryan, Susan A. Moore, and Lynnath E. Beckley. "The Effect of Place Attachment on Pro-Environment Behavioral Intentions of Visitors to Coastal Natural Area Tourist Destinations." *Journal of Travel Research* 54, no. 6 (2015): 730–43.
Triandis, Harry C., and Michele J. Gelfand. "Converging Measurement of Horizontal and Vertical Individualism and Collectivism." *Journal of Personality and Social Psychology* 74, no. 1 (1998): 118–28.
The Trumpeter. Home Page. Accessed December 26, 2019. http://trumpeter.athabascau.ca/index.php/trumpet.
Turner, Derek D. "Monkeywrenching, Perverse Incentives and Ecodefence." *Environmental Values* 15, no. 2 (2006): 213–32.
Uhl, Christopher. *Developing Ecological Consciousness: The End of Separation*, 2nd ed. Lanham: Rowman & Littlefield, 2013.
United States Department of the Interior Fish and Wildlife Service. *Activities of the American Public Relating to Animals*. Phase II of *American Attitudes, Knowledge and Behaviors Toward Wildlife and Natural Habitats*. Stephen R. Kellert with Joyce K. Berry. Washington, DC: U.S. Government Printing Office, 1980.
United States Department of the Interior Fish and Wildlife Service. *Public Attitudes Toward Critical Wildlife and Habitat Issues*. Phase I of *American Attitudes, Knowledge and Behaviors Toward Wildlife and Natural Habitats*. Stephen R. Kellert with Joyce K. Berry. Washington, D.C.: U.S. Government Printing Office, 1979.
Uzzell, David, Enric Pol, and David Badenas. "Place Identification, Social Cohesion, and Environmental Sustainability." *Environment and Behavior* 34, no. 1 (2002): 26–53.
van den Noortgaete, Francis. "Generous Being: The Environmental Ethical Relevance of Ontological Gratitude." *Ethics and the Environment* 21, no. 2 (Fall 2016): 119–42.
van Wyck, Peter C. *Primitives in the Wilderness: Deep Ecology and the Missing Human Subject*. Albany: SUNY Press, 1997.
Vaske, Jerry J., and Katherine C. Kobrin. "Place Attachment and Environmentally Responsible Behavior." *The Journal of Environmental Education* 32, no. 4 (2001): 16–21.
Vucetich, John A., Jeremy T. Bruskotter, and Michael Paul Nelson. "Evaluating Whether Nature's Intrinsic Value Is an Axiom of or Anathema to Conservation." *Conservation Biology* 29, no. 2 (2015): 321–33.
Warren, Karen. *Ecofeminist Philosophy: A Western Perspective on What It Is and Why It Matters*. Lanham: Rowman & Littlefield, 2000.
Warren, Karen. "Ecofeminist Philosophy and Deep Ecology." In *Philosophical Dialogues: Arne Naess and the Progress of Ecophilosophy*, edited by Nina Witoszek and Andrew Brennan, 255–69. Lanham: Rowman & Littlefield, 1999.

Washington, Haydn. *Human Dependence on Nature: How to Help Solve the Environmental Crisis*. New York: Routledge, 2013.

Weinstein, Josh A. "Humility, from the Ground Up: A Radical Approach to Literature and Ecology." *Interdisciplinary Studies in Literature and Environment* 22, no. 4 (Autumn 2015): 759–77.

Wells, Nancy M., and Kristi S. Lekies. "Nature and the Life Course: Pathways from Childhood Nature Experiences to Adult Environmentalism." *Children, Youth and Environments* 16, no. 1 (2006): 1–24.

Weston, Anthony. "Beyond Intrinsic Value: Pragmatism in Environmental Ethics." *Environmental Ethics* 7, no. 4 (Winter 1985): 321–39.

Whitburn, Julie, Wayne Linklater, and Wokje Abrahamse. "Meta-Analysis of Human Connection to Nature and Proenvironmental Behavior." *Conservation Biology* 34, no. 1 (2019): 180–93.

White, Lynn Townsend Jr. "The Historical Roots of Our Ecologic Crisis." *Science* 155 (1967): 1203–7.

Williams, Daniel R., and Jerry J. Vaske. "The Measurement of Place Attachment: Validity and Generalizability of a Psychometric Approach." *Forest Science* 49, no. 6 (2003): 830–40.

Williams, Daniel R., and Joseph W Roggenbuck. "Measuring Place Attachment: Some Preliminary Results." Paper presented at the session on Outdoor Planning and Management, NRPA Symposium on Leisure Research, San Antonio, Texas, 1989.

Williams, Florence. *The Nature Fix: Why Nature Makes Us Happier, Healthier, and More Creative*. New York: W. W. Norton and Company, 2017.

Wilson, Edward O. *Biophilia: The Human Bond with Other Species*. Cambridge: Harvard University Press, 1984.

Wood, Nathan. "Gratitude and Alterity in Environmental Virtue Ethics." *Environmental Values* 29, no. 3 (2020): 1–18. https://doi.org/10.3197/096327 119X15579936382590.

Wright, Jennifer Cole, Thomas Nadelhoffer, Tyler Perini, Amy Langville, Matthew Echols, and Kelly Venezia. "The Psychological Significance of Humility." *The Journal of Positive Psychology* 12, no. 1 (2017): 3–12.

Yina, Jie, Shihao Zhua, Piers MacNaughtona, Joseph G. Allena, and John D. Spenglera. "Physiological and Cognitive Performance of Exposure to Biophilic Indoor Environment." *Building and Environment* 132 (2018): 255–62.

Zavestoski, Stephen. "Constructing and Maintaining Ecological Identities: The Strategies of Deep Ecologists." In *Identity and the Natural Environment: The Psychological Significance of Nature*, edited by Susan Clayton and Susan Opotow, 296–316. Cambridge: MIT Press, 2003.

Zhang, Weizhe, Eben Goodale, and Jin Chen. "How Contact with Nature Affects Children's Biophilia, Biophobia and Conservation Attitude in China." *Biological Conservation* 177 (2014): 109–16.

Zimmerman, Michael. *Contesting Earth's Future: Radical Ecology and Postmodernity*. Berkeley: University of California Press, 1994.

Zylstra, Matthew J., Andrew T. Knight, Karen J. Esler, and Lesley L. L. Le Grange. "Connectedness as a Core Conservation Concern: An Interdisciplinary Review of Theory and a Call for Practice." *Springer Science Reviews* 2, no. 1–2 (December 2014): 119–43.

Index

Page references for figures are italicized

abiotic nature, 75, 88n41
access to nature, 10, 99, 102, 105, 107–9, 127
albizia tree, 54
alienation from nature, 1, 4, 17, 19, 27, 51, 73, 75, 81, 83, 124
altruism, 24, 50, 132
animals, other-than-human, 26, 51, 71, 74, 75, 120, 124; suffering, 25, 26, 70, 74
Antarctica, viii, 26
anthropocentrism, 8, 10, 29, 50, 67, *71*, 72, 73, 128–30, 131–32; biophilic, 124–28; perspectival, 72–74, 88n44. *See also* instrumental value; utilitarian attitude
anthropomorphic projections, 73
Appalachian Trail, 45
assimilation, 38n89, 72–73
Australia, 6, 45, 98, 111, 115, 123
awe, 121, 128, 129, 132

backgrounding, 31, 76
bat, viii
behavior, pro-environmental, 44–45, 48, 50, 52–55, 100, 101–3, 110, 132–33
Bender, Frederic, 4, 19, 22, 24, 35n41, 82, 92n103

biocentric equality, 37n74
biocentric values, 129–30, 132. *See also* biospheric values; ecocentrism
biophilia, ix, 10, 110, 119–33; as evolutionarily adaptive, 119, 122–23, 135n29
biospheric values, 7, 48, 50, 51, 132. *See also* biocentric values; ecocentrism
Bixler, Robert, 102–3
Booth, Kate, 5, 7

Chawla, Louise, 98, 99
Clayton, Susan, 46–48, 50, 51, 53, 54, 63n76, 63n83
climate change, 100
coelacanth, ix
commonality, 22, 24, 26, 27, 30, 47, *71*, 73–75, 89n52. *See also* identification, as kinship
community, viii, 18, 20, *21*, 22, 25, 35n41, 47, 61n60, 69, *71*, 81. *See also* identification, as belonging
connectedness to nature scale, 47, 78–79, 101, 102
connection to nature: affective dimensions of, 43, 77, 83, 101, 102, 103; as background condition,

157

9, 55, 84; behavioral impacts of, 44–45, 48, 63n83, 101–3, 105, 132; as conservation strategy, viii, 1, 132–33; deep ecological thought, forms in, *21*; deep ecological thought, importance in, 2, 4–5, 15; and environmental values, 49–52; and information processing, 51–52; orienting character of, 55, 64n89, 84–85; and outdoor experience, 101–3; and problem-solving, 50–51; recreational activities related to, 100, 104, 106, 116n58. *See also* environmental identity; identification; place attachment

conservation psychology, 8, 41–42, 55, 83, 104, 106

conservation social science, viii, 7, 8

continuity, human-nature, 27, 73–75, 89n52

deep ecology: anti-urbanism in, 106–9; 'death' of, 5–7; early characterization of, 2–3; movement, 2–5, 41; non-dualism in, 4, 82; nostalgia in, 110; platform, 3–5, 15, 41, 67–69, 82, 125; pluralistic character of, 3–5; psychological orientation of, 42, 56n5; *vs.* 'shallow' ecology, 2–3; and significant life experience research, 104

deliberation, 55, 64n89, 83, 93n105

Devall, Bill, 7, 20, 22–24, 36n64, 57n15, 64n86, 104, 105

difference, respect for, 9, 72–75, 79–81

disconnection from nature, viii, 1, 4, 19, 31, 56, 95. *See also* alienation from nature

dualism, 19, 27, 35n41, 76, 83, 88n39

ecocentrism, 48, 50, 60n44, 90n68, 132. *See also* biocentric values; biospheric values

ecological consciousness, 19, 20, 34n29, 54, 76, 80

ecological science, 20–22, 35n40–41, 78, 79, 85. *See also* science, study of

ecological Self, 18, 23, 24, 59n33, 130; indistinguishability account of, 79–80, 91n89. *See also* self; Self-realization

ecopsychology, 41

ecosystem services, 46, 77, 131

ecosystems, value of, 67, 68, 78

education, 6, 93n113, 99, 114n35; environmental, 7, 97–99, 102, 105, 109, 113n34

ego, 18, 19, 29, 104; egoism, 8, 29–31, 49, 50, 132

elk, 70

emotional affinity toward nature, 101–2

empathy, viii, 25, 27, 28, 38n84, 51, 69, *71*, 74, 86n12, 128

environmental identity, 9, 43, *44*, 46–48, 50–54, 62, 63, 63n76, 78, 85, 93n113, 101; behavioral impacts of, 48; scale, 47, 54; and transpersonal identification, 47–48

environmental justice, 100, 114n37

environmental organizations, 6, 79, 97, 99, 132

environmental psychology, 7, 41, 42

epistemic dislocation, 73–75

existential affirmation, 21

extinction of experience, 95

extreme sports, 116n58

fishing, ix, 83, 100, 104

Fox, Warwick, 11n16, 20–22, 26, 35n44, 36n47, 37n48, 42, 47, 49, 52–54, 62n76, 64n86, 64n88, 76, 80

free nature, 49, 105, 108, 109

friluftsliv, 105–6, 108, 109

Gaia, 22, 64n86

Gandhi, Mahatma, 16, 18

gardening, 63n83, 99–100, 127

gestalt, ix, 35n41, 72, 83. *See also* Naess, gestalt thinking

good of its own, ix, 69–70

gratitude, 77

green space, 108, 109
Griffiths, Joanna, 106–7, 109
Gunpowder River, 21

habitat, 79, 97, 100, 120, 126, 127
Hawaii, 54, 58n24
holism, 9, 67, 69, *71*, 72, 76, 78–81, 84, 86n8, 87n31
horizontal collectivism, 51
human distinctiveness, vii–ix, 18
humility, 77–78, 81

identification with nature, viii, ix, 4, 6, 8, 16, 19, 28–32, 42, 45, 47, 48, 50, 55–56, 96, 101, 104, 105, 120, 125, 129, 130; as belonging, 8, 9, 19–25, 27, 29, 31, 32, 44–47, 76–82; as 'conversion' experience, 83; and environmental identity, 47–48; and environmental values, 9, 48, 67–84; as incremental process, 22, 55, 64n88; and interests, 23–24, 28; as kinship, 8, 9, 24–30, 32, *44*, 47, 51, 68–75, 81; personal, 9, 21–22, 24, 26, 36n48, 44, 47, 52–55, 64n86, 103; and place attachment, 43–44; sources of, 22, *71*, 85, 101–2, 103–5; spontaneity of, 21, 26, 83, 93n105; transpersonal, 9, 21, 22, 24, 26, 36n48, *44*, 47, 52–55. *See also* connection to nature
"Inclusion of Nature in the Self," 59n34
individualistic: environmental values, 9, 67, 69–72, *71*, 81, 84, 87n31; sense of self, 17, 18, 20, 48
Institute for Deep Ecology, 54
instrumental value, *71*, 76, 77, 82, 125, 130, 131. *See also* anthropocentrism; utilitarian attitude
interdependence, 5, 15, 20, 22, 46, 49, 61n60, 77, 90n65
International Congress of Conservation Biologists, 132
intrinsic value, 3, 9, 26, 68–72, 76, 81–84, 92n101, 129, 137n68, 138n76. *See also* biocentric values; biospheric values; ecocentrism; nonanthropocentrism
invasive species, 54

Kals, Elisabeth, 101–2, 114–15, 115n39
Katz, Eric, 29, 75, 82
Kellert, Stephen R., 10, 71, 79, 95, 110, 119–32, 135n29; critique of anthropocentrism, 125–26; critique of nonanthropocentrism, 131; ecologistic attitude, 79, *121*, 128–29; moralistic attitude, 71, 138, *121*, 129, 132; naturalistic attitude, *121*, 128, 132; typology of values, 120–22, 128–29
Kheel, Marti, 52, 87n31
kinship. *See* commonality; identification, as kinship

Lal, Sanjay, 74–75
leave no trace, 106
Leopold, Aldo, viii, 35n41, 38n90, 61n60, 64n88, 104

masculinity, 107–9
Mathews, Freya, 20, 24, 36n55
Mono Basin Scenic Area, 45
moral extensionism, 9, 72–75
Muir, John, viii

Naess, Arne: on backcountry recreation, 106, 108; on "beautiful" *vs.* "moral" acts, 24; on biophilia, 124; early formulation of deep ecology, 2–5, 15; ecosophy T, 4, 16, 18, 26, 41–42, 55; flea example, 25, 26, 27, 70; and Gandhi, 16, 18; gestalt thinking, 72, 80; houseplant example, 70; insects killed with spray example, 26, 28, 30; mountaineering, 104; in New Mexico, 109; on outdoor education, 105, 109; penguin example, 26; and Spinoza, 16, 33n11; total-field image, viii, 4, 15; on value of species, 70–71
National Audubon Society, 96

National Wildlife Federation, 97
The Nature Conservancy, 97
nature deficit disorder, 95
nature relatedness, 7, 59n33, 78, 93n113
Ningaloo Marine Park, 45
nonanthropocentrism, 9, 10, 55, 67–69, 70, *71*, 72, 82, 125, 130–32; pragmatic objection to, 131–33. *See also* biocentric values; biospheric values; ecocentrism; intrinsic value
nondualism, 3, 4, 82

oak tree, vii, viii
oceanic feeling, 104
oneness, viii, 18, 80, 81, 101, 105, 115n39
other-oriented, 8, 32, 50, 51, 76, 129
outdoor experience: appreciative *vs.* consumptive, 106; benefits of, 123, 127; childhood, 98–100, 102–3, 105, 106, 113n35; and competencies, 102–3; and connection to nature, 100–105; and conservation commitment, 96–98, 100; decline of, 1–2, 56, 95, 111n3; in deep ecological thought, 103–6; lifestyle impacts of, 103, 105; serious *vs.* frivolous, 102; unstructured, 99, 102–3, 105, 106; urban and rural, 100–103; wild-urban-rural spectrum, 99–100, 109

pelican, viii
place attachment, viii, 8, 43–46, 47, 52–55, 63n76, *71*, 78, 101, 104; behavioral impacts of, 44–45, 46, 53–54, 58n24; civic *vs.* natural, 53; place dependence dimension of, 43, 45, 53, 58n20; place identity dimension of, 43–45, 53, 58n20; Val Plumwood, on, 29, 31, 37n68, 52, 54, 64n88, 79, 80, 88n39
Point Pelee National Park, 45
potential, human/existential, viii, 17–18, 19, 23, 29, 32, 49, 123, 131, 133
psychedelic drugs, 22

purposive character of things, 26, 69–70, 74, 75

relational value, 92n101

science, study of, 9, 22, 41, *71*, 78, 85, 90n68, 93–94, 94n113, 122. *See also* ecological science
self:-centered, 30, 50, 68, 78;-defeating/destructive, ix, 18, 24, 48, 126;-defense, 23, 24, 28, 31, 36n64, 49, 64n89, 130;-determined/motivated behavior, 24, 28, 42, 48, 64n89; distinctiveness of, 9, 31, 79–81, 91n79;-interest, ix, 9, 17, 28–31, 49–51, 52, 125, 128, 129;-sacrifice, 24, 28; social, 18. *See also* ecological Self
Self-actualization. *See* Self-realization
Self-realization, viii, 8, 16–19, 22–24, 27–30, 32, 49, 50, 67, 68, 70, 75; as norm, 1, 16, 30–32
separation from nature. *See* alienation from nature; disconnection from nature
Sessions, George, 3, 7, 15, 20, 22, 36n59, 37n74, 61n60, 67, 68, 104, 105, 116n58, 124
Sierra Club, 97
significant life experiences, 9, 96–100, 103, 104, 106, 114n37; of captive wildlife managers, 112n17; of environmental educators, 97–98; of environmental justice advocates, 114n37
similarity. *See* commonality
simulated nature, 127, 136n52
South African Institute for Aquatic Biodiversity, ix
species, value of, 67, 68, 70–71, 78–79
Spinoza, Baruch, 16
substitution problem, 126–27, 130
surfing, 104, 116n58

Tanner, Thomas, 96–97, 99, 100, 104
Thomas, Emyr Vaughan, 73–75
tree of life, 20

The Trumpeter, 5, 7
Tvergastein, viii

Uhl, Christopher, 19–21, 94n113
utilitarian attitude, 17, 43, 45, 48, 77, *121*, 125, 126, 129. *See also* anthropocentrism

virtual reality. *See* simulated nature

Whale Rock, 21–22, 44
wilderness, 107–9, 116n64, 119
wildlife, viii, 45–46, 79, 100, 120
Wilson, Edward O., 119, 121, 124
wolf, 45, 53, 70
wonder, 77, 109, 128, 132

zoos and aquaria, 127, 112n17

About the Author

Christian Diehm is professor of philosophy and environmental ethics program coordinator at the University of Wisconsin–Stevens Point, where he has taught environmental philosophy for nearly two decades. He has served as a research fellow with both The Nature Conservancy and the Pace Institute for Environmental and Regional Studies, and has spoken on National Public Radio. He is coeditor of two books as well as numerous articles, essays, and book chapters on topics ranging from environmental activism to the ethics of reviving extinct species.

Printed by BoD"in Norderstedt, Germany